Praise for **American Fencer**

"Do you want to know what fencing's really like in the United States? Read *American Fencer*. From the practice room to competition halls around the world, the book is a gutsy look behind the curtain of the sport."

Peter Westbrook

1984 Olympic Bronze Medalist and
13-Time US National Champion, Men's Fencing

"Tim's story is one for the ages. Even after ten years of competing side by side, I never cease to be amazed by his indefatigable will and hunger for improvement. An impossible goal is only impossible if you make it so, and there's much to be learned from Tim's inspiring narrative about finding himself in life and in fencing."

Jason Rogers

2008 Olympic Silver Medalist, Men's Fencing

"I can relate with Tim's story of a small sport athlete trying to fight onto the podium versus well-funded other nations. Tim's personality, perseverance and tales of his fencing matches around the world are a terrific read."

Steven Holcomb

2010 Olympic Champion,
Men's Bobsled, Driver of the USA 1 "Night Train"

"Tim's story is one of passion and perseverance. What he's achieved in his career and what he's done for fencing and outreach for sport embodies what Olympic Spirit is all about!"

Summer Sanders

1992 Olympic Gold Medalist, Women's Swimming

American
FENCER

MODERN LESSONS
from an ANCIENT SPORT

TIM MOREHOUSE
WITH GARTH SUNDEM

ACANTHUS
PUBLISHING

Dedication

To my family, coaches, teammates, teachers, and friends for their never-ending support in the pursuit of my dreams.

Table of Contents

PROLOGUE

Maestro di scherma, maestro di vita
(Master of fencing, master of life)
— Italian proverb

My opponent slashes hard at my Kevlar jacket and his shout shakes the hall as he takes the first point. Did I even move? I'm the second-to-last U.S. fencer in the team saber competition at the Beijing Olympics. We trail 28-36 in a race to 45. The winner goes on to the gold medal match; the loser fights for the bronze.

I've given twenty years, two-thirds of my life, for the right to stand opposite Russia's Alexey Yakimenko on this fourteen-meter strip. Three hundred years ago, fencing was the sport of kings and nobility, and we would have sharpened our blades to draw first blood in a match for honor. Today, though our computerized scoring buzzers and outfits that make us look like high-tech beekeepers, one thing is unchanged: we still fight for honor. Yakimenko and I retake our en garde lines, facing each other from twelve feet away with our sword hands raised. I can't see through Yakimenko's mask but I can feel him, confident and ready.

Since the 1960s, Russia has taken almost every Olympic gold medal in this event. The most recent American medal in team saber was a bronze in 1948. Cameras flash all around us, but inside the mesh of my mask I'm alone, trying to wring the panic from my breath. This is what I work for, I say to myself, as I always do in that moment of stillness before the point begins.

The referee calls, "*En garde. Prêt? Allez!*" and Yakimenko leaps forward to slash past my guard, his saber edge popping against my jacket as I stand there flat-footed and listless. His speed is stunning, but more troubling, Yakimenko has gotten inside my head.

U.S. fencing is a team of scrappy upstarts, thumbing our noses at the natural order of the fencing world by our very presence in medal contention. *Who am I to be fencing Alexey Yakimenko in the Olympic semifinals?* As soon as I think it, I try to stuff it into my lockbox of thoughts for later. I've wrestled with these questions of self-worth, of competence and adequacy and deservedness, all my life. It's only recently that I've learned how to manage them.

I grew up in New York City's Washington Heights at the height of the 1980s crack epidemic. After fencing at a Division-III college, I returned to Washington Heights to work in a middle school with Teach For America while I trained evenings and tried to scrape together enough international points to scratch my way onto the U.S. Olympic Team. I was the underdog with the choppy, unconventional technique since I first picked up a saber to get out of gym class in the seventh grade.

Behind Yakimenko is a Russian machine built for one purpose: to train fencers to win gold medals. They are full-time, paid professionals. There are no professional U.S. fencers.

My coach stands behind me. Unbeknownst to my teammates and me, he's delaying chemotherapy to add his strength to ours on the strip. We are his children and his habit, and he simultaneously runs a fencing club and coaches a college team to support his involvement with this brotherhood of misfits.

The other members of the brotherhood are Jason Rogers, a college student from Los Angeles who switched from skateboarding to saber; Keeth Smart, an African American from Brooklyn who works full-time at Verizon finance; and James Williams, a recent Columbia University graduate. They won their way onto the Olympic strip the same way I did: on a shoestring, while holding down a job, living an invisible, monastic life comprised of training, work, airports, and fencing halls. Always, we fight to the soundtrack of the internal struggle: *Is it worth it? Is it worth giving your life to something that only you know has meaning?*

Can you hold the inevitable defeat and struggle and intimidation inside you and survive physically, emotionally, and financially to fence another tournament? And another? And another? There's no fame or fortune at the tip of an American sword. You have to find it within—you have to own your success and your failure and all the uncertainty in between.

Yakimenko and I square off again in the en garde position, facing each other completely still, standing as mirror images. Our uniforms are nearly identical except for *USA Morehouse* in block blue letters on my back and *RUS Yakimenko* on his. We look equal but we're not. He is the sum of his hours of work, the tournaments he's fought, the lessons he's learned on and off the strip, the people in his life, and the fencers who have come before him. And I am the sum of mine.

"Master fencing, master life," our coaches say. It's true: in the milliseconds that can separate landing a touch and being hit are your goals, your strategies, the way you deal with success and defeat, and, most importantly, what you think is possible.

From the streets of Washington Heights to the Olympic stage, thoughts come before actions, and my evolution has been as much of the mind as of the hand. The strip lays everything bare—your self-worth, patience, precision, aggression, bravery, and perseverance—and only after finding them in your life can you ever hope to bring these qualities to the strip. If not, your opponent slices these deficiencies out of the air.

"*Allez!*" yells the referee, and I jump forward out of the box...

Washington Heights, Apartment 5b

Before I ever picked up a saber, I skated in the 1984 Winter Olympics in Sarajevo, only my blades were socks and my oval was the wood floor of my prewar Washington Heights apartment. While I skated, my dad sat in a rickety rocking chair on a worn green rug, watching the black-and-white television we'd had since before I could remember.

I stood next to him, digging in the toe of my skate, and with the crack of the gun I was off, sliding past the shelf filled with old books and tearing down the hall, careful not to bump the walls where landscapes and watercolors of sailboats hung. In my dirty socks, I chased Russians and those surprising, orange-clad Dutch.

At the end of the hall were two bedrooms: mine, packed with baseball cards and sports gear—messy like only a six-year-old boy's room can be—and my sister's room, with her clothes strewn across her wood-framed bed and desk. She's ten years older than me and by the time my memory kicks in, she was in high school and gone more than she was home. When she was around, she sometimes styled my barbershop bowl cut into a first-grade-cool coif she called a "Superman 'do." When she was away, I would sneak into her room to play and imagine her there amid the piles of clothes.

The thing about speed skating is that, short track or long track, you're still going in circles. My loop took me only as far as the end of the hall before I'd double, or triple, or quadruple back through the living room. I always skated from behind, pulling off a stunning upset around the last turn or crashing spectacularly into the pads. But no matter my speed or how many times I tagged the far wall, I always circled back.

As it happens, I was the only member of that year's Winter Olympic team who also played for the Yankees. One hundred sixty-two evenings a year, I was there at second base in my mind, and when I made an especially awesome diving infield grab, I'd flip the ball around the horn to Bob Meacham at shortstop, who'd lob it to my hero Don Mattingly at first. They'd chuckle to themselves and shake their heads: *Dang, this kid can PLAY!*

From our bathroom window, I could see past a dead-end street to a park where neighborhood kids played, themselves pretending to be Yankees. The mid-80s was the dawn of the crack epidemic in New York City and Washington Heights was its epicenter and, for a while, the murder capital of the city. Parking a car at the dead end was like throwing a cow into the Orinoco River: eventually it would be stripped bare. Sometimes the cars were left there by unwary people who didn't know how the neighborhood worked, but often, the dead end was a dumping ground for stolen vehicles. Once abandoned, the wheels and muffler would go first, then anything else of value, and then sometimes if the city didn't come to pick it up, someone would set the car on fire and the smoke and sparks would carry any trace of the criminals away into the night sky. A burning car smells like metal accidentally cooked in a microwave.

We never, ever parked our aging VW bug at the dead end. Still, the radio had disappeared long ago and we replaced it with a portable cassette player, which we stuck in the dashboard hole where the radio had been.

Before I was born, or at least before I remember, someone had broken into our apartment, so we had a big metal bar—a "police lock"—slung between iron catches on the inside of our door, like the huge beams you see barring castle gates in movies. I remember the metallic screech of the bar swinging open whenever someone entered, and clanging down with finality when someone left. When my mom had to leave me home alone, she would remind me to put the bar down like I imagine mothers in other parts of the country might remind their kids to turn on a porch light.

This is how it was. It never occurred to me that life could be any different. Because our appliances were old and we lived in a bad neighborhood, I thought we were poor. The truth is, everything had once been new—the appliances and the neighborhood—and both had gradually decayed around us. For example, when my mom wanted to make a pitcher of orange juice, she hacked at the ice and sharp frost in our freezer with a metal spoon until it gave up a can of concentrate. But the fridge had at one point been state-of-the-art, as had our eight-track player and rotary phone. Likewise with the neighborhood, which had been a middle class enclave when my parents moved there in the '60s. And just as you would replace an appliance that stops working properly, people saw that the neighborhood was broken and went out to shop for a new one. But while other families had moved away, my parents fought to keep things the way they were—to be the family that stayed.

And so I dreamed impossible dreams of the Olympics and the Yankees—dreams I knew were nothing but diversions from the real world, from the real life that I had lived, was living, and would always live.

What I didn't understand was that every day, my parents were teaching by example. They were setting me up with the qualities and values that would culminate in the power to change my path.

From my dad I learned hard work.

My dad met my mom in the summer of 1960, at a summer camp where they were both counselors. They met when he spilled a can of paint on her while recoating cabins. Once, I found notes that my dad wrote to my mom when he was twenty, describing his dream to be a writer. When he first moved back to New York, he worked as an editorial room copyboy at the *New York Herald Tribune* while taking classes in the evenings at NYU's Washington Square College of Arts and Science. He earned $44 a week minus taxes and $3 union dues, but augmented the salary by staying to work overtime on the under populated second shift. He stayed so often, the people on the third shift thought he was a regular on the second, and so frequently invited him to stay for theirs. The union contract required quadruple-time pay for any work over sixteen hours a day, and so, for a very short time, despite his lowly job title, my dad was one of the highest paid employees in the *Herald Tribune* City Room.

His position restricted him from doing any actual writing, but he found a way: first shift on Sundays, he bribed the early duty city editor to let him write news articles at the rewrite bank—small obituaries and rewrites of news releases. His covert correspondent work lasted until a visiting district reporter caught him at the desk and then sued the *Tribune* through the union.

Dad left, and during the newspaper strike of 1963, he found a job working as a writer at a textiles trade publication called the

Knitted Outerwear Times. After that, he owned a small textiles factory in Patterson, New Jersey for seven years, before taking a job at a factory in Queens, first as a technical engineer, then as a director of engineering.

I wondered what my dad thought about all day while thread became fabric on the huge knitting machines at the factory in Queens—did he still have his twenty-year-old-self's dreams of being a writer? He treasured a baseball signed by Jackie Robinson and the rest of the Brooklyn Dodgers of his childhood. Did he imagine tapping the plate and adjusting his sleeve as he got ready to face a 1957 Warren Spahn, the way I imagined fielding a sharp grounder and firing it to Don Mattingly? I don't know. We didn't talk that way.

Still, on his way home every night, my dad picked me up two packs of baseball cards. And sometimes on Sundays, we'd walk across the George Washington Bridge to Fort Lee, grab a bite to eat, and walk home. Or we'd walk to the ice cream parlor in Washington Heights. I'd get a cone, he'd get a cigar, and we'd walk back to the apartment together, slurping and smoking. I felt safe with him as we walked through the streets of Washington Heights. Instead of having the father-son conversations I imagined other families had, my dad told me about baseball or architecture. He told me the key to playing infield was to keep your body in front of the ball and charge it—"play the ball, don't let it play you," he'd say.

I remember trying out for my first Little League team on diamond six at Inwood Park. With the crack of a bat, I'd charge over the uneven infield, taking bad bounces on my shoulders or chin before fielding them and throwing to first. The coach hit harder and harder, trying to find the pace at which I'd move out of the way. I never did, and I overheard the coach telling my parents that's why I made the team. No matter: I was ecstatic to be playing baseball instead of just fantasizing about it.

As far back as I can remember, I have stood out from my surroundings. In her own way, it was from my mother that I learned being unconventional is an asset, not a liability. I wasn't allowed to play on the concrete baseball diamond by myself. Instead, my mom played with me after work. She'd hit me fly balls or grounders, and she'd throw me batting practice. Her arm wasn't so hot, but one thing I remember crystal clear: my mom could *hit*. Her fly balls were always catchable and she could put a grounder to either side.

My mother worked on bibliographic indexes for the H.W. Wilson Company. Do you want to know about Argentinean penguins or famous first facts about American landmarks or about one of 660,700 famous people? If you go to the library, you can find H.W. Wilson business indexes and online databases worked on by my mom.

My mother's mother grew up in Mannheim, Germany, studied in Heidelberg, and immigrated to the United States around 1937 with the rise of Nazism. My middle name, Frank, is after her family name. Although she was ethnically Jewish, my grandmother had been deeply impressed by the work of the Quakers in Europe after World War I and with her arrival in New York City, eventually converted to Quakerism. Her two sisters who came to America with her remained definitively and resolutely Jewish. The courage to be different and follow your passion is obviously part of my bloodline.

In any case, many Sunday mornings my mom and I would drive the VW bug or take the A-Train to Brooklyn where we went to weekly Quaker meetings. That's not to say my family was especially religious. There's no priest or pastor or rabbi or imam at a Quaker meeting. Instead, fifty or so people gathered in a large meeting room and sat in silence until someone was moved to speak. The meeting lasted an hour, but kids only joined for the last thirty minutes. Still, sitting in silence for half an hour nearly killed me every week. Couldn't I skate in my socks around the meeting room? Couldn't I bounce a ball off the back wall and field it with my mitt? It was on one of these Sundays that a speeding car rear-ended our VW Bug on the FDR Drive. It was totaled, but my mom and I were safe. We spent the insurance money on a used gray Honda Accord.

At the time, the schools in Washington Heights were notoriously bad, so my mom searched around for an alternative and eventually found Central Park East Elementary in East Harlem. In hopes of boosting its diversity, Central Park East was encouraging enrollment from outside its neighborhood, and in this case, increasing diversity meant enrolling white kids like me. The school was at the forefront of education reform—clustered desks instead of rows, collaborative, hands-on projects instead of reading chapters and answering study questions, calling our teachers by their first names, portfolios of art-infused projects of the students' choosing instead of multiple-choice tests... There's a picture of me on the cover of *Power of Their Ideas*, a book on education that my principal, Deborah Meier, wrote. It's not hard to find me: I'm the white kid in the Yankees cap flashing a peace sign in the lower-right corner. Central Park East was the model for the Meryl Streep movie *Music of the Mind*, and I had a couple of lessons with the violin teacher on which her character was based. But holding a violin felt awkward and involved staying in one place for long periods of time, so I quit without adding Carnegie Hall to my list of impossible dreams.

I had started playing chess with my mom and then at an after-school program run by a foundation called Chess-in-the-Schools that brought chess masters to teach inner-city students. When the Russian World Champion Garry Kasparov visited

Manhattan, he came to East Harlem, where he played games simultaneously against fifty of us inner-city kids sitting in a school cafeteria. I was one of the fifty. I remember watching him walk methodically around the room, playing efficiently while easily beating forty-nine of us and allowing one kid a draw. I was not the kid who drew. Playing Kasparov in the Central Park East cafeteria was my first time facing a Russian champion, and let's just say it didn't go well.

Teachers at Central Park East talked with us about the AIDS epidemic and prejudice. They talked about college and we took a field trip to Washington, DC. In the classrooms, we raised rabbits and guinea pigs and we had pen pals in Vermont—mine was surprised (and I think a little disappointed) that I was white. But that's the kind of place Central Park East was: it contradicted the idea that quality education was reserved for the wealthy. In the eyes of nearly everyone outside Central Park East, I was a statistic—one of "those kids"—drowning in the inner city amid a rising tide of crack violence, doomed to academic failure because of where we lived. How can you teach "those kids"? How can you expect them to learn? How can kids who come from these neighborhoods possibly be expected to succeed? In many poor sections of NYC in the 1980s, those kids didn't.

As much optimism and self-directed passion as Central Park East fed its students, we were still poor and often I thought I was the poorest. Picture this: I was the kid in practical Sears pants, hand-me-down shirts, and uncool Puma sneakers—and I blamed my wardrobe for my lack of friends in elementary school. I yearned in the depths of my first-grade soul for a new pair of Nikes! Or even Reeboks. Pumas immediately placed me at the bottom of the food chain. To compound my embarrassment, it took a while to grow into my nose and, until then, I was Nerdy Birdy or White Honky (I didn't get the racial insult and thought the name was because of my nose).

Each school day, I waited for the Billy Baker van service to pull up outside our apartment building and then I'd run downstairs. Billy's wife, Diana, was almost always at the wheel. I'd watch out the window as we made the half-hour drive to school—down the FDR on Manhattan's East side, off at the 125th Street exit, which I always recognized by the huge "Crack is Wack" sign spray-painted on a handball court across the road. Graffiti was everywhere—on the subways, on buildings. Riding in the Billy Baker van, we'd go down through the neighborhood and in the dark mornings before school, I remember seeing homeless people huddled around flaming garbage cans for heat.

In first grade, I had a friend named Albert. He would throw things, scream, fight, and once threw a pair of ice skates at our teacher. That said, he and I got along great. Later, I had a friend named Romain—all we did was play baseball. After Romain came Jamaal. I can count all my elementary-school-age friends on one hand. All were black and I remember the n-word being thrown around offhandedly in conversation. Once, Albert and I were in the ice cream shop playing pinball and when I won, I laughed something like, "Yeah, I beat you, n---er!" and went to slap him a high-five. The ice cream parlor came to a screeching halt with one of those movie scene record scratches. I had no idea what I had said or done wrong, and Albert didn't either. My father marched me home with a look of horror on his face. When my mom explained the meaning of the word, I remember becoming aware of race for the first time, like Steve Martin in *The Jerk*, just then realizing there was something that made me different from my classmates.

I was slow to read. In fact, I've been a slow starter at most things I do. Reading didn't come naturally to me and I remember leaving class for one-on-one lessons with a series of aides and specialists. But I did the scholastic equivalent of keeping my body in front of the ball: I stuffed letters and words and sentences into my brain whether it wanted them or not. It wasn't pretty, it wasn't the way most kids learned to read, and at first it didn't seem to be working, but by the time I was in fifth grade, you rarely saw me without a book in my hand. And instead of reading curriculum, the school allowed me to follow my passions: I read Hardy Boys books—the old ones with the blue covers—or I read sports books about baseball and the Olympics. My favorite teacher, Bruce Kanze, wrote in my remembrance book (the Central Park East version of a yearbook), "Tim will do great things, if he can just learn to be patient."

My parents worked, so after school I would go to the Young Men's Hebrew Association or spend the afternoon in the apartment daycare of an older, Hispanic woman on our building's first floor. She called me *Timoteo* while I ate *platanos* and played with her cats. Once a week, I went to my grandmother's apartment downstairs and she'd spoil me, feeding me hot dogs and ice cream. I sat in a big brown chair, watching a small black-and-white television while she relaxed on an old blue couch behind me.

So there we were, racing through the mid-80s: my dad working in Queens at the textile factory; my mom working in the Bronx, holding down the house, and looking after my grandma; my sister going to high school in Brooklyn; and me skating through Central Park East with my head down, dreaming about baseball and the Olympics but blinkered to the idea that my life could ever be any different than it was.

Here's a somewhat macabre story about frogs I learned in school: obviously, if you throw a frog in a pot of boiling water, the frog will try to leap out. But if you put the frog in cool water and put the pot on the stove, the frog will sit there without struggling in the slowly warming water until it cooks. I've never tested this, but it's how I pictured myself in Washington Heights: all I knew was this pot, warming around me, and I had no idea it was in my froggy repertoire to leap out. As much as the bar on our door kept danger out, the bar kept me in, trapped in the pot behind a barricaded door. Inside, I retreated to fantasies of cooler water, of Olympians or Yankees—they were my superheroes, just as ideal and unreal as the Green Lantern or the Silver Surfer. In all my imaginings, I never thought my life outside the metal bar could match my fantasies inside it. From inside the pot, this is just what life was like on 176th Street, a block from the George Washington Bridge and two blocks from the A-Train in Washington Heights.

My parents fought one hell of a fight to keep the world around them looking like the ideal they'd moved to in the 1960s. And with my grandmother living downstairs, it was hard to leave. But despite their choice to live frugally, they had eyes outside our pot of boiling water—eventually, despite their Herculean effort to resist change, my parents had to admit that we couldn't keep living in a moldering apartment building in a crumbled neighborhood, trapped amid roaches and antiquated appliances by a metal bar across the door.

Finally, we piled into our Accord to search for a new neighborhood. We toured the Bronx, Westchester, Brooklyn, and settled on an apartment in the hilly, quiet neighborhood of Riverdale, where a ground-floor unit in a two-story complex was for sale. In stark contrast to the concrete and graffiti of our Washington Heights neighborhood, the apartment was surrounded by trees and an open grassy area. When the realtor showed us the apartment, I was in a state of shock. A dogwood tree was starting to blossom right outside the living room window. Where was the dead-end street with stolen cars being stripped? The kitchen was filled with new appliances. And there was no metal bar across the front door.

Here's the thing: both my parents had solid, steady jobs.

The secondhand clothes? The black-and-white television? The old green rug and the rickety chair? Apartment 5b next to the dead end that overlooked burning cars and the concrete baseball diamond? The metal bar and the danger that it kept at bay? These were all choices my parents had made and not the way things had to be.

When my parents informed me that this would be our new home, my whole perspective on who I was and the world I lived in was suddenly called into question. For me, realizing that life could include a dogwood tree started to demolish the wall between what I thought was my preordained reality and what I thought were impossible dreams. What? You could simply grab things from your dreams and stuff them into reality? For my family, this was Riverdale, and for me, well, maybe I could be the Green Lantern, or the Silver Surfer—or maybe even an Olympian! I had no idea what, exactly, I would change myself into. In Washington Heights I thought you ate what life spoon-fed you, and now I saw a seemingly limitless menu of possibilities. I saw that you could make something unreal real.

Our last day in Washington Heights, Nelson Mandela toured Harlem in a bulletproof bubble car so that people could see him standing tall and waving as he drove through the streets of New York. He had just been freed from serving a prison sentence for his battle against Apartheid in South Africa. He had been imprisoned for twenty-five years; many people had lost hope that he would ever be released or that Apartheid could be subdued. But there, right in front of us, was proof that the world could change. Thousands of people lined the streets trying to get a glimpse of him. We stood there in the street, waved hello to Mr. Mandela, waved goodbye to Apartment 5b, and stepped into the new reality we'd created.

You Can't Make Me Quit

We bought a grill and stuck it in the five-by-twenty-foot plot of greenery outside our door.

Our apartment was a ground-floor co-op in a series of two-story apartment buildings surrounded by trees. The small yard, which was really more of a patio, was separated by low bushes from a common yard in the center of the complex. Kids and dogs played there, and on weekends and evenings people hung out in lawn chairs. I imagined that bunnies, bluebirds, friendly mice, and maybe benevolent raccoons would emerge from the hedges to clean our house and be my new friends like in a Disney movie. I mean, life was already so strange and new, why not add talking critters?

I didn't have to wait for my mom to get home to hit me fly balls. I could simply walk out the door and play—no metal bar blocking my way—and I could ride my bike around the neighborhood without worrying that it might be stolen.

The apartment itself was originally a one-bedroom with a large living room, but my parents cut the living room in half to give me my own room. We even had a microwave—an astounding leap forward from the eight-track player and rotary phone of our old apartment to what seemed the cutting edge of technology. Every day, I found something to nuke in it.

With the change in latitude came a massive change in attitude—my dad started attending a quaint Presbyterian Church a few blocks from our apartment and singing in their choir. And it turned out that, all along, living inside my dad was a passionate, educated, and opinionated art lover.

My parents started to meet people in the common area. Neighborly hellos turned into barbecues and patio parties. Seeing my parents socialize was like seeing polar bears mingling with penguins. Even stranger, they started puttering in the dirt, planting flowers in our little yard.

When we lived in Washington Heights I saw myself as a scrappy, plucky kid, living on my wits like an orphan in a Dickens novel—the Artful Dodger (or in my case, Yankee) who had big dreams despite his humble surroundings. The move to happy Riverdale challenged the very idea of who I thought I was. Was I a street-smart survivor pulling myself up by my bootstraps, or a rich kid looking forward to vacations in the Hamptons? It opened my eyes to how "poorly" we'd been living in Washington Heights—and not just the socioeconomics, but the tension that we trapped inside that apartment, and inside us, every time that metal bar came clanging down. Then, it had seemed *normal*. Maybe I was starting to learn it didn't have to be.

There's a myth that parents tell children when they move from one place to another: *Sure*, they say, *you can still see your old friends whenever you want—it's not a 'goodbye,' just a 'see you later!'* During the summer after we moved, they engineered a visit from one of my friends from the old neighborhood. In Washington Heights, he and I always imagined we were in the same boat. In Riverdale, it seemed like my boat was a yacht to his dinghy. We tried to play, but it was just… odd. That was the first and last time anyone from the old neighborhood visited. The separation from my old life seemed final.

But the thing is, we weren't rich. My dad kept the same factory job and my mom continued to index reference books. Our new apartment was smaller than our old place.

And the biggest change was still a month away: a new school. With my parents now thinking bigger and better about everything, instead of enrolling me in public school, they had me apply to three private schools in the area, which happened to be among the most prestigious in the country—Horace Mann, Riverdale Country School, and Fieldston, all surrounded by multimillion-dollar mansions. Compare this to Central Park East, which was surrounded by housing projects and graffiti-covered concrete walls, and where on the playground we frequently found crack vials or, if we were lucky, a leftover $5 bill from a deal gone wrong.

I toured the schools. They were like tiny college campuses, each with multiple buildings tastefully arranged among fields, trees, gardens—I couldn't believe places like these even existed! I did poorly on my entrance exams, but they liked my backstory. I got into Horace Mann and Riverdale, and settled on Riverdale because kids left their backpacks outside the classrooms. It seems a fickle detail, like rooting for a sports team because you like their uniforms, but I wanted what those backpacks represented: the confident nonchalance to carelessly toss my bag on the ground. It was a gesture as foreign to me as the grill on our patio and the school campuses themselves, but it seemed to perfectly encapsulate the difference between my old life and my new one.

If you go to the website of the Riverdale Country School,

you'll see a picture of athletic kids playing Frisbee amid red brick and perfectly spaced trees on a lawn that's mowed in rows just like Yankee Stadium. When I checked recently, the scrolling news widget had info about a junior who'd been named a finalist in the Intel Science Talent Search and about the music teacher, Jason Curry, who had upcoming jazz gigs at the Iridium in Manhattan. Simply, it's the best—athletically, educationally, and socioeconomically.

As with most seventh-graders, I was most worried about my clothes. Before classes started, I demanded that my mom take me shopping, and not at Nearly New, the secondhand store where we'd gotten the bulk of my current threads. We went to a department store and I traded my Pumas for Nikes. Not that I started wearing Dolce and Gabbana, but at least in 1990 I no longer looked like a kid from the cast of *The Electric Company*, circa 1979.

On my first day at Riverdale, the headmaster (yes, I learned that private schools call them *headmasters*) greeted me by name. "Hi Tim," he said, thoroughly disturbing me since we'd never met. He had memorized the faces of all the new students from pictures beforehand. I walked into my first class to find a grid of desks, all facing a blackboard. The bell rang—something I'd never heard at Central Park East—and when the teacher talked, kids took out notebooks and started taking notes.

I sat there dumbfounded. What were they writing? How should I know? I kept my mouth shut and did what the other kids were doing. I pulled out a new, blank notebook and started writing… things. But I might as well have been copying Chinese characters. Central Park East had been interactive, built on the backbone of hands-on learning, which took place around clustered desks and cut-and-paste materials. Riverdale had desks in rows and we called our teacher "Mister." While everyone else seemed to know exactly what to do, I sat there without the slightest clue, terrified of being found out.

My next class was science, and my feeling of total inadequacy was just as bad. The teacher was a woman with short blond hair who spoke in a high-pitched voice and talked for forty minutes to the accompaniment of slides on a projector. She was organized, articulate, full of knowledge, and 110% prepared to deliver the lesson with excitement, interest, and aplomb. But it all flew right past me like dollar bills in one of those wind-tunnel cash grabs. At the end of class, she gave us a reading assignment, asked us to memorize a list of terms, and sent us away with about fifteen questions for homework.

And so it went.

I carried all my books home in a fifty-pound backpack, not sure which ones I needed. During the first few weeks, I remember getting home before my parents and spreading them all out on our dining room table. There they were. Sitting there. And I assumed I was supposed to do something with them. Maybe open them? Or read? Or maybe do some sort of homework?

Do you remember that *Twilight Zone* episode in which a criminal dies in a shootout and wakes up in the lap of luxury, unable to lose a bet, with every wish granted? At first he wonders what good things he might have done to deserve an eternity in Heaven. But after a month it turns out to be… the *other* place. It took about two weeks at Riverdale for me to realize that, despite the heavenly surroundings, I had brought with me my own little hell. I brought those barriers with me, building a prison in my mind with the bricks and mortar of *I'm not good enough, not smart enough for this place.*

At school, I turned inward even more. The lectures might as well have been taught in Armenian or Hmong or Elvish. Trying to understand them just made me feel dumber—so I would look around the room or rock quietly back and forth in my seat. The teachers would tell me to knock it off, but I couldn't. When they called on me to answer a question, I mumbled incomprehensibly, too afraid to be heard giving the wrong answer. I got tests back with red Fs on the top and notes from the teachers saying, *Come see me*! Like sitting at my Washington Heights window imagining playing shortstop for the Yankees, I never really sat at a desk at Riverdale—I was safe someplace else in my mind that I had walled off from the pain: an Eden of hard ground balls and Olympic ice.

My first quarter at Riverdale I got charity Cs. In addition to the difficulty I had with the material, I built another wall between me and success: I began to think of myself as a C student. What does a C student do? Well, instead of coming home to study, I started going to the computer lab after school to play video games. By thinking of myself as a bad student, I gave myself permission to stop trying.

On the plus side, I found friends among the other Riverdale outcasts. Ying had come through a summer program called *Prep for Prep*, which pulled a lot of inner-city kids into Riverdale and helped them earn scholarships. (Later, a school counselor let slip that one of the reasons I'd been accepted to Riverdale was their hope that I might bridge the gap between these inner-city minority students and the Riverdale population at large.) Ying wouldn't let other kids visit his small apartment, but after seeing my setup in our converted living room, he started inviting me over to hang out after school. We became inseparable, playing video games on any device with a screen—Game Boys, Nintendos, calculator watches, and computers. Ying was also one of the most frustratingly intelligent people I've ever met. We would goof off in class, play games in the computer lab after school, and then head to his house or mine for *Super Mario*. Then he would get an A on the test the next day and I'd get an F. Ying was brilliant, a geek who deserved Riverdale. I thought I was stupid by comparison, but I bludgeoned the worry away by bombarding it with *Super Mario Brothers, Star Controller,* or whatever awesome Chinese video games Ying's dad had on his computer.

Finally my parents and I had a meeting with the dean, Mr. Berrical. He explained that unlike at a public school, C students were in danger of failing out of Riverdale. After the meeting, I lost one of my midday open periods to a remedial study skills class. The first day, there were three of us, sitting there in a big room looking mortified. Our entire grade had the same period off, and with only seventy kids, word of who landed in study skills traveled fast.

Still, my worst nightmare wasn't math or science or English—it was P.E. It wasn't that I was completely unathletic or small—I was just mentally small. Outside the structure of sit-and-listen classrooms, it was even more obvious that I didn't fit in. I had imagined joining the golden boys and girls who nonchalantly dropped their backpacks in the hallways and breezed into class and through life. In P.E. I had the space to look around and compare myself to these thoroughbreds. I was a mutt. It was obvious. Every minute of every P.E. class reinforced the deep feeling that something was wrong with me.

I lacked something the other kids had. Intelligence? Wit? Ease? Superior genetics?

One day I was walking down the hall feeling bad, off in my own world, when I noticed a sign on the outside wall of the boy's restroom: *Join the fencing team*—get out of gym class! At Riverdale, if you played an after-school sport, you got out of gym. For seventh and eighth graders, fencing was the only sport offered. The coach realized he had to pluck kids early, before he lost them to basketball, football, and the other sports teams that started in ninth grade. I had no idea what fencing was. Maybe it was some sort of blocking game played with balls and nets, or skates, or bats, or… something? There's a Shel

Silverstein poem called "Hurk," in which the narrator would rather play "hurk" than go to work—he has no idea what *hurk* is, but decides it must be better than work. Likewise, whatever fencing was, I decided it had to be better than *gym class*.

That day, I made it my mission to join the fencing team. The first challenge: finding the fencing room. I asked and asked, "Excuse me, do you know where the fencing room is located?" Apparently, not everyone did. As it turned out, the fencing room was hidden away above the gym: a rectangular room with one tiny window and a gray ceiling lined with fluorescent lights.

Stepping into the fencing room seemed like stepping through the looking glass. That first day I gawked from the doorway. Inside, tall, lanky, awkward students wearing glasses and white outfits milled about holding swords. *Okay, swords are kind of awesome. Fencing is sword fighting?* I'd never seen anything like it before. An older gentleman with glasses and slicked-back, graying hair approached with a clipboard.

"Are you here for fencing?" he asked, as if it were more likely that I was lost.

I nodded.

"Okay..." he said slowly. "I'm the coach. Just remember the first rule of fencing..." I looked at him confused, then he smiled and said, "The coach is always right!" He said it as if he'd invented the phrase, smiling broadly, his finger pointing in the air. "I'm Coach Schneider, sign your name here," he said, handing me the clipboard.

"Have you ever fenced before?" he asked.

"No," I said.

"No problem-o," he said, "we'll teach you ev-er-y-thing!" He smiled warmly. As I wrote my name on the roster, I peeked over Coach Schneider's shoulder into the fencing room where students were putting on mesh masks, pairing off, and starting to edge back and forth, poking at each other with the thin swords. In a heartening way, it reminded me of the video game *Street Fighter*.

A week later, Ying and I stood in the fencing room in our shorts and tee shirts, spread out along a line with the rest of the crop of new recruits. We stared at Coach Schneider, who stood facing us, not a blade in sight. *Where are the swords?* I wondered.

First he taught the en garde stance, which looks a lot like a basketball defenseman's crouch, except with your body twisted sideways and your strong-side toe turned 90° to face your opponent. Your back hand stays down and your strong-side hand—which I hoped would soon hold a sword!—comes up in front of you. I looked around the room: some kids leaned forward, some back, some legs were spread wide and others were nearly touching heel to instep; some kids crouched low and others stood nearly straight. The stance was unnatural and I felt like one of those rubber *Gumby* figures bent into a pretzel. Standing there about to tip over reminded me of my short-lived career as a violinist in Harlem. Coach Schneider walked down the line matter-of-factly correcting our positions.

Next he had us step forward with our front foot, and then follow with our back foot to regain en garde. "This is the advance," he told us. Then we reversed it, stepping back with our back foot and then catching up with the front. "And this is the retreat," Coach Schneider said. Fencing is linear—no spinning in circles—and so this forward and back down the narrow fencing strip is the sport's path.

Suddenly fencing practice seemed less *Street Fighter* awesome, but then I thought maybe it was a little bit like *Karate Kid*, which made it okay.

Coach Schneider called out, "Advance! Retreat!" and we struggled to follow, taking one step forward or one step back and trying to punctuate each movement with en garde. After a few commands, we stopped and Coach Schneider surveyed the room: our feet were pointed willy-nilly at the walls as if a net full of shoes had burst at the ceiling.

"Oh-kay!" Coach Schneider said. "Now let's do it again. En garde!" *People actually say en garde outside the movies?* I thought. Coach Schneider told us that you can only launch a maneuver when you're in balance with your feet under you. From this en garde position, we would learn to attack and defend.

"Now, to attack your opponent from the advance, you use what's called a lunge," Coach Schneider explained. He told us to feel the maneuver launching from the power of our back leg rather than trying to step forward with the front. "Your arm sends your weapon, but your back leg sends your body," he explained. As best we could, we followed his instructions.

As with en garde and advance and retreat, lunging requires balance. Coach Schneider explained that lunging too far forward meant giving up the balance needed to recover, thus laying your-self bare to a to an opponent's counter-strike if you missed. So we tried to land our lunges in balance, bringing our front knee only to 90°, ready to cock back into balance. It was speed and power, but under control. At least that was the goal.

"Don't worry, you'll get it," he said as we ratcheted forward and back in our wavering line.

"Fencing an opponent is a lot like a pitcher facing a batter in baseball," he explained. "It's *mano-a-mano*." Unlike basketball, in which you score on and defend a hoop, or football, in which the goal is the end zone, in fencing, you attack the opponent's body as you simultaneously defend our own. "Each fencer is a challenge," Coach Schneider explained. We would be building the skills we needed to face these very individual challenges, using different sets of tools each time, but always picking them from the home base of these positions of balance.

The thing is, despite the overarching strangeness of the sport as a whole, it felt *good* to be molded from scratch along with a bumbling line of other beginners. In Riverdale's classrooms, I had no idea how to act—what was the procedure, or even the posture, for sitting at a desk and taking notes? In contrast, Coach Schneider expected us to be beginners with no prior knowledge of how to stand like a fencer. When he asked us to step our feet into the en garde position, he knew that he had just set a lump of clay in the middle of a wheel. Even in this first fencing lesson, I felt myself relax into the structure of being told what to do by someone who expected me to be able to do it.

The day I had first found the fencing room and peeked over Coach Schnieder's shoulder, the sport had looked fairly effortless. I thought maybe under the equipment, fencers might not even break a sweat—that it might be the athletic equivalent of golf or billiards. After these footwork drills, however, Ying and I were soaked through our gym clothes, and I knew I had been using muscles that had never burned glucose at quite that pace before. Later I would learn that during a point, a fencer's heart rate gets up to about 180 beats per minute.

The crop of recruits was grateful to sit around a fencing strip where Coach Schneider had captains from the high school team demonstrate the three fencing weapons: foil, épée, and saber. Foil, he explained, was the traditional practice weapon of kings and nobility and as such, it has the most civilized and restrictive rules. You can only score with the foil's tip and only on your opponent's torso. If both fencers touch at the same time, the fencer who initiated the action is awarded the point—this is known as right-of-way. It means that if your opponent attacks, you have to parry or dodge the attack before you can score with an attack of your own.

As we sat and watched, the foil captains, dressed in masks and fencing whites, took the thin fourteen-by-one-meter strip where they stood four meters apart, facing each other behind the en garde lines. The captains saluted each other and Coach Schneider started the point, saying, "Fencers ready?" They became perfectly still. Then he yelled, "Fence!" The captains edged toward each other, probing tactically with their foils for the angles that would allow their tips to sneak through their opponent's defenses. Rather than going for a knockout punch, foil fencing seemed like a series of controlled jabs—a fight between territorial hummingbirds.

The foil captains fought to 5 touches—standard for a high school match—and then Coach Schneider explained the next weapon. Épée, he said, was a dueling weapon, and because duels were traditionally fought to first blood, the épée is slightly heavier than the foil—meant to wound, not just touch. Rather than scoring only on the torso, the scoring zone of épée is anywhere that could draw blood—anywhere on the body.

The épée captains took the strip, saluted, and we saw that épée points are much different than foil. The small scoring zone and right-of-way rule of foil means that you can stand across from your opponent and depend on blade work to keep his point off your torso for forty-five seconds or more. Not so in épée, where it's impossible to block a blade from your entire body for long. Instead, épée fencers tend to hop forward and back, depending on footwork rather than blade skills to steal a touch or retreat out of range. There's no right-of-way in épée—if both fencers land valid touches, both are awarded points, so épée fencers practice evasion in the midst of attack, in hopes of scoring without also being scored upon. If foil fencers are hummingbirds, then épée fencers are mongooses bothering cobras—hopping in and out to worry their prey while keeping themselves safe from strike.

Saber, on the other hand, is the midair collision of F-15s. Coach Schneider explained that the saber originated as a cavalry weapon, meant not for practice and not to draw pinpricks, but to kill. Due to its cavalry origins, the scoring zone in saber is from the waist up—intending to kill the rider and not the horse. And in addition to the weapon's tip, you can score with the side of the blade. Whereas foil and épée fencers poke, saber fencers slash. It's fast, vicious, and, to the untrained eye, messy.

Peter Kim and Taka Sudo were our saber captains. When it was their turn, they flew at each other down the strip with sabers flashing. Points were scored in the blink of an eye, either with a successful attack or with a parry-riposte. When one of them landed a touch, Peter or Taka spun with a clenched fist and let loose yells that made the walls of the fencing room pulse like a speaker membrane. There was a rhythm to it—the sound of their feet slapping hard on the wood floor, the metallic clink of blades or the clang of a blade against a bell guard, the pop of a saber connecting with a Kevlar jacket, or the *tink* of a saber hitting a mask. When Taka and Peter fenced for the class, even behind the masks, their eyes made it clear that this wasn't a game. It was a battle—not for practice or first blood, but for death and honor.

Coach Schneider had an intuitive way with kids, and he intuited from the start that Ying and I had an exponentially greater potential to goof off together than either of us had on his own. Ying went to saber and Coach Schneider put me in foil. I think he also saw that I was wild, and thought the restrained discipline of foil would do me more personal good than the seeming reckless aggression of saber.

Whatever the case, I was underwhelmed the next day to be holding a peashooter foil rather than a high-caliber saber. Still, there was a two-week probationary period after signing up before you could officially drop gym class, and so there I was.

As the probation weeks went by, I got into the flow. While captains from the high school team led footwork and blade drills, Coach Schneider pulled kids aside for short, individual lessons. I remember that in our first one-on-one lesson, Coach Schneider explained that at the beginning of a lesson or a match, you salute your teacher or opponent by bringing your foil handle up vertically in front of your face and then swiping outward. At the end of a match, you shake with your ungloved, non-sword hand to show respect to your opponent. These were the protocols I lacked in the classroom—social norms that came naturally to my classmates but that I had somehow missed.

Coach Schneider showed me how to hold a foil, closing my hand around the foil's straight handle in what's known as a French grip, the fingers curling under the bottom of the handle and the thumb closing over the top. Coach Schneider wore a heavy, black Kevlar jacket that made him look barrel-chested, and in that lesson I learned why. Standing a foot apart in our basic stances, he taught me to send the tip of my blade to his chest so that when it hit, it arched upwards and not sideways or down. Then he showed me the two basic blocks, called parries in fencing. There are two foil parries: one in which a tick of the wrist puts your blade in place to block an opponent's blade sent to the weak side of your body; and another, in which the wrist rolls in the opposite direction to keep the blade off your sword-hand side. Slowly, Coach Schneider pointed his foil to my left torso. I parried and then counter attacked—called a riposte in fencing—ending with my foil to his chest, arching upward. We sped up, shortening the time between the *clink* of my parry and the *thwak* of my riposte landing on his jacket until we were nearly at match speed.

Coach Schneider had started fencing in New York public schools, back when fencers earned scores for form as well as touches. He'd gone to some unnamed city college, which, while he was there, was acquired by NYU. By default, Coach Schneider found himself on the NYU fencing team. His senior year, he finished second at the NCAA Championships, but then moved straight from college to coaching and teaching.

First, he went back to his old neighborhood, taking a job at Taft, an inner-city school in the Bronx. Soon, he started shuttling over to Riverdale in the afternoons to make some extra cash. Since going full time at Riverdale in the 1960s, Coach Schneider had kept a hall of fame bulletin board with tacked-on notes showing every outstanding season or fencer who'd won tournaments, like the Mamaroneck Invitational. Coach Schneider was never explicit about taking scholarship kids under his wing, but in hindsight it was obvious that he did. And because he didn't cut anyone from the team, the fencing room became a haven for kids who didn't quite fit in at Riverdale. Still, outside the one-on-one lessons with Coach Schneider, I didn't immediately sink into the persona of a model fencer. I goofed off during footwork drills and at the end of practice when fencers sparred, I would run over to grab a saber and wail on Ying. Neither of us knew any moves, but it was fun to beat on each other with swords.

The second Coach Schneider signed us out of gym, Ying and I starting cutting practice to play video games in the computer lab.

I thought I had quite a racket going. Staying within the wall of safety I had built as a C student, I got a C+ my first quarter of fencing. As I cut practice more frequently, and spent more time goofing off when I actually went, I became that seventh grader no teacher wants—the one who slips through the cracks of a place like Riverdale and into some other school, to become somebody else's problem somewhere else.

My decision to quit fencing was helped along by a junior foil fencer I'll affectionately call Malfoy. To Malfoy, fencing was deadly serious, and slacker seventh graders who goofed off during practice caused him some sort of very personal and egregious pain.

Malfoy was my assigned mentor—the older kid who had personal responsibility for me as a fencer.

His bullying started with shoves in the hallway between classes and the growl, "You better come to practice today, shitwad." When I showed up, he made me look like an idiot, as if I misunderstood easy drills and couldn't possibly copy even the simplest positions. We sparred, and when I opened my defense or took a bad angle, he landed vicious hits as punishment for failure.

Malfoy was careful to keep his bullying secret, and it took me a long time to say anything to my parents or to Coach Schneider about what was happening, and even then I never told them the full extent. Partly I didn't want to be a tattletale, partly I was embarrassed to admit to Coach Schneider that I was the kind of kid that got picked on, and partly I felt like I deserved it. See, I *was* a slacker, goof-off shitwad who had no business fencing at Riverdale. I belonged at diamond six in Inwood taking grounders off my chin, and Malfoy was just the harsh voice of realism creeping into my short-lived fantasy.

As I cut more and more, I knew what was coming. Finally Coach Schneider asked me to come see him before practice. I considered just drifting away, showing up for gym class the next day and letting my name fall quietly from the fencing roster sheet. But for whatever reason I showed up to see Coach Schneider and hear the bad news.

He didn't cut me. Instead, he told me that I could be an excellent fencer. Somehow, he'd seen through the façade of failure that I'd built around myself and into the dreams of confidence and success that lay inside my wall. He promised to make these dreams come true.

"Here's the hard part," he said. He would help me, but any more skipping and I'd be off the team.

I showed up early the next day and in my awkward, untrained

way, I fenced as hard as I could. But for whatever reason, my new-found focus made things *worse* with Malfoy.

One day, Malfoy told me to meet him at the track before prac-tice. I didn't dare not show up. It was freezing, I was in jogging clothes, and Malfoy held a foil.

"Start running, shitwad," he said. I started and he kept pace behind me. "Faster!" he yelled, and I felt a sting as he hit me in the shoulder with his foil. I sped up. "Faster!" he yelled, and I tried to speed up but my lungs were burning. He loped along easily behind—my sprint was his jog. When I slowed down, he hit me, hard. I imagined stopping. I imagined turning around and landing a hard right to his perfectly white smiling teeth be-fore he had any sense that his trained tiger had turned against him. But it was only another fantasy, like playing for the Yankees, like making the Olympics—*Maybe he's right about me, maybe I am a shitwad*. Maybe I deserved it. Of course I did. We ran and he whipped me with his foil. I ran harder.

Finally, I couldn't run any more. I bent over, gasping for air, red stripes hot through my tee shirt. Malfoy grabbed me and started hauling me back toward the fencing room, up a long flight of stairs from the track. I was sore and humiliated, but the worst part was that I was quiet and accepting. This was the natural order of things. We stopped in the stairwell and he slammed me against the wall.

"I want you to quit," he growled. "You're a waste and you'll never be any good and I never want to see you in the fencing room again!" He threw me against the wall one more time and marched upstairs. I heard the gym door open and briefly the noise of fencing leaked out before the door clicked closed and all was quiet in the stairwell.

I slunk into the locker room and sat on the double-slat wooden bench in front of my locker. I was alone in the locker room and the click of my combination lock opening echoed off

the cement floor and metal lockers. It seemed like such a whimper. Because I could, I kicked the lower locker, which made a
much more satisfying noise. I took off my shirt and looked in the
bathroom mirror. On my back were raised stripes where Malfoy
had smacked me with the foil.

Of course I cried for a while. A couple people came into
the locker room and I darted between banks of lockers so they
wouldn't see me. I was ready to quit. I would quit.

When my teachers called on me I mumbled incomprehensibly, and when Malfoy hit me I bowed my head and closed my
mouth because for some reason I deserved it. But slowly, in the
locker room that day, sitting on the wood bench, the dam I had
built between the shitwad self that everyone saw and the little
core of me that lived at second base in Yankee Stadium and at the
Olympics sprung a leak. This dammed-off part of me knew that
day that if I quit fencing, I would be a shitwad forever.

Slowly, my fear turned to anger and my anger turned to rage.

"You can't make me quit!" I screamed into the cavernous
locker room. "You can't make me quit!" I yelled again. It's funny
to think that the defining moment of my life happened when
I was twelve.

I closed my locker, and instead of a whimper, the clicking lock
sounded like a declaration. I walked upstairs to the gym. I wasn't
the worthless, talentless shitwad everyone said I was, as I'd come
to accept. Rather than my C-student façade, I was something that
Coach Schneider alone at Riverdale had seen.

That day, I opened the door and I walked into fencing practice.

Dragon Slaying

In the book *The Fencing Masters* by Arturo Pérez-Reverte, set in Madrid in 1868, a young female pupil wants to learn "the unstoppable thrust" from the fencing master. But like in life, there is no silver bullet in fencing—there is no *one thing* that solves every problem easily. You will get hit, and how you take a hit is as important a skill as the ability to avoid one. Instead of an unstoppable thrust, the pupil's answer is a constant evolution—a learning process in which you take hits and learn from them; then when you strike successfully, you learn to replicate it.

On the Riverdale fencing team, my first hit was Malfoy. Overcoming this challenge was the first of many times I learned a move on the fencing strip and then took it as a metaphor that I applied to life. The disengage, in which you circle your blade mid-lunge to slip around an opponent's parry, is the first deceptive move you learn in fencing. I never told anyone what happened that day on the track, but the day after learning the disengage, I asked Coach

Schneider to move me from foil to saber, thus skirting the road-block that was my mentor and tormentor, Malfoy.

Truth is, I'd been fascinated by saber from the start. The same way I wanted to join the Riverdale students in throwing their bags nonchalantly in the hallways, I craved our saber captains' assuredness and flare, the bravery and confidence to spring forward toward an onrushing blade, or to hold my ground and hit or be hit with my eyes open. It was still the opposite of who I was in Riverdale's classrooms but, there in the Alice-in-Wonderland enclave of the fencing room, with other beginners and other misfits, maybe I could reinvent myself as someone different—someone competent and powerful.

My first day in saber, I remember putting on my fencing whites, grabbing one of the team's sabers from the walk-in equipment closet and thinking, *Finally, I can just run and slash!* I held the saber above my head to admire the large metallic guard, which, unlike foil's small circle, covers the entire outside part of the hand. Though I had yet to speak a sentence to a girl at Riverdale, now I had suddenly become Zorro; could swooning be far behind?

Coach Schneider assigned the saber captain, Taka Sudo, as my new mentor. On the first day, Taka took me aside to help me transition from foil.

I got in the en garde stance and Taka adjusted my hand position on the grip so that my thumb lay straight down the length of the straight handle, with the rest of my fingers balled around the grip in a loose fist. This way, the thumb and index finger guide the saber's movements while the rest of the fingers hold the blade steady.

In foil, only the chest and back are targets. In saber, the entire upper body, including the arms and head, are fair game. In saber, you can slash and hit with the sides of the blade; the thrusts are called cuts. Taka showed me how to attack an opponent's head. From my en garde stance, Taka had me lunge at his masked head, and I liked the satisfying metallic *clank* of the saber landing. He had me repeat the cut, each time pushing me to straighten the path of my arm, and thus the point of the blade from start to target.

"No hitching back with your arm—straight arm," he told me. Without cocking my arm, my cuts felt weak, but I followed his instructions as best I could. When finally my arm was reasonably straight, he had me advance, double-advance, and triple-advance lunge to his mask.

Then Taka opened up the right side of his body, moving his saber to guard his left. In this drill, when Taka moved his blade left, I cut straight to the right side of his body—over and over, slowly at first and then speeding up. These cuts landed with a less satisfying *thwap* on the fabric of Taka's long-sleeved, white fencing jacket. He then had me cut to his left side as he stood in his en garde stance, which requires reaching a bit further, since your opponent's body is sideways to you. Finally, he taught me the belly cut. He'd raise his saber above his head and I'd slash across his belly. Like the head cut, this one recharged my enthusiasm. "Smaller," he'd tell me, "don't hitch."

Finally we put these cuts together. Taka would advance and retreat, and I would match with the opposites, trying to maintain the distance between us until Taka opened a scoring zone and I would lunge to hit him. Each cut he wanted small and precise. Where were the Zorro slashes?

After he showed me the cuts, we switched to saber's three basic parries. Unlike foil parries, which work to keep only the tip of an opponent's blade off your body, saber parries have to stop the weapon's entire length. In my en garde stance, Taka had me turn my wrist counterclockwise, rotating the guard and blade to block cuts and slashes to my right side. "This is parry three," Taka told me, the third of saber's three basic parries, which block the scoring zones of the head, right and left sides of the body. The others are parry five, which guards the mask by bringing the blade up parallel to the floor and slightly above the head, and parry four, which defends your non-sword-hand side.

Standing behind me, Taka guided my hands through these parries, helping my wrist and forearm glide through the minute change between parries. He showed me how to rotate my arm, leading with the blade to keep it at the best angle to block, but also under control, able to recover.

Then we put it all together, with me first parrying Taka's slow attack and then riposting to whichever scoring zone he left open. These ripostes, he told me, had to be straight and fast to take advantage of a successful parry. Finally, at the end of his work with me that day, I was exhausted but ecstatic.

I noticed that while the foil and epee teams filtered out right after practice, the older saber guys stayed behind to fence a couple extra minutes. I told Ying it was time to *battle!* It had been a while since Ying and I had fenced, and our previous matches had consisted of us swinging wildly at each other. And even though everything Taka had taught me involved small motions, I still couldn't believe that Ying's budding precision was any match for the slashing power of Zorro.

On the first point, I charged at Ying, saber held high, ready to deliver a mighty blow. But instead of trying to escape or parry (like Zorro or Errol Flynn in *Robin Hood*), Ying simply stabbed me in the chest, long before I could deliver my blow. Take note: if you ever find yourself in a real-life sword fight, don't channel the movies.

Even later in this match with Ying, when I tried to Zorro my best friend into sashimi, he snuck inside my overblown slashes, hitting me long before I could land. This, I learned later, is known as hitting an opponent in preparation. Looking back, the term might even be too kind: I'm not sure I even knew what I was preparing *for*, with my sword cocked behind my shoulder like Conan the Barbarian.

After fencing Ying (if you can call it that), I stood back and watched Taka and the older saber fencers—slashing, flying, and yelling, but somehow maintaining precision. I wanted to feel that confident. I wanted to be Taka Sudo, who modeled not just a new skill but a whole new way of being.

I started imitating not only the movements of his blade and feet but the angle of his back arm as he took an en garde position, the way he saluted before a match... in short, the entire demeanor that he brought to the strip. I tried to become Taka Sudo, because I wanted his persona as much as I wanted his skill.

Again mimicking Taka, I started showing up early to sneak in a couple extra tips and maybe a little extra face time with Coach Schneider. Because of those two—Taka and Schneider—I started wanting to be good, and unlike my experience with Malfoy and the foil team, they expected that someday I would be.

Practice each day started with the whole team jogging around the room, and then we'd line up for footwork drills—advance, retreat, lunge, advance-lunge, double-and triple-advance lunge—while intermixing calisthenics like jumping jacks and push-ups. Then we'd split up by blade, or into "weapon squads".

While we did blade drills, Coach Schneider roamed the room giving pointers—maybe he'd adjust my elbow or loosen my grip on the blade, which allows more flexibility and finesse with the wrist. He had a sportscaster's list of idiomatic phrases, and when he'd say things like, "The way to get strong is to lift your girlfriend thirty times every night!" or he'd yell, "To the moon!" we'd all chuckle, mostly *at* him, but we loved it and he did, too. Coach Schneider was fifty-nine at the time, with slicked-back white hair, but another one of his bits was insisting that he was twenty-nine, and when he picked up a blade, he looked it.

Along with Taka, Coach Schneider worked to teach me the

basics—the beat-attack (hitting your opponent's blade to throw off his defense before attacking), the *prise de fer* (searching for an attacker's blade to beat it away and thus reclaim right-of-way), the stop cut (landing to an attacker's wrist if he hitches before a lunge). Coach Schneider would teach a lesson and Taka would reinforce it, pushing me to do each action over and over until I got it right. Don't get me wrong: Taka was a taskmaster. But in contrast to my experience with Malfoy on the foil team, Taka *expected me to get it right*. I had moved from a culture of failure to one of success.

The one thing I couldn't imitate was Taka's yell, the "Apppaaaa-YA!" he screamed after landing a touch. I'd tasted that scream briefly in the locker room on the day of my beating on the Riverdale track, and I wanted to taste it again. But, for now, the closest I could get was channeling Taka Sudo's movements on the strip.

I started to feel safe in the fencing room. My mom picked me up so I could stay a couple minutes later than the kids who had to catch the sports bus, and in the time after practice when I used to flail at Ying and goof off, Taka had me running through parries over and over until the motions became second nature.

As I found confidence on the fencing strip, my grades started to improve. By the end of seventh grade, Cs became C-plusses and Bs, mostly due to the academic equivalent of being the last to leave fencing practice or throwing myself in front of bruising groundballs. By the beginning of eighth grade, I even started to learn some of the intricacies of the game of school. For example, I learned that I didn't have to lug my entire library of books home every night—just the ones in which I actually had homework. I learned the process—if not the love—of memorization. It seems silly now, but I also remember becoming aware that certain topics or facts were more likely than others to be included on a test, like maybe I should spend a bit more time on Lincoln than on the obscure names of his generals.

And just like the expectations of Coach Schneider and Taka made me want to fence and believe that I could pull it off, in eighth grade I finally had a teacher who made me feel like I could learn. Mr. Caldwell actually expected me to do well. It was a U.S. history class, and I remember getting our first big test back. As Mr. Caldwell handed them back to the class, I saw my grade flash in the top corner: a B-plus! I ended up with a B in the class, but more than that, I gained the feeling that maybe I could succeed at my new, rich, intimidating, overwhelming school. Around this time, I remember seeing a story about fencing on the TV news one night. The piece was about an Olympic fencer, Peter Westbrook, who had recently started a fencing foundation in Manhattan with the mission of helping inner-city kids succeed socially and academically through the discipline gained by fencing.

Westbrook is an American fencing legend. He started fencing in Newark in the 1960s when his mother bribed him with $5 to try the sport, imagining that fencing would keep him out of trouble. Westbrook would go on to qualify for six Olympic teams. The son of a Japanese-American mother and African-American father, he had long been one of the only fencers of color in a sport known for its upper-class, mostly European participants.

The Westbrook Foundation held free Saturday clinics.

That week I talked my mom into driving me to the Fencers Club on 71st Street, between Broadway and Amsterdam in Manhattan, which donated space on Saturdays to the Westbrook Foundation.

When we showed up that day, I spent a couple minutes watching through the ground-floor window. Three strips lay on the worn wood floor, separated by pillars with chipping paint and surrounded by dirty white walls. Fencers in whites worked the strips—it was the first time I'd seen adults fence, and it made it seem even more like a serious endeavor than a game.

As other kids arrived, I went inside.

Long fencing bags that looked like golf club cases were piled next to a ratty green couch in the foyer, and everything smelled like sweat. This wasn't the Wonderland of Riverdale's fencing room—it was something more adult, more visceral, and maybe more dangerous. I climbed the stairs to the locker room, changed, and stashed my clothes in a broken, battered locker. Next to the locker room was another fencing gym, with rubber strips and a ceiling low enough that tall fencers sometimes scraped it with their overhead attacks.

Stepping into the New York Fencers Club was to step into one of the city's oldest and most successful traditions. Fencing first landed in the States in New Orleans with the French in the 1700s, but it was the melting pot of New York City where it stuck. In 1893, after learning to fence in military school and then graduating from Yale, blue-blooded New Yorker Charles DeKay founded the Fencers Club at 426 Sixth Avenue at 9th Street. DeKay was a literary critic for the *New York Times*, a poet, and sometimes a diplomat, who also founded the National Arts Society, the Author's Club, the National Sculpture Society, and the National Arts Club, most of which are active today.

In thirty years, the club moved eight times before erecting its own ten-story building at 320 East 53rd Street between 1st and 2nd Avenues. The ground-floor fencing room was paneled in oak, with a gallery of weapons hung around the walls. The second story was locker rooms, showers, and living quarters for the resident fencing master. The rest of the building, the club leased out as apartments.

Rather than reporting scores, the *New York Times* reporter assigned to the fencing beat (yes, there was a reporter dedicated to fencing) reported on matches as if they were society events, focusing on who was in attendance. Frequently, the names included Vanderbilts and Astors.

In 1894, the *Sunday World Newspaper* ran the headline "Society Women Who Fence," writing, "Any woman who poses as being ultra-fashionable this winter must go in for fencing." To join Fencers Club, the board had to vote you in. On the floor, members were only allowed to speak French, fencing's official language. National Championships were held onstage at the Waldorf Astoria. Around the country, thousands packed opera houses to gamble on professional fencers who dueled to first blood.

Fencing's popularity came tumbling down along with Wall Street in October 1929, and to save itself, Fencers Club was forced to sell the building. Its demise was effectively complete when General Broadcasting Systems started regular television service in New York City on April 26, 1931. With its invisible blades and even more invisible touches, fencing wasn't telegenic.

Who knows what the state of fencing in the United States might be today if Fencers Club could have held the building, or if the sport, like football, had found ways to play to the camera.

In any case, the club had struggled along since the 1930s, falling into obscurity and disrepair but continuing to produce at least one Olympian in every Games. On the club walls, alongside pictures of these Olympians were black-and-white photos of women fencing in dresses. Women's foil had been added to the Olympics in 1924, but it wasn't until 1996 that women were allowed to fence épée—the dueling weapon. When I was in seventh grade, there weren't any women's high school saber teams, let alone a women's saber event in the Olympics. Culture changes slowly in fencing, and many of its rules and assumptions are still based on a very nineteenth-century European conception of honor and ethics, including gender roles. Basically, until women's saber was added to the Games in 2004, the fencing world thought that women were too demure for the aggressive and sharp-edged weapon. It's ironic that, later, it was the women's foil and saber teams, not the men's, who would lead the United States' charge back into the international consciousness of fencing.

That day as a seventh grader, I lined up in the Fencers Club along with about thirty other (mostly African-American) kids and went through the basics of warm-up and footwork. Just as Coach Schneider would have at Riverdale, Peter Westbrook pulled kids aside, having them fake to his head and cut to his side—a move known as a feint cut, and something that, for whatever reason, I've always struggled with.

In my fantasy world, I had grown up skating alongside Dan Jansen and fielding with Don Mattingly, but this was the first time I had ever stood in the room with one of these heroes—an Olympian! Being in the room with Peter Westbrook, listening to the running commentary of his colorful stories, and doing a simple drill with him humanized the idea of being a top fencer. Westbrook expected his foundation to train the next generation of U.S. Olympic fencers, and there we were.

Though I only attended a few of the Saturday clinics, with Westbrook, Coach Schneider, Taka Sudo, and Mr. Caldwell, I suddenly found myself surrounded by the new expectations of a new norm—that I would succeed in school and in the fencing room—and these expectations started seeping into my own beliefs about myself.

Every day during the Riverdale fencing season, a little mind worm started whispering in my ear as I walked past Coach Schneider's bulletin board showing the achievements of past fencers, and I realized that *I* wanted to be on the board, too. Finally, imitating Taka, I worked up the courage to admit to Coach Schneider that when I was a senior in high school, I wanted to win the Mamaroneck Invitational—our league's most prestigious competition. At the time, the skills to win Mamaroneck were light years ahead of me. Still, rather than treating it as a surprising and comical revelation, Coach Schneider assumed that *of course* Mamaroneck had been my goal from the start. Aiming high was simply the norm.

Through most of eighth grade, Malfoy and I had passed like ships in the night. I avoided him and, now that I wasn't his problem, he was generally content to keep a disdainful eye on me from afar. Then one day near the end of my eighth-grade season, his senior year, he walked over to the saber group and challenged me to fence. He was a senior—a foil captain!—and he towered over me. When he said I was nothing and that he would beat me at my own weapon, all the confidence I had built in the last year slunk away like a kicked dog. I got ready to make some sort of excuse. But before I could run away, Taka told me to fence him. The way he said it made the intention clear: Taka expected me not just to take my beating with honor—he expected me to win. And even more than that, he expected *me* to expect to win.

Whatever the case, there was no slinking away now.

After practice, the saber, épée and foil kids all gathered around. Taka would referee. Suddenly it wasn't practice—it was an eighteenth-century duel for honor. We were fighting for blood. Coach Schneider couldn't have been unaware that one of his captains had decided to slaughter an eighth grader in front of a crowd at the end of practice, but in my memory he was absent. Looking back, I imagine he knew perfectly well what was going on and what the outcome would be.

Taka started the match and Malfoy danced around me, holding a saber but moving with foil technique, which now looked totally unfamiliar to me. I was paralyzed. Adopting the aplomb of saber, Malfoy slashed me hard across the stomach. Padding or no padding, it hurt like hell. I had a mark just like last year on the track. "See!" laughed Malfoy. I looked over at Taka—he wasn't laughing.

Taka started the second point and I stayed frozen—that boy on the track taking a silent beating. Malfoy danced left and right, knocking my blade back and forth before lunging as I back-pedaled, completely off balance. Smack! I was down 0-2 with a second welt across my forearm to show for it.

Taka asked for a moment, the picture of calm. *Holy hell*, he still expected me to win! He grabbed me by the shoulders and put his face up to my mesh. "Fight!" he said. "When your mask is off you can be whatever you want to be, but in the mask, *you're a warrior!*"

I nodded.

"Ready, fence!" said Taka.

I have stepped outside my body to look down on my fencing from above only a couple times in my career, and it means one of two things: either I'm freaking out, totally panic-frozen and transfixed, unable to get back into the moment on the strip and hoping my opponent will offer a quick, merciful end; or it's the opposite—I've surrendered control to my body and my training; I'm completely *in* the moment, so much so that my mind can kick back and watch from the rafters.

The first time this happened was on the Riverdale strip that day with Malfoy—Taka and the rest of the team watching. Right then, I lost myself and looked down from above.

And when I lost myself, I lost my insecurities, my doubts, my years of shuffling through life with my head down, mumbling through classes while my classmates and even my teachers expected me to fail. Taka expected me to win. Westbrook expected his foundation kids to be Olympians. Coach Schneider expected I would win the Mamaroneck. Mr. Caldwell expected me to know the answers.

When Taka said fence, I charged. It might not have been the prettiest display of footwork and technique, but I landed a belly cut across Malfoy's chest that, with a sharper sword and a little less padding, would have spilled him right there on the floor. And when I connected, I yelled Taka's, "Appaaaa-yaaaa!" I'm not sure anyone in the room noticed, but I did: it was the first time I yelled.

Malfoy was pissed now, too. The score: 1-2.

He charged the next point, but an onrushing opponent was something you see every match in saber. Not so in controlled, precise foil, and coming full bore, Malfoy had little in the way of attack other than a full lunge. I raised my saber to parry away his lunge and then landed a riposte to his head, unleashing an even louder scream. Who *was* I in that moment? I didn't know him, but I think I liked him. The saber kids were laughing and I realized that it wasn't at me.

The next point, Malfoy landed past my parry, 2-3. Then we battled to 4-4. Malfoy took off his mask to wipe his face and I could see he was sweating, worried—he wasn't used to this style, this pace, this new person he faced across the strip. For the first time in my fencing life, I tapped directly into my opponent's feelings—as if we briefly shared a mind and, because of it, I knew his weakness. One more point. One last point to five, with the winner of this touch leaving as a whole person and the loser leaving some piece of himself on the strip.

"Ready, fence!" Taka said. I charged forward and Malfoy lunged to take me as I stumbled onto his blade. But I had set a trap, stopping short as Malfoy's saber fell short and swept through the air, leaving him completely unguarded. I lunged and hit.

"Apyaaaaaa!" I screamed, twirling and ripping off my mask.

I don't remember Malfoy's reaction, or really anything about him after that point. He walked out of the fencing room and slipped from the story of my memory. I had new expectations of myself, and they didn't include him.

Inside and Outside
the Mask

Before the start of ninth grade, my friend Ying transferred to Stuyvesant High School on the Hudson River, just below the Holland Tunnel in Manhattan. Then, during freshman baseball tryouts, after almost a full year of fencing and no throwing, I tried to gun the ball to first and something in my elbow popped. I made the junior varsity team, but I could tell I'd lost a lot of throwing power. Maybe it was the injury or maybe it was the fear that throwing hard would do more damage, but whatever the reason, I stopped being able to throw straight. It's hard to watch a dream go by the wayside, but that's what happened to my Yankee aspirations my freshman year at Riverdale Country School.

I quickly replaced it with another dream.

I continued showing up early to fencing practice to get a few extra minutes of private instruction with Coach Schneider, and I started staying late to fence bouts with whoever was still floating around the room. Thursdays were alumni nights, and after high school practice, Coach Schneider would run a practice for whichever alums were in the area. Some alumni brought their kids, as much for initiation into the emotional centering of Coach Schneider as for the fencing skills, it seemed. I started staying and joined Coach Schneider and the alums for hot dogs afterward. From the start, it seemed that I didn't have the talent and natural fencing athleticism that other kids had—I wasn't inherently fluid or quick or precise—and I tried to make up for this by working as hard as possible.

But my fencing dream wasn't necessarily a cool one according to the unwritten (but very real) rules of Riverdale Country School. In middle school, getting out of gym was a socially acceptable excuse to be on the fencing team; in high school, now with the option of other sports, the get-out-of-jail-free excuse dissipated and people knew you were on the fencing team because you *wanted* to be. Wearing a football jersey to class was awesome. When, one Halloween, a teammate wore his fencing outfit as a costume, I remember students snickering, and even I thought it looked out of place outside the Wonderland of the fencing room.

One year ahead of me at Riverdale was a student named Cliff Bayer. I knew him only in passing, and he slid fairly unknown through the high school halls. The year after he graduated, I read a New York Times profile of him as a foil fencer on the 1996 Atlanta Olympic team. Cliff had fenced in clubs rather than on the high school team and had kept his fencing to himself. Apparently even being an *Olympic* fencer at Riverdale didn't make you cool.

In short, we were a team of misfits, more likely to supplement fencing with chess club than with another off-season sport. On our team, one student was a Westinghouse Science Talent Search finalist and another was a classical pianist. One fencer's parents were both brain surgeons and another baker's dozen were scholarship students who, like me, found a safe haven at Riverdale in the fencing room with Coach Schneider. Did you know Facebook founder Mark Zuckerberg was a fencer? So was eBay founder Jeffrey Skoll. I bet they weren't cool either. We were Riverdale's second-largest team behind football, but no one knew about us. In the fencing room, we trained and fought and yelled. In the classrooms, lunchroom, and halls, we were invisible.

What was this new thing I now loved to do?

In step with my uncoolness, my last name morphed into the nickname *Whorehouse*, which I'm sure is as funny now as it was then. "Hey Whorehouse!" kids would shout, and like taking my beating silently that day in seventh grade on the track, the sad thing is that I answered to it. In fact, I didn't even think kids were being mean, I just felt like they were noticing something wrong with me that I hadn't quite figured out yet. I was tall but I felt small, like Chief Bromden in *One Flew Over the Cuckoo's Nest*, and I walked around the school with my head down, always feeling like I was wearing the wrong thing, saying the wrong thing, but unsure of what the *right* things were. The only place I felt confident was inside the fencing room, inside the mask, and so I threw myself more and more into the sport. Both the name and the mask were artificial veneers and I wasn't yet sure what they covered.

So on winter Saturdays, when the Riverdale football team donned their shiny maroon helmets and played in front of half the student body, we boarded buses early in the morning for tournaments where a smattering of moms cheered from the bleachers. In a high school tournament, a team's top three fencers in each weapon—saber, foil, and épée—fence 5-touch matches against each of the other team's top three fencers. So there are 27 total matches, and the team competition is a race to 14.

Freshman year, I was our third varsity fencer, behind Taka, who was a senior, and another teammate. I remember my first varsity meet, held in the basketball gym of Mamaroneck High School—

the home of the tournament I had made it my goal to someday win. I jumped off the bus vibrating with nerves. We carried our equipment into the gym, helped tape down and equip a fencing strip, or piste, on the wooden floor, and eyed the other three or four teams warming up. To fence at national competitions, you're required to have your name across the back of your fencing jacket, so we looked between competitor's shoulder blades to gauge how worried we should be. Most high school fencers at the time wore general tennis shoes, so we looked for the opponents with fencing-specific footwear, or at the shine of their weapons. On our team, only Taka and a talented foil fencer named David Liu had their names on their jackets.

Like Coach Schneider, some of the other coaches had been around for twenty years or more, and over that time rivalries developed as much between coaches as they did between schools. We felt like it was our duty to win for Coach Schneider, especially since that day at Mamaroneck an opposing coach conspicuously left his scouting notes near our bench. Next to our second fencer's name was the note, "Stupid. If he falls for something once, he'll fall for it over and over again." The scouting report for our third saber fencer read, "Morehouse is clumsy. Move him around the strip and he'll fall apart."

Maybe leaving the notes where we could read them was an accident—but I doubt it. Before the match, we huddled with Coach Schneider. He pulled us closer, looking at everyone's faces, and said, "Move your feet. Use your *brains!*" On the count of three we yelled *Riverdale!* Then Taka—our A-strip saber fencer—walked to the reel at the back of the piste and plugged a wire into the body cord attached to the back of his jacket. With no barricades, the rest of the team edged closer and closer to the strip until we stood almost shoulder-to-shoulder with the referee.

Taka met his opponent in the middle of the strip to test their equipment. Taka touched his saber to his opponent's jacket, getting a loud buzz and a green light from the scoring machine that sat just off the strip at its center. Taka's opponent did likewise, turning on the red scoring lamp. In addition to red and green, the fencing machine had two white lights, which, along with a buzzer, went on if either scoring wire came unclipped or there was another malfunction. The buzzer stayed on until someone mercifully turned it off or until the problem was fixed. We put a man on the moon in 1969, but in 1992, when saber had just "gone electric," it was typical for a saber match with two minutes of fencing to take twenty minutes due to technical delays, during which various coaches and referees checked and changed wires, pushed buttons, and intermittently shook and swore at the $2500 fencing machine. It was a simple circuit, completed when a metal saber touched the metal fibers woven into an opponent's scoring zones, but *c'est la vie*: metal saber to metal jacket was apparently more difficult than rocket science.

Interestingly, this fencing machine single-handedly retired many of the older fencers who'd been surviving on reputation. Who scored the point? Well, certainly it was the fencer with the better reputation and the loudest victory yell (who happened to be friends with the referee)! In fact, in fencing's pre-electric or "dry" history, these subjective touches were beholden to referees' whimsy to the point that a fencer's street cred could be as important as his performance on the strip any given day.

For example, in his thorough history of fencing, *By the Sword*, Richard Cohen tells the story of Csaba Pallaghy, an up-and-coming Hungarian fencer trying to qualify for the 1956 Melbourne Olympics. In the Hungarian national championships, Pallaghy, in his mid-twenties, reached the semifinals, needing only to beat one veteran fencer to qualify for the Games. They fenced to 3-3 in a match to 5, and then twice Pallaghy hit his opponent in the head as his opponent parried late. Twice the referee gave the point and thus the match to his opponent.

Any American fencer, especially in the pre-electric era, knows how Pallaghy felt.

That day in the Mamaroneck gym, with Taka now plugged in, the referee said, "Ready? Fence!" and Taka quickly dismantled his opponent, 5-2, with form, speed, and grace.

Then it was my turn to plug in. Taka patted me on my back as I walked onto the piste, and whispered, "You can do this!" I fumbled nervously to clip the scoring wire to the back of my jacket, and then, like cowboys in *Tombstone*, took my en garde line where I faced my opponent across the strip. We saluted with our sabers and I brought down my mask, closing out the insecurities of Whorehouse. Here, completely still in the en garde position, I waited for the referee to give the signal.

As a freshman at Riverdale, I had exactly two moves. When the referee said, "Ready, fence!" I charged off the line like a bull and lunged at my opponent. That was my first move. Unfortunately, high school fencers in their team's third position *tend* to only have two moves, and my opponent had the same idea. We met in the middle of the strip—a mess of untrained arms, incidentally smashing blades and guards as we tried to catch each others' scoring zones. It was like middle-schoolers kissing with braces. Sadly, this isn't uncommon in high school fencing, and when it happens, usually both beginning fencers scream in victory and both coaches yell *Nice point!*, trying to sell the touch for their fencer. Then everyone looks at the referee—usually an underpaid college student—to sort it all out.

That's how it went for our first 6 points: "Ready, fence!" and we'd charge forward, sabers crashing, people cheering, lights going on or not—and suddenly it was 3-3 in a race to 5 points.

This is how I had won junior varsity matches the year before:

I beat my opponents with a blind charge that left them the deer in the proverbial headlights. But not so with varsity, apparently.

The coaches called time out simultaneously and as Coach Schneider walked over to me, I raised my mask. "Listen, you're doing GREAT," he said. "But you've got to SLOW DOWN." This was a habit of his—speaking a couple words in all-caps so that even in the midst of a charged match, we had at least a chance of internalizing his bullet points.

And so I unleashed my second move. The referee said, "Ready, fence!" and I again charged like a bull off the en garde line—only before lunging, I stopped. My opponent, who had started his own lunge to meet me in the middle, swept through open air, and as he did, I flicked my saber upwards to parry away his attack and then riposted to his body. Without the car crash of blades and guards, my opponent nearly fell onto my saber point in the vacuum between us. "Apaaaa Yeah!" I screamed. It was 4-3. I did it again to win my first varsity match, earning a "Great job! Now do it again!" from Coach Schneider.

I won two of three that day and we beat Mamaroneck 15-12. Victory: it seemed like the top of the world! I don't remember how we did against the tournament's other two teams, but I remember the drive home on the bus, feeling happy, and in a way, powerful. I also remember that when my parents picked me up, Coach Schneider told them I had helped the team. My father beamed, saying, "The more Tim fences, the better he does in school!" My mom smiled right along with him.

At school the following Monday, I was Whorehouse again, ducking through the halls.

When we didn't have school competitions, I started going to competitions at the Fencers Club and the New York Athletic Club—the two most dominant clubs in the country. A mostly cordial rivalry had developed between the two clubs. Vassil Etropolski, a Bulgarian former world champion, coached for NYAC, and Ukrainian Yury Gelman coached the Fencers Club saber team along with the top students from the Westbrook Foundation. The NYAC fencers were mostly white and affluent. Like the Yankees buying talent, the club was known to offer top fencers money to fence there. The Fencers Club was similarly well heeled. Then there were the Westbrook students, who tended to be socioeconomically challenged. I must have seemed like the stereotypical white fencer from a prestigious private school, but maybe because of Washington Heights and Central Park East, I felt more at home with the Westbrook/Gelman/Fencers Club crew. Once when I finished a match and took off my mask, I heard a surprised, "You're white!" from a spectator, who had apparently failed to notice my white back hand showing and associated my last name with the traditionally black Morehouse College.

Incidentally, I knew Westbrook fencer Akhi Spencer-El from Central Park East. He was a year behind me but big and strong. At Central Park East he'd been wild, a constant fighter, and the type of kid you didn't want to cross. But when I re-met him as a freshman, he was completely transformed—he walked up and shook my hand, said a soft-spoken hello, and made me feel welcome at the weekend club comps where he was a regular and I was nearly new.

I also remember meeting siblings Keeth and Erinn Smart who were at Westbrook, too. Erinn fenced foil and Keeth was in saber. While I was battling to win high school matches, Keeth, Erinn, Akhi, and a handful of other high schoolers at the NYAC, Fencers Club, and the Westbrook Foundation were already turning heads on the national level. Compared to these club fencers who were taking private lessons from Eastern European coaches and being told they were the next crop of Olympians, my two moves looked like amateur hour. You see, a charging bull can't see. And like a bull that goes blindly for the cape, when I charged, opponents like Keeth and Akhi simply pulled themselves out of the way and hit me on riposte. When I faked my charging bull and then pulled up short, they weren't fooled and calmly stepped around my flailing blade into the space I left open to hit me.

And these club fencers had an athleticism you didn't see on the high school circuit, where fencers tended to be the students who couldn't make the basketball, baseball, or football teams. At these club tournaments, I remember Keeth coming at me with blazing speed, running down the strip, flying and intense. I remember people whispering about Akhi being the next star—Peter Westbrook had claimed Akhi as his protégé, saying, "This kid is just like me—he can move, he can parry!" Peter always loved people who, like him, could parry.

While I had been mimicking Taka at Riverdale, Keeth and Akhi had been fighting college fencers, Olympians, and immigrants from elite fencing countries every evening at the Fencers Club. I was looking forward to three more years of high school, hopefully punctuated by a win at the Mamaroneck Invitational, and maybe college fencing. Keeth and Akhi were already looking ahead to the 2000 Olympic Games.

At one of these weekend competitions, the Fencers Club coach, Yury Gelman, passed me a business card and asked in his thick Ukrainian accent if I would like to study with him. He said in a very matter-of-fact way that I needed a lot of work, but that he could help me. As a freshman I never followed up with him, not ready to trade Coach Schneider and my burgeoning confidence in the safety of the Riverdale fencing room for a new start at the lowest rung on the ladder of club fencing. My commitment to high school fencing ensured I remained an outsider at the club comps, but Keeth, Akhi, the other Westbrook fencers, and the fencers from the NYAC always ensured I felt welcome, as if I had a toe in that other world of fencers who were aiming straight at the top ranks of international competition.

Due in large part to this toehold, by the time I was a sophomore I was starting to win more than I lost at the high school level, adding some mild subtlety to my "charging bull" and "faux charging bull" moves.

After my freshman year, the Riverdale fencing team graduated a strong crop of seniors, and so as a sophomore I was suddenly one of the experienced saber kids, now setting the culture as opposed to surfing it. My mentor, Taka, graduated and went to Yale, and his younger brother, Mitsu, started Riverdale a year behind me. While Mitsu was new to fencing as a freshman, he had already spent a handful of years practicing the Japanese sword-fighting art of kendo, and quickly proved to be the saber team's rising star. Unlike me, he was a natural—fast, quick, and confident—and my hours and hours of hard work barely outweighed his natural ability to the point that a couple months into the season, we fought tight bouts at the end of practice.

My junior year I was elected captain over a handful of seniors, but outside the fencing room I was still Whorehouse. Two personalities: one created by a mask and one created by a nickname.

And by my junior year, now with fencing shoes and my name on my jacket after competing at the regional Junior Olympic qualifiers (I didn't make nationals), I was confident enough on the strip to join our foil captain, David Liu, in a bagel competition. He and I were frequently winning 5-0—"bagelling" opponents. So at tournaments that year, whoever blanked the fewest opponents had to buy the winner fresh bagels the following Monday. It was silly, but it marked a confidence I had only on the fencing strip.

Because there weren't enough high school fencing teams in the area, we augmented our schedule by fencing college JV teams, including those from Yale, West Point, and Columbia. These informal high-school-versus-college comps allowed college coaches to get a sneak peek at promising high school fencers and we were happy to put our skills on display. (With a crackdown on NCAA recruiting rules, these get-togethers are now a thing of the past.) College coaches loved what they saw in Mitsu and in David: athletic fencers grounded in basic techniques that provided a foundation on which college coaches could build.

In contrast, I wasn't even on college coaches' radar. The comment from the "misplaced" scouting report from my first varsity match had proven prophetic, and my technique remained ungainly, depending as much on aggression and resolve as on skill to overcome my opponents. These attributes worked in high school tournaments, but college coaches didn't see them carrying me through the next level. The UPenn coach put David Liu on his recruitment list and not me. Henry Harutunian, the coach at Yale, was in love with Mitsu's fencing and wanted him to join his brother, Taka, at the school. I was the third-best fencer on a high school team and the recruitment talk didn't extend to me. And even with talk aside, Mitsu and David had something I always thought I didn't: raw talent.

Without interest from college coaches, I started to wonder if maybe I was a good high school fencer without a future in college. I questioned whether my commitment to fencing was born of my love of the sport or of my love for Coach Schneider, and without him at the next level, did I even want to continue fencing? The fall training season of my senior year came and went, and then it was time—the Mamaroneck Invitational—my goal since I'd first held a saber and my last chance to impress college coaches.

Like most high school tournaments, the Mamaroneck Invitational was held on a Saturday morning in a basketball gym converted for the day, though there was one important difference: this was not a team tournament. We would fence for ourselves and ourselves only. Twelve or so rubber strips were laid down on the wood floor, and there were another couple strips taped down in a long hallway outside the gym. The bleachers were pulled out and soon strewn with the fencing bags and warm-up clothes of the 100 or so fencers who came to compete from our cluster of schools, including Hopkins, Concord-Carlisle, Bishop Feehan, Guilford, Cheshire, North Haven, and St. John's Prep.

We started by splitting into pools of 6 and fencing round-robin style. Then the two fencers with the worst pool records were cut and the remaining fencers formed new pools. The cutting and reforming continued until only a final six-person pool remained.

In the small pond of our conference's high school saber fencers, either Mitsu or I was expected to win, and so we were seeded high and set to meet only if we both made the final round of 6. When I wasn't fencing, I rooted for Mitsu as he blew through his opening-pool matches—his perfect technique and great speed tearing through his first five opponents—then the second pool, and then the third pool, without losing a match. He rooted for me as I did the same.

At Mamaroneck, Whorehouse was nowhere to be seen—I was Tim-inside-the-mask, and this Tim took no prisoners. I attacked, I defended myself, and when I scored points I screamed. My technique wasn't always as pretty as Mitsu's, but my aggression carried me through 5-touch matches, which ended before opponents could see through my fury to the holes in my technique.

If teammates met in a pool, they fenced each other first to keep fencers from throwing matches later in the competition when it was clearer what wins and losses would mean. So Mitsu and I faced each other in the first match of the six-person finals. While we would go on to fence the remaining four fencers in the final pool, most people thought the tournament would be decided right there.

I'm not sure what Mamaroneck meant to Mitsu at that point. There was a big trophy with the names of the twenty five or so past winners, but few of the listed fencers went on to do much on the national stage. At the end of the day, when the masks came off, it was just a high school tournament—the first one of the year—and despite its history, it was probably about as nationally important as a weekend get-together at the Fencers Club. Mitsu was already a near lock at Yale. But for me, Mamaroneck was both the crowning achievement of my high school career and the only doorway that I saw leading to fencing at the next level. For me, it was everything.

When teammates fence, the coach stands aside. And without Coach Schneider's belief, in that first match of the final pool against Mitsu, my confidence evaporated. My self-talk turned to Whorehouse's running commentary of *I'm not good enough*, and Mitsu beat me 5-3.

It's amazing how light your body can feel when you're fencing. When things are going right, your legs, your arms, and your torso become a vehicle for the edge of your blade, and it feels like your whole body dips and dives like a swallow with that edge. But it's amazing how heavy that same body can feel with its energy removed. After losing to Mitsu at Mamaroneck, it was as if someone had poured sand into my whites, or injected it straight into my veins, where it pooled in my low parts and dragged me down.

I sat in the bleachers and watched the fencers I'd beaten in earlier rounds, who suddenly looked strong, fast, and fierce. For me, the tournament was over and I still had 4 more matches. Looking around the stands, I realized that the match hadn't even mattered in the first place—one and only one college coach had come to watch me fence. Coach Bill Shipman from Brandeis had made the three-hour drive from Waltham, Ma. I was sorry to disappoint.

I remember Coach Schneider telling me to keep fencing, to

stay in the moment of each match, and play out the tournament with honor.

But Mitsu had unmasked me and it was Whorehouse who stood reluctantly on the strip facing my second fencer of the finals. I was ready to meet his incoming blade with halfhearted retreat, to strip my whites and head home, to continue ducking my head through the rest of my senior year, into a non-fencing college, and maybe straight through life. I was ready for defeat, ready to be Whorehouse.

I lost the first point, sand weighing me down.

There was nothing to win, nothing to lose. No bright lights or big expectations. No cadre of college coaches giving me one last shot. No chance for my name on the trophy or achieving the goal I'd set in seventh grade.

But in that short space between points, I started thinking about that seventh grader—the one who took a silent beating on the track, mumbled in class, and then obliterated the pain of incomprehensible homework with video games—and internalized others' opinion of my hopelessness, my worthlessness. I thought about Whorehouse. But there was another kid in me—the one who had screamed that day in the locker room, the one who had strong SAT scores and who was a captain of the fencing team. Which one was I?

I realized there was nothing to win or lose but myself.

I don't remember the four fencers who joined Mitsu and me in the finals at Mamaroneck. But I ripped through them all. I imagined my opponents as the teachers who'd written me off, as the kids who assumed I would answer to *Whorehouse*. Did I lose a couple touches? Probably. But I don't remember them. I went 4-and-1 in the final pool and ended Mamaroneck as *Morehouse*.

Mitsu went to 4-and-0, and I watched him in his final match— the younger brother of my mentor, Taka, bound for the Yale fencing team. To my high school eyes he was masterful, gliding the strip and nipping points with the precision of a modeler building a boat in a bottle.

But fencing is a fickle sport, with the edge in skill and speed giving the favorite maybe a seventy-five percent chance of taking any given point from a slightly weaker opponent. And with high school matches being a race to only 5 points, it doesn't take too much luck to gift a couple touches to the underdog.

That's exactly what happened in Mitsu's final match at Mamaroneck. Somehow, despite his previous dominance and the obvious fact of being the better fencer, he lost 5-3, giving us each one loss in the final pool. He and I would fence a sudden-death playoff to decide the champion.

Mitsu had beaten me within the hour, and let's admit it—he was the better fencer at that point. But things had changed. He carried the sand born of an unexpected loss, and I had the energy independent of a magic mask. For the first time, I fenced as myself and felt my own confidence, and I blew through Mitsu 5-0 to take the Mamaroneck!

This was my Olympics, albeit in a high school gym with a plaque that probably cost $5. Standing there in the moment, I imagined it was the high point of my career. More than that, standing there with my ribbon and medal, I tasted a self-confidence that I didn't want to let go.

That Monday at Riverdale, I started asking people to stop calling me Whorehouse. Many didn't realize I found it insulting, and unfortunately, as is the way of things, the ones who did were the ones who continued. But I started seeing that there were actually a lot more outsiders than insiders at the school. It always sounded like the whole room was laughing at me, but I realized it was just a handful.

A month later at a school assembly, a few members of the

football team got up during announcements and ripped our grade about not having school spirit because students weren't coming to their Saturday football games. When other teams took the podium to ask students for their attendance, the football players goofed off. Encouraged by one of my friends, I wrote an editorial for the student newspaper that I titled "Arrogance Personified," which included gems like, "no one really cares what a bunch of jerks do on their Saturday afternoons." Okay, maybe going from Whorehouse to immediately taking on the whole football team was going a bit overboard, but I was just learning that I could fight back without a mask.

The reaction was interesting. Not only did the football team graciously refrain from kicking my ass, but people I'd never talked to before stopped me in the hall to thank me. By the end of my senior year, I had all but stopped people from calling me Whorehouse. Then, in our caps and gowns at graduation, with Riverdale alum and then Philadelphia Mayor Ed Rendell waiting in the wings to address our class, a kid called me Whorehouse as we waited in line to get our diplomas. My reaction was immediate—like my fencer-self parrying and riposting—and I shoved him to the ground. He looked at me a bit stunned. "What's your problem, Tim?" he said, as if he had no idea.

I'm not especially proud of my ham-handed and disproportionate response, but it was the end of Whorehouse and a step toward healing the divide between my selves—inside the mask and out. I didn't quite know how to live in this new skin, but at least I would go to college as Morehouse.

Proving Myself,
Losing Myself

By the second semester of my senior year at Riverdale, I had two choices for college fencing: Penn State, where I could try to walk onto a national-caliber fencing team, or Brandeis, whose coach Bill Shipman was the only college coach to recruit me—the one coach who had sat in the stands to see me fence at Mamaroneck. When I visited Brandeis on a recruiting trip, I was encouraged to see a fencer named Elliott Clinton. He had grown up fencing in Rochester, moved to Portland, Oregon to train with a top coach (a Polish immigrant named Ed Korfanty), and had just won a junior-level national competition. If small, Division-III Brandeis was good enough for Elliott, I figured it was good enough for me.

As it turned out, I'd made a mistake—it was Elliott's twin brother, Colin, and not actually Elliott on the Brandeis team, but I didn't know it at the time. But more than (mistakenly) being encouraged by the presence of strong peers, I was encouraged by Coach Shipman. Unlike every other college coach I had approached, it seemed as if Coach Shipman shared Coach Schneider's rare faith in my potential. Shipman wasn't much of a talker, but in his southern drawl and with many-seconds-long gaps in our conversations, we talked at length about what my time at Brandeis would look like. When I was faced with the decision to stick to high school vs. club fencing, I opted to stay a big fish in a small pond. I would have to make a similar call in choosing a school—start fencing right away as one of the top three at Brandeis, or fight my way onto Penn State's bench and hope to eventually make it into competitions.

After spending the summer working as a camp counselor, I started Brandeis in the fall. Arriving at Brandeis was almost exactly what I'd imagined from every college movie I'd ever seen: orientation week parties in the basements of dumpy frat houses, pick up basketball with guys from my floor, my closet-sized dorm room decorated with Yankees posters, my classes about 100 yards away from my dorm so I could be in class with a bagel and a banana in hand ten minutes after rolling out of bed. The school itself was only about fifty years old. Albert Einstein had been a founder, and it was meant to be a nonsectarian, Jewish Harvard, just down the street from Boston College and twenty-five minutes from Boston proper. The buildings had housed a veterinary school—a castle on a hill—and the visitor's center still held onto its castle-themed kitsch. Unlike Riverdale, I had no problems making friends at Brandeis. Everyone seemed so nice! And though I'd been horribly worried about the academics, if anything I thought the classes were easier than what I was used to from Riverdale. It looked as if I'd left my insecurities behind.

NCAA rules limit the length of sports seasons, so the start of fencing practice was pushed six weeks into the semester and then, rather than being directed by Coach Shipman, they were "captain's practices" led by foil fencer and team captain Alex Banks. Alex was the quintessential geek—a physical chemistry major doubling up his class load to earn a B.S. and a Masters in four years. To compound matters, Alex wore glasses and was neither tall nor fast. I was a cocky freshman straight from captaining a strong prep team and winning the Mamaroneck Invitational. Thus, I assumed I'd soon be running the show.

A couple weeks later, Coach Shipman's practice replaced the light jogging and ultimate Frisbee games of captain's practice and we started to get ready for the season, meeting in the impeccable basement training facility in the newly built Gosman Center from 4:00-6:00pm five days a week. At the time, the Celtics used the gym as a practice facility, and every once in a while I'd luck into a pickup game with guys from the team—not that I was anything more than a 6'2" speed bump for David Wesley and Rick Fox. The fencing room had a dance studio's wall-length set of mirrors opposite windows that looked into the hallway and over squash rooms below. The walls were Brandeis' light blue, one painted with a wall-length school name shot through with a sword.

It felt modern and light, like a place where winners were born, and I jumped headlong into proving I was the best fencer in the room. At practice, I fenced to win and often I did, frequently beating down the saber upperclassmen. One senior—last year's number-one guy—freaked out when he saw he couldn't beat me and started avoiding practice. But that's fencing. It's not a sport about holding back, right?

I didn't know it at the time, but I was going overboard. Instead of leaving Whorehouse behind and correcting to the centerline, I'd overcorrected and brought with me to college the persona that had published the "Arrogance Personified" article in the Riverdale school newspaper and pushed a kid during graduation. Without the cowed mutt persona that kept me in check, who was I? As a freshman, I was a jerk.

In gaps between classes, fencers scheduled individual lessons with Coach Shipman, and I had a block from 11:00am to 12:00pm on Tuesdays and Thursdays. Coach Shipman had fenced at North Carolina, and despite the blue northeastern blood coursing through Brandeis, Shipman had maintained a very southern demeanor. He didn't talk unless he had something to say, and then in a slow, measured drawl. I immediately took to his calmness and felt at home in the Brandeis fencing room, the way I had felt a safe sense of belonging at Riverdale.

In short, academically, socially, and in fencing, I rolled into a charmed life.

That is, until one day at practice when I was doing reaction drills with Alex Banks. I held out a hand steadily in the air and, starting from about a foot away, Alex tried to slap my hand before I could pull it away. Like gunslingers, the goal was to react quickly. Only that day, Alex slapped my hand and about a full second later, I'd react. I was slow to the point of cartoon humor, feeling like I was pulling my hand through thick syrup. After practice I noticed my glands were huge. When I went for a checkup at the student health center, they admitted me. I'd picked up mono in the usual way as a camp counselor the previous summer, but it wasn't until two months into the semester that it laid me low.

The doctor wanted me to go home, but I refused. Leave this charmed life behind? No way! So I spent two weeks in the infirmary, fighting the fevers and generalized horror that comes with the lowered immune system of mono. I was too tired and too sick to do any coursework, but at least I got to watch the Yankees beat the Braves in six for their first World Series win since the year I was born. I called home from the infirmary and I remember communicating with my dad via my mom. I'd hear him in the background asking about me or telling my mom to tell me something. My mom urged me just to get on the phone with him and eventually she'd hand him the phone and my father and I would share a stilted conversation.

Despite making friends easily at Brandeis, it was still early in the year and I'd spent more time in the gym than with my hall-mates, so only a few people stopped by the infirmary to visit. One of the exceptions was Alex Banks, the team captain I'd written off as a geek. He visited every day to bring me videos or just to hang out. Alex might not have been the most athletic fencer on the team, and in practice he didn't come off as the most talented, but I was surprised to learn from other teammates that the year before he'd been the leading point-winner in the Brandeis team competitions. Coming to the infirmary every day, videos in hand, was an extension of the persona he brought to the training room and to the strip—in what seemed like an individual sport, Alex was a team player through and through.

His visits helped me stick out mono in the infirmary instead of going home, which would've meant failing the semester and missing my freshman fencing season.

It's probably a good thing that when I finally got out of the infirmary, my enlarged spleen still meant I couldn't fence—I was desperately behind in my classes and needed those four afternoons a week to play a massive game of catch-up in the library. My teachers were spectacular, helping me troubleshoot all the work I'd missed. Still, it would be the one college semester I wouldn't make the dean's list. I'd come a long way since being slow to read and a resource-room student in middle school.

My first tournament back was a Northeast League match against Brown, Boston College, MIT, and Vassar. The only fencer on any of the other teams I had heard of was Luke Mountain from BC, whom I'd met at a national competition. Other than him, the tournament looked to be a cakewalk, and I told my teammates I was going to crush it.

The morning of the tournament, the Brandeis team board-ed a bus for the trip from Waltham to the Boston College campus in Newton. We wore light blue warm-up suits with our mascot, Ollie the wise old owl, holding a gavel over his head for the Brandeis Judges (which perhaps rivals only the Evergreen State College Fighting Geoducks for the country's most quizzical mascot). The tournament was held in the BC field house, where, like at high school tournaments, strips were taped down for the day. The room was effectively without spec-tators and we found a corner of the room to stash our fencing bags and then started warming up. Like I had at high school tournaments, we eyed the competition. I now had "Morehouse USA" across my back—I'd never been to an international com-petition, but added the "USA" for intimidation.

We huddled. "Well," Coach Shipman said and then, as was his way, paused for what seemed an eternity, "do what you've been practicing. Take this team seriously."

And then Alex Banks led the team in our huddle cheer. "Roll 'Deis!" we yelled. I was ready to prove my practice results were no fluke and trotted out to my strip opposite a tall, skinny kid from Brown. We plugged in and took our en gardes.

"Ready, fence!" called the ref and I rolled out my best new move, checking into the center of the strip and then retreating. My opponent bit, chasing me down the strip—as I moved back-ward, I left my body tantalizingly close, goading him to attack. The theory was this: weak fencers tend to take three or four steps at most before lunging out of fear that any more footwork would lead to a technique nosedive. I hoped he would lunge from too far away, allowing me to jump into the space behind his ill-fated attack to take the point.

There's a basic drill called the "get away, go" that's just like it sounds: you retreat away from your opponent's attack, then turn on a dime to land an attack of your own. My retreat was good, and here came his lunge—*whiff!*—through the air in front of me as I stayed just out of range. But while my "get away" was good, my "go" was weak. In the time it took me to turn the corner from retreat to attack, my opponent redoubled his own attack and caught me in transition.

In high school, I'd never seen a fencer able to redouble. In college, I was down 0-1.

Stick to my plan, I told myself, only I promised that this time, I'd recover more quickly. But my opponent wasn't stupid— he watched me go back, and knowing I couldn't turn the corner, he threw himself headlong into his attack and chased me down as I backpedaled, landing a hard slash to my chest. He turned, screamed, pumped his fist, and the Brown bench went wild.

When the ref called the start of the third point, I lunged to my opponent's head, and my Brown opponent quickly rose to parry-five and then riposted for the touch. I was down 0-3, frustrated and confused. "Come on!" I yelled, and slapped my legs. What was the rhythm, the speed, the tactic, the move?

I crouched down lower in my en garde stance, ready to make a fake charge and then parry. "Ready, fence!" called the ref, and I launched, stopped, and swung my saber through the air where I expected his weapon to be. Only, he hadn't bit on the fake. Instead, he waited for my parry to sail past and then as I desperately tried to retreat out of range, he landed a cut to my belly and screamed. I was down 0-4. Nothing was working. I was desperate and he knew it. Hell with it, I decided, and the next point I charged, but he pulled away easily and just as I had attempted in the first point, he backpedaled until my technique broke down and I was forced into a desperate lunge from a too-far distance—only, he turned the corner and caught me before I could redouble.

In what should have been the match in which I justified my

top-recruit spot, I lost 0-5 to a fencer I'd never heard of.

I lost to Brown's second fencer, too, and after 2 rounds we were tied with Brown, 9 matches to 9. There was 1 round left—9 matches, 3 competitors each in saber, foil, and épée. "Come on," Coach Shipman said, "we need some help from saber!" My saber teammates had fared as dismally as I had.

I lost my third match. My saber teammates lost theirs too, and on aggregate we lost 14–13 to Brown, having lost all 9 of our saber matches. Under the leadership of Alex Banks, our foil team won all 9 of theirs, and epee had split 4-and-5 for the fatal, deciding point.

Next match: MIT. They were coached by Polish former World Champion Jarek Koniusz, but warming up it looked like no amount of coaching could do them any good. I thought Alex Banks looked geeky, but he was Brad Pitt compared to the MIT team.

My first match was against Brian Bower and I towered over him. His en garde stance looked skinny and awkward, and I thought that while maybe I hadn't been able to outmuscle Brown, I could roll over MIT. But as I advanced into the center of the strip against Bower, he nipped me under my sword-hand wrist to go up 0-1 on a one light stop-cut. It's a subtle hit that makes the initial attacker (me) look stupid and unprepared, and the initial defender (him) look like a genius, which, in hindsight, I guess he probably was. He was patient, too, and on the next point, he worked me slowly down the strip until I was in danger of stepping off the back, thus gifting him the point. When he noticed my nervousness, he again nipped me in the wrist—you didn't see this precision blade work in high school.

I lost all 3 matches to MIT. Again, saber got swept, Alex and the foil team swept, and épée lost the split for a 14-13 loss to MIT. Dear God, what was happening? I was reactive, behind the curve, not knowing where the curve was exactly, and bobbing around like a ship with a broken mast in line of what now seemed like the cannons of pirate captain Sam Bellamy.

After losing badly to BC's Luke Mountain, I turned it around against the other two BC fencers and against a weak Vassar team, but the damage was done: we'd lost two team events because I couldn't salvage one win.

My freshman season came and went, and rather than the star recruit I seemed in practice, I proved to be an albatross around the team's neck, losing points more often than winning them. Despite frequently being smaller than his opponents, Alex Banks was the exact opposite, winning at least 2-of-3 in all but one tournament.

Like always, my evaluation of my fencing talent was tied to my self-worth, which was tied tightly to my results, and at the end of my freshman season, I started to think maybe I wasn't such hot stuff after all. Where was the cocky freshman who'd rolled into the Brandeis fencing room intent on dominating his teammates?

I fenced a bit better as my freshman season progressed and I brought a humbled self to the postseason Intercollegiate Fencing Association tournament—the longest-running NCAA tournament in any sport. Now, instead of expecting to dominate, I wondered if I could be halfway decent. My first opponent was from Princeton— they weren't in our Northeast League and I didn't really know their fencers, so I was surprised after winning my first match over Maxim Pekarev when someone congratulated me on beating the previous year's NCAA champion! I managed to advance to the eight-person finals, where I had a rare win against my old Westbrook friend and rival, Keeth Smart, who was now attending St. John's on a fencing scholarship, and ended up finishing 5th.

The next competition was the NCAA Regional Tournament. Results at Regionals would in large part determine who advanced to the NCAA Championships—the results being combined in some BCS-Bowl-esque formula with your regular season record. And at Regionals, the new, humbler me made the final pool again and finished 7th. Twenty-four fencers from each weapon make the NCAA Championships and regions are allotted a certain number of these twenty-four spots, based on their calculated strength in past tournaments. The Northeast region had seven spots for saber and I had finished 7th at Regionals, but due to my dismal season record, I didn't advance.

Not so for Alex. In individual college fencing events, competitors from Division- I, II, and III schools fence together. Generally, these individual NCAAs are dominated by fencers from St. John's, Penn State, Notre Dame, Ohio State, Wayne State—schools with scholarships that frequently go to talented foreign students. Schools like D-III Brandeis can't offer scholarships and frequently fill out their fencing rosters with walk-ons and even first-time fencers who pick up the sport as freshmen. Competing for little Brandeis, Alex Banks took 10th at the NCAAs that year, earning the title All-American. I spent the summer collating and contemplating, working at a bookbindery connected to the publisher my mom worked for. Basically, I stood at a spot along the path of the huge bookmaking machine, which would spit me a stack of pages 51 through 100. I wore a weight belt and would pick up the stack and feed it into another mouth of the machine. If you come across reference books with a 1997 publication date in which the pages 51-100 are upside down, that was me.

I thought a lot about Alex Banks that summer—about how he fenced, but also about *why* he fenced, where he got his motivation and energy. I realized where I got *mine*: channeled aggression and the need to prove my self-worth through results. I had used fencing my freshmen year as a way to force people to accept me, to bully my way into respect and a top dog's form of camaraderie. I fenced from a place of insecurity translated into anger, from an outsider's perspective, chipping my place among the in crowd with the blade of a saber.

I really don't think Alex cared about how he was perceived. He certainly didn't fight for the alpha dog spot in practice, where he frequently lost bouts to younger teammates. Instead of letting the world define him, Alex Banks defined his world—he had the two clear goals of helping the team win and being an All-American. At Riverdale, I'd set similar goals: to help the team win and to take first at the Mamaroneck Invitational. These goals drove me at practice and helped me make decisions about training that ultimately let me go from goal to reality. While methodically moving pages that summer, I realized that in my first year at Brandeis, I hadn't set a clear goal for myself and, as a result, *the goal had set me.*

On the strip, your arm goes straight to the target or you lose; off the strip it was the same. I hadn't picked a target and so I went cockeyed toward the subconscious goal of proving myself, being the best fencer on the team. It wasn't a goal I had set. It was the default—the punishment for failing to set any goal at all. And by letting myself slip into trying to beat my teammates in practice, I had remained woefully unprepared for matches against other teams.

Standing at the bookbindery, I decided very consciously that instead of making the complete break with high school that I had coveted, I needed to keep from throwing the baby out with the bathwater—to keep the lessons that had made me a successful high school fencer. Like I had copied Taka, I decided to copy Alex Banks. I made his goals mine: to help the team win matches and to be an All-American. In neither the first nor last time I've reinvented myself, I unwrapped a very new Morehouse my sophomore season at Brandeis.

6

Underdog

Through Washington Heights and Riverdale, I'd gained access to a fierce place in my heart and, even now, it serves me well at times. But my sophomore year at Brandeis, I tried my damnedest to direct this aggression outward, away from my teammates. I worked hard and I played to win, but *winning* started to mean something different. I knew that to meet my goals of helping the team win and being an All-American, I'd have to change how I did things.

For example, my freshman year I had scored points in practice by noticing and exploiting my Brandeis teammates' weaknesses—a fencer's inability to parry-five, or a minuscule hitch in another's transition from advance to lunge, or the general fact that Brandeis saber fencers tended to pull their arms just a bit too far back when preparing for an attack. I'd hit them with the fencing equivalent of a jab as they wound up for a haymaker.

Sophomore year, I worked with my teammates to correct these problems, which meant that instead of scoring points in practice on quick, preemptive attacks, I found myself on the defensive—parrying while being driven backwards. And at this point, my retreat tended to look more like an off-balance and disorderly rout. And so with my teammates' faster attacks, I started losing in practice.

But while I was losing, I was learning. I worked with Coach Shipman on converting a retreat into an attack, turning the corner in the "get away, go" drill—the weakness that had doomed me in my first match against Brown the previous year. If there's anyone to be ugly with, it's your teammates. And by relying on parlor tricks to win in practice, I'd failed to develop the parts of my game that would have allowed me to win in competitions. My sophomore year, I got clear with my goals and ugly with my teammates and, as a result, we all improved.

At the Boston College tournament that opens each season, instead of going 0-6 against Brown and MIT, I went 6-0 then went 2-1 against Boston College, losing only to Luke Mountain (who continued to decimate me). It was a major swing from the depths of my freshman year to the highs of this new sophomore season.

But while my results skyrocketed along with my skills and goals, my mindset was slower to turn the corner. Suddenly, on the strip, no one doubted my skills, and in the dorms and classrooms, my Brandeis peers were fun, kind, smart and inclusive. I wasn't bullied, I wasn't doubted... something was missing. I had grown so accustomed to people shoving me into the box of low self-worth that now, with these external pressures removed, I didn't know how to be without them. I became my own worst tormentor.

Days before a fencing match, I would start withdrawing, blocking out the world with earphones, playing sad music. I wrapped myself in dark thoughts and let myself get frustrated with schoolwork. When finally the competition came, I started matches listlessly, going down 0-2 to less skilled fencers. I'd made myself into the underdog again; from that perspective, I could start believing that my opponent didn't respect me, thought I was nothing. Suddenly, I'd get the flash of anger I needed and roar back to win 5-2 or 5-3. Each bout was a microcosm of my life. If I lost, I felt horrible not just about losing but about myself as a person. When I won, it almost felt like a relief. After the meet, I would be back to normal again, able to reengage with my friends and teachers, as if I'd punched away a bully I knew would be waiting for me around the corner tomorrow.

By midwinter, the melancholy had crept into the corners of my everyday existence. I'd go into practice at 3:30 most days and when I got out a little after 6:00pm, it'd be dark. I would eat, study, and go through the motions of the evening, but I started to get the feeling that something was missing. Again, in some ways, I almost reveled in it, putting on sad music and moping around. Then I'd feel guilty about feeling down and it made the melancholy worse.

Was I just being a brat, having jumped the fence from the struggle of Washington Heights and then (in its own way) Riverdale, to the life of a whiny, privileged kid at a private liberal arts school?

Maybe I needed a girlfriend.

There was a girl on the women's fencing team I had a major crush on. She wasn't a star—she played piano, was a good student, and had picked up fencing her freshman year at Brandeis' open tryouts. Being generally fit, she'd made the squad. I started strolling through the cafeteria when I wasn't hungry, hoping to bump into her. Finally, on a fencing trip, I told her I liked her (!), and we held hands on the airplane home (!). I remember her hand being surprisingly clammy, but maybe it was just the airplane.

Does this sound like a middle school romance? Wait, it gets better: we dated through second semester freshman year and before going our separate ways for summer break, I made her a mix-tape—really, it was a cassette tape packed with romantic fa-vorites. It had been a typical, silly college relationship—we dated and broke up, usually hanging out more when we were broken up than when we were together (why is that?). On the day before summer break, when I tried to hand her the romantic mix-tape, she dumped me.

I still cry a solitary tear when I hear the song "Nightswim-ming" by R.E.M. Curse you, Michael Stipe!

And so it went through my sophomore year, both in my per-sonal life and in my fencing. I needed my on-again, off-again girl-friend to provide a constant problem that I could fight against in order to motivate myself to do well in school; I needed to go down 0-2 in 5-touch matches before I could roar back and win. For a couple days before matches, I needed the ritual of turning inward with my Walkman headphones blasting sappy songs, totally re-moved from campus life, in order to have an artificial haze to rip myself out of when I hit the strip.

All this is to say that a girlfriend wasn't the cure for my melan-choly. Every night that winter I'd fence from 4:00-6:00pm, come back to the dorms in the dark, and wonder what the hell I was doing. The feeling grew inside me that something wasn't right, but damned if I could pinpoint exactly what it was.

The campus psychological services were housed in a building between the gym and most of the classrooms. It was the only thing in the building, so you knew that anyone heading in the door was pretty much hiding a dark and twisted internal life beneath the thin façade of a functional college student. My first visit, I hid behind a tree outside the building and waited until no one was around, then I snuck in the doors. It was all very ninja. Of course, four of five people I knew were sitting in the waiting room. When I worked as a Resident Advisor, I found out that about a quarter of all students used the campus psych services. Rather than some stigmatized secret, counseling was nearly the norm.

It was in a Brandeis counseling office that I first made the overt connection between my actions as a fencer and my life as a whole. Here I saw for certain that I had been trying to master fencing in order to master life—and that I would need to master life if I wanted to be a better fencer.

Unlike the previous year, as a sophomore I rode my new-found goals and skills, plus my emotional M.O. of self-inflicted underdog-ness, to the national NCAA tournament. Twenty-four of the best NCAA fencers would fight 5-touch matches, with the top twelve earning All-American honors. In matches on the tournament's first day, I again went down 0-2, in order to ignite my underdog aggression. But with national-caliber fencers, giving up two points meant that instead of clawing my way back to a win, I was clawing my way back to a 3-5 or 4-5 loss. After the tournament's first day, I'd won 5 matches and dropped 9, putting me in 18th place.

It felt like Mamaroneck all over again. I was effectively out of the tournament with another half still to fence.

That evening, in pragmatic Shipman style, Coach asked if maybe I didn't have to give away 2 points to start every match. Maybe I could start a match imagining that I'm already down 0-2? If the phoenix rising from the ashes to victory was the only sto-ryline I knew, couldn't I sprinkle some metaphoric ashes around the strip before the match started rather than spending 2 points to buy ferocity? Couldn't I trick myself into it?

The next day, I stood on the strip, chanting to myself inside the mask, *I'm down. He's beating me. He doesn't respect me.* It was the first time I remember being aware of self-talk. *I'm down. He's beating me. He doesn't respect me,* over and over. And when the referee said *fence,* I roared off the line. I won my first three matches, went 5-2 in my first 7, and suddenly found myself at 10-11 overall with two matches remaining. I thought to myself, *Win these two, and you'll be in range of making the top twelve.* All-American honors were within reach.

As fate would have it, my final two opponents were my friends and former Riverdale teammates, Taka and Mitsu Sudo, both now fencing for Yale. *I'm down, I'm down, I'm down*, I told myself. I traded points with Mitsu and ground out a 5-4 victory—against his skill, I certainly didn't have any points to give.

With an 11-11 record, only Taka Sudo—my Riverdale fencing mentor—stood between me and being an All-American. I knew Taka well.

When the referee said *fence*, he liked to take a step forward and then watch. If it looked like his opponent planned defense, Taka would fake like he was cutting straight, baiting his opponent into a misguided parry before launching into his opponent's mistake with a long series of additional feints to disguise the location of the final cut. Or, if after his first step an opponent looked like he wanted to attack, Taka would bait him with a fake parry that seemed to momentarily leave open a target zone. When an opponent would lunge for this zone, Taka would be ready to parry away the blade and take the point.

Quite cleanly, I was Darth Vader and he was Obi-Wan Kenobi.

Sure enough, on the first point Taka checked into the middle and I faked as if I had bit, playing the card of willing defender. Taka feinted his attack and I feinted a retreat away from it—but then I reversed to cut into his body as he came forward with his saber blade feinting. As had been my mistake in my first match against my Riverdale friend Ying, Taka's movement had been too big. He assumed I was on the defensive and let his arm travel too far back.

Next point, Taka checked again and I played the offense card. He opened a target zone, baiting me into an attack that he could parry. Instead, I ignored the trap and launched into a series of feints, driving him backwards down the strip and eventually lunging to take the point. Even ahead 2-0, I kept saying to myself, *I'm down, I'm down, I'm down.*

When I scored the last point, I ripped off my mask and screamed as I dropped to my knees. It probably wasn't the celebration spectators expected of a fencer with an overall record of 12-and-11 who'd finished 10th, an honorable mention All-American, but for me it was huge. I'd learned to use self-talk to drive the rollercoaster of my emotions to the level I needed. Also, I had proved that the quiver of lessons I was carrying on my back actually paid off. The year before, I had learned to set concrete goals and now I had glimpsed the rewards.

I also saw the next level. My sophomore year, the NCAAs were dominated, as they always were, by fencers who had come up through the club system. Keeth Smart had won the NCAAs the previous year and that year took 6th. New York Athletic Club fencers had a great day, with NYAC's Luke Lavalle beating NYAC's Michael Golia for first, and another NYAC fencer, Patrick Durkan, beating an Italian fencer who had been recruited to Columbia for 3rd.

At 10th, my goals, skills, and mindset had made me the highest finisher who'd learned in a high school program. But I still had a long way to go.

Fifteen Touches

Many of the fencing coaches who escaped the former USSR in the 1980s tried to continue coaching in the States, and at the time, almost all the fencing jobs in the country were at the college level. Then, when the Berlin Wall came down in 1989, the self-starting seeds of Soviet Bloc coaching talent blew on the wind of unrequited dreams into the U.S. system of club fencing and began to expand it. Now in the 1990s, these seeds were starting to grow at places like Fencers Club and the New York Athletic Club in Manhattan, at Nellya Fencers in Atlanta, at the Oregon Fencing Alliance in Portland, and at several clubs in Kansas City. These primarily Eastern European coaches brought with them both the secrets of Soviet fencing and the attitude that we Americans could use these secrets to fight our way to international respect.

It was an uphill battle. In the 1904 St. Louis Olympics, American Albert Van Zo Post won gold in fencing's "single stick" event, which is no longer competed. In 1948, the U.S. took the bronze in the team event of men's saber. And in the heavily-boycotted 1984 Los Angeles Olympics, Peter Westbrook won the individual bronze medal in saber. The U.S. program had won a smattering of medals in épée and foil, but no gold, and nothing since 1984. We simply weren't a fencing nation.

In the summer between my sophomore and junior years of college, the 1996 Atlanta Games were a time of sweeping change for American fencing. At forty-four years old, Peter Westbrook had competed in his sixth and final Olympics and he switched his focus from competing to his foundation—discovering, motivating, and training the next generation of talent. Also, Peter had made the Atlanta Games without traveling to one international competition. It would be the last time that would be possible.

In addition to Westbrook, Peter Cox and Tom Strzalkowski fenced saber in Atlanta, and only Peter Cox had made an international result, winning one match in one round of 64 at an international world cup competition. This result—making the round of 32 at a world cup—was considered shocking and had earned Peter Cox the qualifying points he needed to vault past his competitors onto the U.S. Olympic Team.

This team was an old guard, or, more appropriately, the final U.S. Olympic Team powered by the idea that simply showing up to international competitions was enough. And into the void they left (Peter Westbrook, especially) stepped a new group of young fencers with very different goals who soon started to create a whole new set of expectations.

For one thing, the U.S. Olympic Committee only offered funding to sports they considered to be in medal contention. And so just before the Atlanta Games, the U.S. Fencing Association decided that we would try to win medals—just like that.

With no real understanding of how to actually make this medal contention happen, the USFA turned to the man who formerly ran the most powerful fencing program in the world. Vladimir Nazlymov had come to the U.S. in 1991 after being fired as head coach of the Soviet Union's fencing program. On a visit to Colorado Springs, Colorado, one of his top fencers had defected; Nazlymov had shouldered the blame and taken the fall.

In the world of U.S. fencing, Nazlymov is nothing short of mythic. Despite an eye injury that left him with a lazy eye (the result of stick fighting as a child), Nazlymov had won ten world championships and several Olympic team gold medals for the Soviet Union. After his fencing career, Nazlymov was given the title of Colonel in the USSR Army, coached the army fencing team, and for a time was the head of the entire USSR Olympic program. When Nazlymov could no longer stay in the USSR, he immigrated to the United States, settling in Kansas City, where he started a fencing program at an inner-city sports magnet school. For a time, the FBI and CIA kept tabs on Nazlymov, wondering what a former colonel in the Soviet Army was doing teaching inner-city kids in Kansas City.

Soon Nazlymov became the U.S. National Team coach, bringing with him skills and the Soviet focus on medals. Nazlymov wasn't used to losing, and when he said we could win medals, the establishment listened. Never one to dip a toe, his first step toward this goal was to launch his young fencers Terrence Lasker and Jeremy and Tim Summers into international competition. He also changed the Olympic qualification process, making it more dependent on international points. Remember how Peter Westbrook made the Atlanta Games without traveling internationally? When Nazlymov took over the U.S. program, that quickly became impossible.

With Nazlymov sending his fencers overseas, others couldn't help but follow—including the Manhattan clubs. So young fencers like Keeth Smart and Akhi Spencer-El packed their bags and started hopping planes to competitions around the world.

Westbrook's Hungarian coach, Csaba Elthes, had always pushed Peter to win national championships and qualify for the Olympics—those were the goals. Peter had met these goals with flying colors, winning thirteen national championships and making 6 Olympic teams. But Westbrook's coach and the fencing world at large never expected that American fencers could compete with the top European talent. "Fencing isn't an American sport," went the prevailing wisdom, and the Europeans were professionals with skills that no upstart American could understand. Who knows what heights Peter Westbrook might have reached if he'd come up under Nazlymov's focus on international experience?

In any case, in 1996 it was out with the old, in with the new. The year after the Atlanta Olympics, the four members of the U.S. National Saber Team who would fence at world championships included Nazlymov's young high school fencers Terrence Lasker and Jeremy Summers, along with the two Westbrook fencers Keeth Smart (coached by Hungarian Aladar Kogler), and Akhi Spencer-El (coached by Ukrainian Yury Gelman). For the previous twenty years, a small group of American fencers and coaches had dominated the sport. Now everyone on the team was twenty years old.

Outside Manhattan and Kansas City, former Soviet Bloc coaches were pushing local programs into the national spotlight. Under the Soviet system, Arkady Burdan had been the head coach of Ukraine, based in Odessa. But as a Jew, he wasn't allowed to travel to international competitions, and so was forced to give up his best talent. Burdan immigrated to Atlanta in 1990 and started out by giving fencing lessons in his driveway. Eventually he started a club in a creaky room attached to an Atlanta school. In the late 1990s, his young saber fencers, Colin Parker and Chip Crane, were pushing up the national rankings.

Likewise, Ed Korfanty, a former head coach of the Polish team, had missed his chance at the Olympics when Poland boycotted the 1984 Games. Soon after, he immigrated to Portland, Oregon, where from this home base on the left coast, he was pushing young fencers up the national rankings.

Perhaps driven by inspiration from the influx of passionate Soviet coaches, several American-born coaches started to step up, too. In Rochester, New York, young American coach Buckie Leach was producing female foil fencers who made international results, including Ann Marsh, who made the quarterfinals at the Atlanta Games.

While the Soviet Bloc coaches had left their countries behind, they hadn't left behind their ambition or their connections with the world of international fencing competition. With their expectations alone, they raised the bar.

Finishing my sophomore year at Brandeis, I was almost completely insulated from these changes. Just as I had dipped a toe in club fencing while in high school, I dipped a toe in national competitions while in college, traveling to North American Cups (NACs) mostly as a way to get an edge on my NCAA competitors.

One of these NACs was in South Bend, Indiana, where I fenced in the under-20 junior division. Of the many differences between an NCAA meet and an NAC, the most dramatic was that NAC matches were fought to 15 points instead of the 5-touch matches of NCAA tournaments.

At the time, the now-defunct airline TWA offered college students a ticket four-pack for $100 each, and so I flew to South Bend and stayed by myself in a hotel across from the convention center that held the tournament. As I walked across the enclosed footbridge from the hotel to the fencing venue, I saw faces I recognized—there's a lot of overlap between NCAAs and junior NACs.

I walked into the convention hall's main room a few hours before the start of the tournament. The room was mostly gray—not many sponsor banners—just metallic strips around the room, with scoring machines and wires everywhere and a large raised table in the center of the room for the bout committee. Equipment bags were everywhere.

I looked at the seeding lists. The first sheet showed fencers with U.S. ranks. Akhi and Keeth from Westbrook were at the top of the ranked sheet, along with Terrence Lasker and Jeremy Summers, who fenced with Nazlymov in Kansas City. Other names I recognized included Patrick Durkan and the brothers Luke and David Lavalle from the New York Athletic Club, Colin Parker and Chip Crane from Nellya Fencers in Atlanta, and Adam Skarbonkiewicz, a strong Polish junior fencer who now fenced for the Oregon Fencing Alliance with Coach Ed Korfanty. It was a roll call of the new superstars of U.S. fencing.

Keeth and Akhi wore black and gold and warmed up with Peter Westbrook in a corner of the room. In another area, the New York Athletic Club fencers wore red and were getting loose. Another group was jogging around the room, following a thin man with white hair and small, circular glasses. It was Vladimir Nazlymov.

Wearing my Brandeis warm-ups, I went by myself to an open section of wall, did a couple jumping jacks, and started stretching.

The tournament started with six-person pools. In these pools, fencers fight 5-touch matches against every other fencer in the pool, with the results affecting how you're seeded for the start of the tournament's direct elimination rounds to 15 points. Because high seeds are matched against low seeds, fencing well in the pools would earn you easier opponents later. I had calibrated my mental game to these 5-touch matches and I fenced well, earning a beatable opponent in my first 15-touch match.

In my second junior division match I drew Ahmed Yilla, a lefty high-schooler from the Westbrook Foundation who had only started fencing two years before. *I'm down, I'm down, I'm down,* I chanted to myself, whipping myself into a froth that I rode to a 2-0 lead... before Yilla decimated me 3-15. He moved fast, his arm parrying my every attack—I couldn't find a way through. When I didn't attack immediately, he'd tear down the strip with lighting speed, leaving me nowhere to go.

In the senior competition the next day, I again did well in the 5-point matches in the pools, only to be completely outclassed in my first 15-touch match. I could fence 5, but extend it to 15 touches and I was cannon fodder.

I was stunned. I went back to my hotel room confused, unsure of what happened. Worse even than losing was being completely bewildered by *why* I had lost. I'd always known there were fencers more talented than me out there, but until then I thought I could close the gap with hard work. In 5-point college matches I knew how to bottle and dispense aggression in a way that allowed me to overwhelm opponents. But in these longer national bouts—maybe 6 or 7 points into a 15-point match—stronger opponents discovered the angles through my defense and exploited them, burying me in an avalanche of points toward the win.

In high school, I hadn't worried about competing with the club fencers—my world was the high school team and I was content to lose in the clubs, sure that I was learning tricks that would help me win for Riverdale. My first two years of college I'd thought only about college fencing and losing at national tournaments hadn't bothered me much—I was doing it for the experience. But now, after finishing 10th at NCAAs and fencing strong in the 5-touch pools at NACs, a thought crept into my mind: what would my name look like alongside Keeth, Akhi, Jeremy, and Terrence? What separated me from these top fencers? Just like the U.S. Fencing team in the pre-Nazlymov era, I was thinking small. Could I think bigger? I needed to know what these fencers knew.

The next day, I tracked down Ahmed Yilla's coach, Yury Gelman, the same coach who'd given me his card when I was a freshman at Riverdale—the coach I'd never followed up with. I asked what I'd lost on.

Gelman paused and then said in his thick Ukrainian accent, "Many things." He was ready to leave it at that but I was still standing there and he saw I wanted more. "Many things, but mainly the footwork… and many other things. Yes, but footwork especially bad, but many things bad," he said.

This time I followed up. I asked Yury if he'd train me in the summers when I was home from Brandeis. He said he would. Coach Shipman was helping me reach my 5-touch college goals, and I hoped that Yury Gelman could dovetail with this instruction to give me the tools I needed for the longer, national matches.

Climbing the Mountain

My junior year, in addition to setting the goal of being a second team All-American, I spent time reflecting on the subconscious barriers I had set for myself, and realized that I had internalized the idea that I couldn't beat Boston College's Luke Mountain. "You gonna climb the Mountain?" my teammates would ask before every BC meet, and of course I said *Yes!*, nodding and feigning confidence. But once I got on the strip across from Luke, I knew deep down I didn't stand a chance.

We added another strong saber fencer to the Brandeis team that same year. Mike Topper was a 5'2" vegan computer science major with tattooed stars spiraling up his arm. Mike and I were the fencing height equivalent of the NBA combo Larry Johnson and Muggsy Bogues of the 1990s Charlotte Hornets. Because Topper was from Michigan, and maybe because of his height, he had flown under the radar (as it were) of major fencing colleges. I knew Topper from national-level junior tournaments and when he visited Brandeis on a recruiting trip, I gave him the hard sell. His first day on campus, I took him out to eat and Topper got food poisoning—it was awful—but despite the inauspicious start, we were soon good friends.

The first time he fought a match for Brandeis, I remember Topper standing there on the strip with a guy a foot taller. Topper's opponent took his en garde, looked at Mike, and then looked back at his teammates on the bench with a laugh that said, *Who are you kidding, having this little guy fence?* On the first point, Topper's opponent came at him, three steps and a lunge. In the beat of a bees wings, 5'2" Mike Topper parried away the attack and nailed his opponent on riposte, pumping his fist up at the opponent who'd laughed at him and yelling, "Wow, wow, wow!" The guy wasn't laughing anymore and my teammates were stunned: Topper was so quiet off the strip!

Over and over I saw this same scenario play out, with Topper using his quick hands to block his small target zone, creating an impenetrable fortress from which he decimated opponents who underestimated him. Once he fought a 6'7" fencer and literally had to jump upwards to hit him after he parried. That's fencing—sometimes you have to improvise, and Topper was as creative as they come.

As in years past, the first tournament of my junior year was at Boston College against a handful of other Northeast League teams. A funny factoid about college fencing: you frequently had some of the country's top fencers like Keeth Smart squaring off against guys who'd picked up sabers three months earlier to fill an open spot on their team's roster. Some college competitors fenced like I had in my first high school varsity match, diving headlong and out of control into the center of the strip with their sabers flashing and visions of Zorro dancing through their minds with no technique to back it up. Meanwhile, other college fencers were flying to international world cup tournaments. You'd never have Division-I Ohio State play football against Division-III Carleton College, but fencing disregards divisions, sometimes to the detriment of poor D-III fencers, some of whom could just as easily be on the ultimate Frisbee team or the science Olympiad as the fencing strip.

At that year's tournament, I tore through the other Northeast League fencers before we reached Boston College and Luke Mountain. "You gonna climb the Mountain?" my teammates asked, trying to pump me up. As always, I nodded, feeling unconfident.

In every unsuccessful match for two years, Luke Mountain had baited me into his traps. I'd usually go on the offensive, driving Mountain backwards down the strip. But at some point he'd fake as if he were cutting into my attack, and I'd lunge right into his trap: Mountain would parry, closing the scoring zone he'd showed me, and then riposte for the touch. Every time. When he scored, he roared like a mountain lion. My freshman and sophomore years, he'd beaten me badly.

Mike Topper fenced him first. The opening looked familiar: Mountain hanging back until Topper came at him, driving Mountain backwards. Then came Mountain's fake. But instead of lunging into the trap, Topper kept going, waving his saber almost in Mountain's face, in a series of fakes that left Mountain searching desperately for the parry—position three to four, three to four, backpedaling and looking for Topper's blade. Topper watched for Mountain's retreat to disintegrate and when it did, Topper landed the touch, followed by his fist pumping "wow wow wow," like a Chihuahua barking at a pit bull. That match, Mountain crumbled. Topper's win looked effortless.

When I asked what the hell he'd just done, Mike shrugged his shoulders like it was nothing and said in his usual low-key way,

"I just kind of did a wavy-wave with my blade each touch." He demonstrated by waving his blade in the air like he'd done during the match. As you can probably guess by now, "wavy-wave" isn't necessarily a technical term—it was Topper's creativity solving a problem that I'd beat my head against for two years.

The next round, I rolled out Topper's wavy-wave against Luke Mountain, and it worked like a snake charmer's flute. *It can't possibly be this easy*, I thought. But it was. I took the first point, then the second, then I finally, magically beat Luke Mountain—badly. From then on, whenever one of us took the strip against Mountain we'd say, "And don't forget to do the wavy-wave!" The glib move was the key and after Topper solved him, I never lost to Luke Mountain again.

Before, I had given Luke Mountain a mythic status that he didn't necessarily deserve (not to impugn Mountain—he was a very good college fencer). Until Mike Topper ripped them off, I had been wearing silly glasses that made Luke Mountain bigger than he was—Mountain was a molehill!

The thing is, I was pretty sure that I could have figured out Mountain myself—if only I'd thought it was possible. By putting Luke Mountain on a pedestal, I'd given up any chance of beating him, and it took someone with similar blinders to kick-start my belief.

I rode my new belief to another strong regular season, and a 6th-place finish at the NCAA Championships—2nd Team All-American. That year, Topper and I helped Brandeis finish as the #1 D-III school in the country.

Only one male Brandeis fencer had ever made 1st Team All-American—Mike Mayer—and his plaque hung in Coach Shipman's office. I made it my senior year goal to join Mayer. That year, suddenly, I was winning almost all my regular season matches and qualified easily for the NCAA Championships. Just before traveling to the tournament, I surreptitiously unscrewed the Mike Mayer plaque from the wall and packed it in my fencing bag for inspiration. Thanks, Mike, for being my travel companion that week!

That year, the NCAA Championships were at Stanford. I was nervous. But I had packed the previous four years with skills, life lessons, problem solving, and, just as importantly, belief. I believed I could beat anyone to 5 points. Early in the tournament, I showed it, blazing to 20 wins, which included beating the tournament favorite, Ivan Lee, another strong Westbrook fencer then on a full ride at St. John's.

Then in the finals—1st Team All-American sewn up!—the format changed: the remaining four fencers fought 15-point rather than 5-point bouts. I lost 10-15 to a Polish fencer, and then lost 12-15 to Ivan Lee to finish fourth.

It wouldn't dawn on me until later, but why hadn't I set the goal of winning NCAAs? If I'd thought it was possible, might I have been able to do it? And if I'd set the goal of winning as opposed to just *making* the finals, might I actually have won?

And so like high school, as I finished college, I had a reputation as a hard-working fencer who had ridden his hard work as far as it could take him—I was a good, 5-point collegiate fencer who couldn't go the 15 points needed to compete on the national or international stage. I had learned to manage my aggression and use one-move parlor tricks that beat good fencers, but these strategies could only take me so far—5 touches, to be precise. To make it to the next level, I would have to add the skill I needed to last 15 touches.

This is where most fencing careers end. I was a Division-III fencer, nowhere on the national radar, and with few prospects for *getting* on said radar. But somewhere in the back of my mind, I wondered where my real ceiling was. Maybe—just maybe— could that ceiling be as high as the Olympics? What did that even look like? I imagined getting to New York City and studying with Yury. I wondered if I could find a way to climb the biggest mountain of all—the logistics of post-college fencing.

Deciding to
Teach For America

In the spring of 2000, as I got ready to graduate from Brandeis, I was ranked 19th in the country. I wasn't even nipping at the heels of those people who were nipping at the heels of Keeth Smart and Akhi Spencer-El, who would go on to compete in the Sydney Olympics. My grandfather, a lawyer, had attended Brooklyn Law School and, lacking another clear direction, I applied to BLS and was accepted. My dad was overjoyed. I sent away a deposit for room and board.

It was at a crossroads in my fencing career. When I somewhat sheepishly mentioned my pipe dream of making the 2004 Athens Olympic team, people said I was crazy—everyone except for Steve Mormando, a coach from NYU. He was a three-time Olympian of the Westbrook era and he put it this way: "You have your entire life to just work, but something like going for the Olympics you can only do when you're young... Why not take a chance? What do you have to lose?"

He explained how, during his Olympic years, he'd eked out a meager existence while he trained and traveled and tried to make the team. He assured me that it had all been worth it. Of course, he *made* the Olympics, which I imagined went a long way in justifying the years of monastic living. I wondered how the others felt—the ones who'd put their lives on hold for a shot at the Games only to fall short.

If I go to Brooklyn Law School, I thought to myself, *I can fence recreationally at the New York City clubs*. That, I knew, would be a sidestep at best on the path to the Olympics. And going to law school would mean living on loans—not nearly the income I would need to pay for training and the now-necessary international trips.

Taking an entirely different path, my college housemate, Larkin, had applied to a program called Teach For America, which placed talented college graduates in teaching positions in struggling schools around the country. I'd picked up a red application packet at the student center a few months prior and then left it sitting in my room. After Larkin applied, I flipped through the materials. *Apply yourself*, it said. I liked the sound of that. I also liked the idea of making a difference in the life of a young version of myself who hadn't gotten to whack the lucky teleportation button to Riverdale Country School. Unlike some of the people I had met at Riverdale and Brandeis, I knew exactly what the education alternative looked like—especially in Washington Heights—and exactly how lucky I was to attend Central Park East and then Riverdale.

Serendipitously, I was in my car later that week and I heard Wendy Kopp, the founder of Teach For America, on talk radio. She described the shortage of teachers in low-income areas and the difference in educational quality between rich and poor schools in the United States. The show got a lot of calls—people criticized

Kopp for the faith she was willing to invest in what many callers described as "a bunch of inexperienced, white, idealistic suburbanites" and their ability to "waltz into the ghetto and save the day."

What I heard was this: Kopp was a person of action, tackling a huge problem with idealism, diligence, and passion. To me, the naysaying callers were the equivalent of the people who told me I was crazy for having an Olympic dream.

I couldn't shake the idea. Even if the whole fencing thing didn't work out, it seemed like TFA offered the chance to make a difference—a chance I might not have as a lawyer. I knew I had to give it a shot or I'd forever wonder what could have been.

I went home, ripped open the Teach For America application on my desk, and found it was due the next day. I stayed up all night re-crafting all the essays and recommendations I'd used in my law school application and postmarked my Teach For America application by noon the following day. If I got in, I would do it; if not, I still had a deposit on file at Brooklyn Law School. For neither the first nor the last time, my fencing career was in the hands of the Fates.

I got an interview, which was scheduled (of course!) for the last time slot of the last day of hiring. I drove to Boston and, with five other New England-area seniors in the room, taught a five-minute sample lesson. We discussed education, answered interview questions, and listed our geographic preferences. I wrote New York City, Kansas City, and Atlanta—all places with the top fencing coaches. Then, a month later, I found out I'd been accepted and placed to teach in New York City.

Suddenly the future looked clear: I would train with Yury, fence with Keeth and Akhi, live at home to save money for travel, and do my best to help inner-city kids get the education they deserved (ah, the naïveté!).

The end of college brought finals, graduation, goodbyes, and a road trip with my friend Abe through California. The whole time, all I could think about was my next step.

Then I had a few weeks at home before the start of the intensive Teach For America summer training institute, and in that time TFA asked all incoming "corps members" to observe schools. I went to a handful of high schools in Yonkers and New York City, and felt like I was more qualified to be a slightly older friend than a teacher. I felt as though I was somehow moving in the wrong direction—from high school, to college, and then back to high school. *What in the world made me think I wanted to be back in high school?*

Soon enough, I arrived at the training institute in Houston along with 1,000 other new teaching recruits from around the country. The airport was like a party—there were balloons, cheers, and an overwhelming atmosphere of energy and idealism as we boarded the yellow school buses that would take us to the summer institute housing. I remember freezing in the air conditioning of the bus, then immediately beginning to sweat as we unloaded at the University of Houston, then instantly freezing again as we entered the University's Moody Towers, where we'd be living for five weeks.

After a week of intensive classes, TFA assigned me to be the eighth grade Social Studies teacher in a four-person summer school teaching team at Jefferson Davis High School in Houston.

To prevent gang violence, the kids at the school had to carry clear backpacks so they couldn't conceal weapons in them, wear white shirts and white shoelaces so no gang colors could be displayed, and every classroom was equipped with a panic button. A huge security guard with a drug-sniffing dog patrolled the hallways. When students arrived for the first day of summer school, the security guards made it a point to pick out the biggest kid and berate him in front of the school. It was a message: *We can take the biggest kid, so the rest of you better toe the line.*

It was as far as I could possibly be from Brandeis and from my fencing goals.

My teaching team was given a tiny room in the building's voluminous interior, so we made papier-mâché windows with whimsical outdoor scenes to make it seem less like a closet. The first Monday morning, my team taught reading and writing to a class of about twenty students. After getting their writing samples, it turned out that a quarter of our students couldn't spell basic words and almost all were reading far below grade level.

That Wednesday, I taught my first solo class. I had four weeks to teach *the causes of the American Revolution.* Mimicking my overconfidence as a freshman fencer, I thought the four weeks sounded like a forty-five-minute lecture—what would I do with the remaining three weeks and four days of class time? Rather than the raucous class you imagine from movies like *Dangerous Minds* or *Stand and Deliver,* my class was completely silent. There was no paper rustling, no pencils scratching, no clicking binders, no popping pens—just the sound of my voice intoning the causes of the American Revolution.

I was a gravedigger his first night on the job, suddenly struck by the silence of the dead. I stood and lectured for forty-five minutes and at the end of the period I asked the class why the colonists were upset with the King of Britain. No hands. Silence. Finally, I called on someone and he asked, "What's a colonist?" I called on another student and she asked, "What's Britain?"

There's a point at which every torture scene must end, and for me the end finally came at forty-five minutes—after which my corps advisor, Jen Koyzk, read me the riot act. She asked me if I realized that not one student learned one thing about the cause of the American Revolution during that class. I remember stammering that it was the students' fault—maybe they *hadn't* learned, but it wasn't my fault because *I'd taught the material*.

Jen disagreed and she said something important: "If the students didn't *learn*, then what you did *wasn't really teaching*."

By the second week I was in crisis mode, scrambling backward to find a place in the curriculum where I could pick up the thread. Every day, I stumbled from the cafeteria to the yellow school bus at 5:30am, then to teaching, to evening classes, to grading and planning, to the Kinko's late at night to make copies, and then to bed by 1:00am. By the third week, I had reached the point that only a failed teacher truly knows—that feeling of confusion, frustration, and overwhelmed despair, mixed with the certainty that the next day would bring more of the same. Gone were the carefree college days of classes, fencing, and a social life. I had flipped a switch as surely as I had with my move from Washington Heights to Riverdale. I was in a totally new world.

The weekend before the last week of Teach For America summer institute, I peeled out as quickly as my rented Neon would take me to that year's fencing National Championships, which happened to be nearby in Austin.

I hadn't practiced in months, but I'd qualified for the tournament by making the top thirty-two at a couple of North American Cup tournaments (NACs) that year and thought a little fencing would be a nice distraction from the pummeling I was taking daily in summer school. Even when I was in top form, I had no expectations at these national tournaments. I had figured out how to solve northeast fencers in our collegiate 5-touch matches and in this short format I could sometimes beat fencers like Keeth Smart or Ivan Lee. But I knew this wasn't enough to survive the 15 touches of a national tournament. To go 15, you not only have to solve your opponent, but you have to keep solving him as he evolves. Then you need to outpace your opponent's evolution, changing and improving your game as the match progresses to avoid being solved yourself. My ill-preparedness notwithstanding, a weekend off was just what I needed. I talked a couple TFA friends into joining me and splitting the cost of gas and a hotel room for what promised to be a raucous weekend in Austin.

Shaking off the rust and stress of standing incompetently in front of twenty eighth graders, I blew through my seeding pool and then my round of 64 and round of 32 matches—something I had never done before—scratching my way into a round of 16 match.

There I met Steve Mormando, the NYU coach who had encouraged me to continue fencing after college. He might have been a couple years past Olympic shape, but he was still massively intimidating—6'2", bald, and built like a bull. Mormando had the reputation of beating opponents with his mind as much as with his saber. For example, he'd come forward almost to his opponent's body, sweep his saber through the air to block, and then continue the sweep to riposte by swinging his saber around behind his back. It was a trick maneuver, but if it hit, it left opponents totally baffled. How could they handle someone willing to open the entire bag of tricks? I'd never seen it before and haven't seen it since.

Sometimes instead of attacking, at the start of the point Mormando would backpedal to his end of his strip and stand there with his saber "point-in-line." It's like a stationary attack, holding the blade straight out, and if an opponent's sword is point-in-line, you have to make contact with it, "beat away" the blade to claim the right-of-way before you can score with an attack of your own. But was Mormando's blade really point-in-line? Or was his elbow bent just a degree? Could you attack and win the touch, or did you have to beat his blade away first? Mormando did this to create uncertainty, and he turned his opponents' hesitation into points. You didn't see this on the college circuit.

Mormando might have been past his days of a long athletic

attack, so one successful strategy against him was to camp just out of his reach and wait for him to launch a slow attack, then parry or dodge and riposte for the touch. Mormando countered by dancing backwards away from his opponents and taunting them into attacking. I watched Mormando tempt opponents into launching ill-fated attacks time and time again. Occasionally, he would launch an attack of his own, just to keep his opponents honest.

He loved a show, and before our round of 16 match, he took his time warming up and otherwise delayed until all the other round of 16 matches had ended and spectators had no other option but to watch our match. He even called people over to watch.

I knew Mormando couldn't move with me, but I also knew he was wily—an old-schooler with old-school tricks. I went in patiently, attacking the line occasionally, but more often waiting him out, forcing him to attack me and then scoring on my defense. I jumped out to a 9-5 lead. Mormando held up his hands, taking time. Apparently, his underpants were askew and in the middle of our match he dropped trou to adjust them. I looked down at the ground, trying to stay focused on fencing. Mormando spent five full minutes adjusting his underwear and then his fencing knickers, as the crowd chuckled.

Finally we resumed. Mormando advanced then danced backward to his side of the strip and straightened his arm. Point-in-line? I attacked directly, landed my saber to his body, but impaled myself on Mormando's outstretched blade. *Whose point was it?* If his arm was straight, Mormando had right-of-way and thus the touch; if it was bent, then I had initiated the first attack and even though he'd speared me, the point was mine.

The ref gave me the touch. It was a turning point and Mormando knew it. Without a sympathetic ref, he wouldn't be able to game his line.

A saber match usually lasts three or four minutes. Ours went half an hour. But once the tide turned, I pulled out the win 15-10.

It felt good to have my warm-ups on in the final round of 8 while the bleachers were populated with eliminated fencers in their street clothes. Despite making 1st Team All-American and training with Yury Gelman for the past two summers, I had never been on the radar screen of national fencing. Making the quarter-finals at Nationals would start to change that.

And there I met Keeth Smart.

In high school, Taka Sudo had been my role model and Coach Schneider had been my teacher. Then at Brandeis, I had watched our team captain, Alex Banks, and learned from Coach Shipman. Now with my sights set on the Olympics, I knew I had to surround myself with the best. In the U.S., that was Keeth Smart as a peer and Yury Gelman as coach.

When I fenced Keeth Smart in high school, he had been fast but wild and a bit of an also-ran to Akhi's amazing technique and ability. Now at the 2000 National Championships, Keeth still didn't have Akhi's technique or a great parry, but he'd honed his speed and especially his footwork and ridden them to the #1 national ranking.

Keeth took his garde against me with a bit of a laid back swagger. He looked languid and relaxed, a skinny, six-foot left-hander whose footwork gave him the reach of a seven-footer.

I had fenced him enough to know that while he looked calm on the en garde line, it was the calmness of a lion stalking zebra. When the referee said *Fence!*, Keeth exploded with liquid speed, landing the first point before I could even set up my first move. On the second point, I tried to match Keeth's speed and when the referee said fence, I jumped forward and faked, expecting Keeth to whiff with a parry, thus opening a line. But after my fake there Keeth stood, still at his en garde line—my fake had all the effect of shadowboxing, and in the milliseconds after I finished my move, I had time to think *Oh crap* as Keeth easily launched and landed his attack.

The rest of the match became a desperate fight not to win, but to prevent being shut out. Keeth seemed so close and I would lunge but then—poof!—he was gone, retreating backwards down the strip with an uncanny prescience. Then, while my head was spinning, he would follow with neat, nimble slashes across my belly. The more I tried to get down the strip after him, the more lithely he retreated, always acting a split second before I attacked. Was I cocking my shoulder? Was I changing the rhythm of my charge? It was like playing poker with an opponent who could see my cards. I lost 6-to-15 and it could have been worse.

It felt like losing to Ahmed Yilla at NCAAs all over again. Would I ever be able to compete with someone of Keeth's caliber? Keeth wasn't even doing that well on the international level—how good must these international fencers be? I had put my eggs in the basket of the Olympics but my skills were nowhere near what they needed to be. How do you maintain high expectations when you know you are so far away?

Just as I had done after being outclassed by Yilla at NCAAs, I turned to my coach, Yury Gelman, for answers: *What went wrong?* What was it about Keeth? He was fast—that was obvious—but there was something else. Was he psychic?

Yury said this: "Keeth? He have thousand more 15-touch matches, hours more time spent on footwork, he travel to world cups, he fence every day with best in country." The gap, Yury explained, first and foremost was one of experience and training.

At the National Championships, the top eight fencers get medals. And because it was technically Olympic trials (though that year the results had been preordained by the season's points), we got certificates with Olympic rings. Though Keeth had laid bare my lack of skills, standing on the finals strip with the rest of the top eight for the awards ceremony still made the Olympics seem close, doable. Making the finals boosted my national ranking from 19th to a respectable 10th. As organizers announced Keeth and Akhi as the official men's saber team for the 2000 Sydney Games, the small crowd of maybe 100 fencers and parents cheered.

When the weekend ended, I went back to Jefferson Davis High School in Houston, unsure that any of my eighth graders had grasped a single cause of the American Revolution. Keeth and Akhi went to train for Sydney.

Teaching a Bear to
Feint Cut

What does a strong collegiate fencer do after college? In a hold-over from the time when the Olympics tried to be exclusively amateur, young Italian fencers become "Carabinieri," a kind of police officer, though the fencers never need show up for work. Likewise, Polish fencers get "factory jobs" in the coal mining industry—again, jobs they're paid for despite never showing up. Other countries like France and Germany have massive complexes where fencers live and train—free room, board, coaching, and training while they hone their skills.

In the old Soviet system, the government paid eight members of a national fencing team, an additional ten fencers were on the Army payroll, and ten fencers were on the police payroll. Soviet fencers made even more money in commerce. Fencers would buy caviar in the USSR for the equivalent of $10 per can. When they traveled for tournaments to a country like West Germany, they could sell it for $40. Then they would use the $40 to buy

Sony Walkmen and other items not available in the Soviet Union, which they'd bring back to the USSR and sell for a small fortune. Even with the fall of the Soviet Union, the tradition of professional, government-funded athletes continued.

In the U.S., fencing can help students get college scholarships, but graduation is where the perks end. All but the very best quit, and even some of the very best choose a life over the monasticism of work, training, and the never-ending string of fencing halls that is the life of a do-it-yourself American fencer.

For example, the Riverdale foil fencer Cliff Bayer finished 10th at the 2000 Olympics, and then retired at age twenty-two so that he could start a life. My Riverdale/Yale friends Taka and Mitsu Sudo both came out of college with bases solid enough to start competing internationally and—who knows?—maybe elbow their way into world cup points and a run at the Olympics. In another country, they might have. But the life of a U.S. fencer is one that requires massive amounts of time spent training and traveling, with little recognition and no financial reward. Staring at that stark choice, both Mitsu and Taka took jobs in finance.

The U.S. system had and has leaks—we lose top fencers like Cliff Bayer or potential talents like Mitsu and Taka to the desire for a life. But our bottom-up system also presents opportunities to those of us willing to make our own way. In the Soviet system, only the best fencers were allowed to move up at each level, and if you weren't among them, there was no backdoor to rejoin the system. In the U.S., if you're pigheaded enough, you can fight your way into the ranks at any point—at least that's what I hoped.

When I returned to New York City from the Teach For America summer institute, a TFA friend and I toured schools looking for the places we'd spend at least the next two years teaching. There were two schools within a couple blocks in Washington Heights, both with openings for middle school Social Studies/

English teachers. Intermediate School 143 on West 182nd Street faced the challenges you'd expect of an inner-city public school. At Intermediate School 90 on 168th, our interviews with the principal each lasted four minutes and consisted almost solely of one question: "What would you do if kids were fighting in class?" The message was obvious: if either of us wanted the job, it was ours.

We flipped a coin and I lost. My friend took the job at IS-143 and I landed at IS-90. I'd grown up in the neighborhood and knew the streets like I knew the smell of a fencing bag. Two blocks downtown is the theater where Malcolm X was assassinated; a little further south sat a mansion where George Washington had lived part time. On my way from the subway station at 168th I walked past six-story walk-up apartments similar to the one I'd grown up in, a couple other neighborhood public schools, a handful of bodegas, and the semi-frequent car blaring salsa music. In the nine years since I'd left, I'd been to both Riverdale and Brandeis, but walking from the subway to IS-90 still felt like coming home.

So that fall, there I stood in the classroom as my new alter ego, Mr. Morehouse, seventh grade Social Studies and English teacher in Washington Heights. I wore a short-sleeved collared shirt and a tie, khaki pants and black shoes. I held a clipboard, my back was perpetually covered in chalk dust from leaning against the board, and I said things like, "Maturity, everyone! Maturity!" and "Okay, students, please focus on your assignment!"

Being a first year teacher is hard enough at any school, and it didn't help that IS-90 was on the brink of collapse. There were sixteen- and seventeen-year olds in the sixth and seventh grades. Within the first month of school, IS-90 was featured in the New York Daily News under the headline "School in Chaos!" Hundreds of kids cut class and wandered the hallways during the day instead of sitting in classrooms without desks or books.

In the breaks between classes, I wondered how the Russian and Italian fencers were spending their days.

That first month, I taught, went home and collapsed, woke up in the evening to grade papers and write lesson plans for the next day, then collapsed again before getting up in the morning for school. For a month, I didn't touch a saber—my big dreams had met reality. One day after school, frustrated, I drove out to Riverdale Country School and sat in my car on the street and cried. I imagined the seventh graders in those classrooms reading Shakespeare and learning chemistry and joining the fencing team while less than a mile away, my students were on average reading at a fourth grade level and falling further behind every day. My resources as a struggling U.S. fencer in comparison with those of the Italians and Russians were the equivalent of my IS-90 students' resources in comparison with those at Riverdale. Were my dreams—and my students' dreams—of catching the privileged people ahead of us doomed?

I didn't realize it at the time, but in both teaching and fencing, I was making excuses that made success impossible. On the fencing end, I wasn't going to practice because I'd decided I was too tired and overwhelmed from the school day. At school I was doing the equivalent in the classroom by accepting the idea that my students' challenges were too large to overcome. On the outside, I was working doggedly, but subconsciously my growing belief in the impossibility of my goals allowed me to ease up on both. Really, if I tried and failed I was a failure—but if I didn't really try, I could blame failure on circumstance. What would it mean if I put all of myself into trying to be a great teacher and an Olympian and neither happened?

It took seeing this corrosive mentality in my students to see that I had to change it in myself. Early in the year, several of my students took to writing a long series of stories in which I was a vampire and the young science teacher they all had crushes on was a damsel in distress, pouring out page after page on their own time to create these wonderful and humorous stories. I quickly realized that they were as brilliant and smart as any student at Riverdale; why couldn't they be learning and doing the same things? Why, during our structured lessons, would they rather misbehave to the point of earning detention rather than show they didn't know an answer? I realized that maybe bigger than their fear of failure was the fear of exposing themselves—being seen as unintelligent, or untalented, or just plain bad.

My students were living the self-fulfilling failure prophecy of the culture that surrounded them. Their whole lives, my students had been told they were failures. Even if it wasn't said overtly, many teachers, administrators, and other officials expected failure—these adults made excuses and placed the blame on the poverty in the neighborhood, on the students' families, and on any other number of socio economic reasons to explain, and thus, in a way, permit this failure. The students, who were unbelievably perceptive, accepted that perhaps their challenges were too great. Why even try?

U.S. fencing as a whole suffered from the same combination of steep challenges, self-disbelief, and a culture of low expectations. We couldn't possibly compete with Europeans, the prevailing wisdom went, so why even try? As a result, just like my students' unwillingness to answer questions and my inability to go to practice, U.S. fencers often skipped international competitions, making failure inevitable.

But despite the prevailing failure of IS-90 as a whole, some teachers succeeded. For example, when you walked into Ms. Winnett's room, you would swear you'd walked into a different school. She taught and her kids learned—despite facing the same challenges as everyone else. Ms. Winnett owned her students' results with no excuses.

Our fencing equivalent was Vladimir Nazlymov's insistence that we could compete, and he willingly threw his students into international competitions with no excuses for failure. Preordained defeat was unacceptable to him. The results weren't immediate and there were a whole lot of U.S. fencers getting their butts kicked. But it was educational butt-kicking—the kind that teaches you valuable lessons even in failure, a necessary precursor to success.

Eventually results started to follow. Though fencing at the 2000 Games wasn't televised, in September I followed the results on the internet as Cliff Bayer lost by one point to the eventual gold medalist and the U.S. women's foil team came within 2 points of a bronze medal. These results were signs that the excuses had been just that: excuses and nothing more, mountains in our minds.

During my senior year at Brandeis, the Fencers Club had moved from its cramped uptown digs to a cavernous floor in a factory building on 25th Street, between 6th and 7th Avenues in the Garment District. (The old Fencers Club space became a fertility clinic.) Inside the new space was a main training room with nine white practice strips painted on a blue floor. In a second room, coaches gave lessons. A third room sat empty. The Fencers Club had rented the whole floor and planned to sublease the empty room, but then membership boomed. The Club cannibalized the empty room, painting it with strips and opening it to the burgeoning crew of fencers who were flocking both to the sport and to the Fencers Club itself, which had fast become the Mecca of American fencing.

Finally, no longer allowing myself to be road-blocked mentally by excuses, I took the train down to the Fencers Club for a lesson with Yury, who was fresh back from Sydney. And that's where I found myself at 6:30pm, asleep on my feet.

"Team! What are you doing!" Yury shouted in his thick Ukrainian accent. I looked around. The other fencers kept working and I noticed that Yury was only speaking to me. His accent turned "Tim" into "Team."

I looked back at Yury and watched as his hand flew up to his black coaching mask. He ripped it off and stared at me with cold eyes, his arms spread wide, his saber in his right hand and his mask in his left.

"Tell me, Team! What are you doing?" Yury spoke each word slowly, deliberately. Then he waited. Yury sees everything—it's what makes him so good. A cut one centimeter too far, a blade that momentarily arches back or one that doesn't take the shortest possible route to the target, lazy footwork—Yury sees it all and demands that it be made perfect.

I leaned on my saber blade, pushing it downward as I answered, "My arm? The feint isn't good?"

We had spent fifteen minutes working on my feint cut, an attack maneuver in which your blade moves first toward one scoring zone, drawing your opponent into a parry, then redirects to catch your opponent in the zone left undefended. It's the equivalent of a pump fake in basketball, getting a defender to jump at the wrong time to block your shot. And my fake wasn't working—not in practice and not in matches.

Yury saw it all.

Yury is from Kiev, the capital city of Ukraine, which had been part of the USSR when he was growing up. He's the son of a schoolteacher and a colonel in the Soviet Army. As a child, he'd seen the *Three Musketeers* on TV, so when a Soviet sports official visited his class one day and asked who wanted to be a swordfighter, Yury volunteered. He started fencing foil at a local club and showed immense promise from the start, eventually working his way into a sports university in Kiev. His goal was the Olympics.

Eventually he represented Kiev at the Soviet Army Championships and looked forward to showing his talent on the national stage. Yury knew that if he could beat Moscow fencers, he could hope to move to the Moscow team himself, and then maybe on to the Olympics.

Then his coach told his team to throw matches. Yury was the only person to speak up, asking what would happen if he refused. "Then you can go to the regular army," his coach told him. Honesty was a one-way ticket to Siberia and then to Afghanistan, where the Soviet Army was fighting a brutal and bloody war against the Taliban. Yury acquiesced. What choice did he have? He continued to fence, but he realized that with the system set against him, his dream of fencing in the Olympics was over.

He moved to coaching, eventually at the Kiev Institute of Physical Culture, a sports academy for high-level athletes. Among his students were the preternaturally gifted Vladimir Kaluzhny and Yury Keznetsov. Yury started to believe that his coaching goals could succeed where his personal fencing goals had failed.

But there was another barrier: Yury is Jewish, and Jews were forbidden to travel outside the USSR. Yury couldn't take his students to international competitions, so rather than hoarding his talented pair in Kiev where they would be doomed—as he had been—to forever be provincial talents, he talked both fencers into leaving him and moving to Moscow, where they had a shot at moving up through the system instead of being restricted by it.

Yury settled into a program aimed at preparing young fencers for the Soviet Union Championships. He worked hard and excelled as a coach, but in the back of his mind lingered his Olympic dreams.

Then Chernobyl changed everything.

On April 26, 1986, there was an explosion at the nuclear reactor in Pripyat, Ukraine, which sent radioactive smoke and debris spewing into the sky like a plume from a volcano. Yury's daughter,

Julia, developed a rash on her arm and Yury knew he had to act quickly. He had long thought about moving his family out of the Soviet Union, and now was the time. Fearing for his daughter's safety, he sent his wife and daughter to Lithuania by train, staying so that he could work and send them money.

Finally, Yury was granted refugee status due to the health concerns surrounding Chernobyl, and with his family he immigrated to the United States... where he got a job making doughnuts. Even now, gravely seriously, Yury will say about that time, "I make best doughnuts."

In the back of his mind was always the Olympics.

That day at Fencers Club, we'd started the lesson like every other lesson, with a salute, me wearing only a glove and a mask for protection, and Yury in full padding with a black-visored mask that obscures his eyes. If anyone at Fencers Club met Yury on the strip, they'd beat him, but that's not what the lesson is about. Sometimes the best guys can't teach a basic move. Yury had started slowly, raising his saber to rest it underneath mine. Then he opened a line, bringing the tip of his saber parallel to the floor: the signal to attack to his "five"—his head. Boom, boom, I double-cut straight to the top of his mask, tapping twice to show control and then leaving my position. Yury examined my shoulder, my arm, the angle of my blade. When I bounced haphazardly off his mask, we did it again; when I was in control, we progressed. Yury moved his blade deliberately toward one of my scoring zones and parried, freezing so he could check the position. Then we were back to resting, his blade under mine, facing each other from a couple feet away. Yury opened the right side of his body and I straight cut to the zone, arm relaxed, direct to target.

I was stressed, tired, and emotionally mangled from school and Yury saw it—he saw everything. When I double-tapped and started to return my arm back to en garde, Yury saw it and we did the move again. Yury never felt sorry for me or let me off the hook, as I imagine he could easily have done—*Tim's working too hard at school to be an Olympian, Tim's fencing is so far behind everyone else's, he can't make the team.*

I tried to take the lesson. I tried to keep excuses from creeping into my work with my students at IS-90. I would fence toward the Olympics, they would learn toward reading at grade level, both despite circumstances that seemed designed to keep us from our goals.

Next, we added footwork. Yury lowered his blade, I double-cut to his head—boom, boom—and he started walking toward me. I maintained my distance, arm outstretched, keeping a saber's length between us until Yury cut slowly toward me and I parried, again leaving my angles for inspection. We increased the speed, increased the complexity. Neither of us talked. In addition to his head, right, and left sides, Yury started to show his wrist. I beat his blade, then cut under his wrist, cut over his wrist, cut to his head—*beat, tap, tap, tap, touch* was the rhythm of our conversation, slowly speeding, staying relaxed, using my fingers, as if rolling Chinese medicine balls, to drive my blade's tip.

Fencing has a circle of actions—parry an opponent and you can make him scared to finish. Then you catch him in preparation on the next point, in those milliseconds of hesitation born of the doubt you've forced into his attack. Then when he focuses on fixing his attack, you counter with a direct attack of your own. Then defense. Each move has a logical follow-up based on how you predict an opponent will adjust. By outthinking your opponent, you stay a step ahead in this circle of actions.

On the strip with Yury, we built through this circle toward the complexity of false-action-parry-riposte, me checking forwardthen retreating as Yury sent a cut. I parried and riposted for the touch. We sped up. "Double retreat make fake action stronger, parry, riposte," said Yury and we did it. "Fake parry four, parry three, riposte," said Yury, and I briefly opened my four, he cut to my three, I parried his blade and then riposted. Yury started going for my blade as I attacked and I manipulated my fingers to snake my blade around his parries.

I kept my arm relaxed. I finished my steps. I went straight to target.

We continued a little further, a little further, extending toward the bleeding edge of my technique. Until it broke down.

"Do it again," growled Yury, referring to my feint cut. He put on his mask and signaled with his blade. I advanced and he retreated. I advanced again and sent my blade rocketing toward his head, shifting mid-flight toward his flank. Yury calmly defended my attack, which landed harmlessly against his guard with a metallic clang—in every way the equivalent of a basketball clanging the rim. Yury shook his head again as a couple fencers glanced over in our direction.

"Team! Matt can do this better than you!" Yury shouted, referring to a high school fencer who was standing close by. Matt spun and yelled, "Hey!"

We tried it again, the frustration boiling inside me. I moved forward, launched into the maneuver, and failed again. The moment my blade fell, Yury began stuttering as he looked for the perfect words to vent his frustration. "I… I… Team, I can teach bear do this better than you!"

"A bear?" I asked. Behind me, I could hear Matt and some of the other fencers snickering. Yury breaks us down so that he can rebuild us—technically, emotionally—but it's a grueling process. Simultaneously, he pushes his fencers to the breaking point and roots for them to overcome. Enemy and ally—Yury is both. He pushes you, heckles you beyond the end of your skills in that dangerous unknown where every day you succeed or fail.

"Yes! A bear can be taught to ride tricycle. Bear can do feint cut! Just not you!" Yury's eyes were wide open now. He sees everything.

A smile crept across Yury's face. "Can you tell me what is the secret of fencing, Team?" I knew him well enough to know it was a rhetorical question—a misdirection as sure as a feint cut. Yury was a step ahead; he already had the answer.

"Um, hard work?" I answered.

"Team," Yury said, "imagine you are at party and there is beautiful girl there. What is most important thing if you want to get her?" So far I was with him… At least, I'd heard that people with more time and more panache did that kind of thing.

"A good pickup line?" I answered.

"No!" said Yury, delighting in my springing his trap. "You can't shout pickup line from across bar. *You have to be at right distance.* Even if you a little bit incorrect, it still has chance to work. Wrong distance, it can never work. That," he said, "is the secret of fencing."

I nodded at Yury and we pushed our masks down, paused, and then he signaled with his blade. I moved forward. Feeling anxious, I forced myself closer, closer, closer, and launched into my feint. This time, Yury's blade rose to defend his mask and my blade cut back towards his flank, landing before he could pull away. We both froze. I stayed in my lunge, maintaining my balance. Yury stood still, examining my final position.

"Woo woo!" he said, which is his typical noise of approval. "This is better, Team!"

He lifted his mask and saluted. We shook hands. The lesson ended.

Like most of Yury's lessons, the right distance was more than a position on the fencing strip. In the following days, I put myself at the Fencers Club alongside Keeth, Akhi, and Ivan, and I put myself with Yury—in the right distance.

Practice Like You Play

After school, if I sat down on a park bench or if I stopped at home even briefly, I'd pass out. A couple times on the train down from 168th, I fell asleep and woke up at the terminal just across from Brooklyn. Once I woke up on the way uptown again—I'd slept through the turnaround.

Unlike the others at Fencers Club, I had graduated from college without ever working with an international coach, and this (plus perhaps stubbornness) meant that I'd developed a style through a mishmash of trial and error. In college, there were enough fencers with frumpy styles that I didn't stand out, but now, surrounded by the country's top fencers, I was an eyesore.

I took my en garde in a forward-leaning crouch with my blade circling in the position known as a four-parry. The unconventional stance not only shrank my target zone but because it was simply strange it also gave me that edge of inscrutability. When my opponents eventually attacked this weird position, they tended to do so hesitantly, and with my saber already circling I was able to pick up their blades and riposte for the touch. This worked against mid-level fencers and I had used it to solidify my NCAA results.

An extension of this circling four-parry was that my strategy tended to focus on opponents' blades, constantly searching for their sabers. I held my own blade somewhat extended so that if I saw an opponent's blade go back, I could quickly tap the fencer on the head while he was in preparation. If his blade stayed even or came forward, I'd beat the blade, then attack. And so, really, I was fencing against the saber rather than against the opponent. It worked well in college, but it proved little more than a parlor trick against the best Americans.

Perhaps my strangest technique was a maneuver my college coach Bill Shipman affectionately named "dog peeing on a fire hydrant." As the name implies, it wasn't beautiful. Basically, when an opponent attacked, I'd wave my body sideways and take a whack at his wrist so that I was essentially blocking and counter-attacking at the same time. I don't know why—it was just something I did. Adding to the visual of a micturating canine, my back leg would come off the ground, often leaving me in danger of pitching sideways off the strip.

It was these skills I brought to Fencers Club.

Yury gave group lessons from 5:30-6:30 on Mondays and Wednesdays—variations of the footwork, attack, and parry drills that make up the all-important basics of the sport. Outside the group lessons, most fencers took two or three individual lessons per week, and committed fencers showed up pretty much every day to free fence on the open strips.

On any given night, the open strips of the Fencers Club were home to the country's best fencing. In addition to Keeth Smart, Akhi Spencer-El, Ivan Lee, Herby Raynaud, and Ahmed Yilla, there were strong kids from teams at St. John's, Columbia, NYU, and St. Benedict's Preparatory School in New Jersey. Like shooting pool, the winner stayed on the strip. The first trick was choosing your strip—if you picked Keeth Smart's strip or got behind him in line, it could mean a quick exit and a forty-five-minute wait before you could fence again. But if you picked a lame strip, you'd end up fencing underpowered opponents all night and not get anything out of it. So you had to pick your sweet spot: an opponent you could beat, but who would challenge you.

Strips as well as fencers gained reputations. Did you dare challenge Keeth Smart on strip #1? Some fencers were less gracious than Keeth—a top fencer didn't want to see a wet-behind-the-ears high school kid next in line. It just wasn't worth their time. Still, fencers like Keeth and Akhi were a big reason I kept coming back for more—beating me every time and willing to even offer a tip here or there. It felt good to fence them, even when I lost, since every point I scored meant another thing I'd learned.

In this big pond of fencing's top national talent, you either sank or swam—and there was no one passing out life jackets. But if you took it seriously, fought hard, and trained even harder, the competitive environment took on a collaborative hue. Everyone was still trying to kick your ass—black or white, rich or poor—but we were like siblings who fought tooth and nail at home but stood shoulder-to-shoulder against the world.

Now fifty years old, Peter Westbrook himself came to fence, he came to talk, and he came to win. When he walked in, the room's spotlight turned to him automatically and the talk would start: "Morehouse, Morehouse, you gonna beat me today?" I remember once when I was fencing an up-and-comer from Notre Dame who was visiting the City, Peter came to watch, keeping up a running commentary of, "Which one of you guys is better? Which one of you guys is better? Let's see who wins." Peter was like that: gregarious, hilarious, and more than a bit impish, stirring up rivalries, poking for insecurities, and always testing, testing, testing fencers to see if they could take the heat.

Say I was ahead 13-8 against him—he'd start a commentary like, "Wow, man, what's that: you only need 2 points and I need 7? Shoot, that's gonna make it hard for me, man." Then he'd shake his head, feigning a hopeless look, then score the next point and say, "Oh man, what's the score now?" He damn well knew the score! The commentary continued until he'd win and say, "Shoot, you can't let me back in the match like that!" If you took a point, he'd shake his head and say, "Nice point, nice point, man!" in an amazed, over-congratulatory way that implied it wasn't the norm—it must have been a *really nice*, maybe lucky point if you'd scored.

Still, we all loved to fence him—at fifty, he beat me nearly every time. He'd been known for his cobra-like speed, and now maybe he'd lost a couple milliseconds in his strike, but you could see its fluid power as he glided around the room—the same warm-up every day and then to the strips where he more than held his own against fencers less than half his age. Once I won a match against Westbrook and then went maybe three months without fencing him. When we met again, he remembered every point, talking his way through how he was correcting the last match's mistakes. He destroyed me that day.

Once, a retired big-name Russian fencer visited Fencers Club and was holding a strip, mowing through New York's top talent who quivered at his feet, taking their beating as if it were cake—just the chance to stand on the strip with Russian talent was enough of an honor to make standing in a long line worthwhile. Westbrook saw our awe and cut the line. Peter still had a world-class parry, so fast he spent practice matches goading younger fencers into attacking him. When they did he'd simply deflect their blades and then rather than attacking for the points, he might let them attack over and over again for the fun of it, safe behind his parry. Against this Russian fencer—like many Russians, known for his blinding, powerful long attack—Peter turned to all of us watching and said, "Watch this, I'm gonna take parry four this point." The match started and Peter came forward, letting the Russian lunge and then, with a whole lot of attitude, parried him with a lightning-quick block and immediately riposted to his mask. Peter held out his arms in the air as he turned to us with an expression that said, "*See how easy that was?*" He continued calling his parries, saying, "See what I'm gonna do now is take parry three," as if the Russian fencer were a student in an instructional drill and Peter were demonstrating technique.

It was demeaning, it was rude, it was funny as hell, and when Westbrook took 15 points and the strip, he ripped all the stars from our eyes and showed us that not only could we compete with top international talent, but that we didn't have to kowtow to the presumed world fencing order that put us at the bottom. Peter might be standing at the other end of the strip, but even before the first point, he was in your head. Could you take it? If not, you couldn't take Fencers Club and you certainly couldn't take international competition—better to know it now, before throwing your life and your bank account at a pipe dream.

The same head-worm was true of Steve Mormando, only in a less gregarious way. You hated to fence Mormando. He'd done things like the point-in-line he'd pulled in Austin. If you tried to argue with the ref, Mormando would get in your face, put his fingers in your chest and tell you the point was his. Or he'd go for homerun maneuvers like his behind-the-back riposte that, if they actually landed, could put the room on his side and take the wind out of an opponent's previously full sails.

Archrivals in the past, Mormando almost never fenced Peter Westbrook at Fencers Club, and when they refereed each other's matches, they helped each other out. They might have lost a step on the young guns, but they had a mental game we lacked.

It's a game you can't learn in the fencing rooms at Riverdale or Brandeis, and American fencers don't have big enough sponsorships to spend the time and money learning these lessons in international competition. Simply, without meaning to, Fencers Club created a cutthroat, competitive, tournament-style atmosphere every night of the week. It was like standing in the on-deck circle swinging a weighted bat—by the time Fencers Club sabreurs got to a competition, they'd seen it before. Fencing against Westbrook, we learned how to stay in our own space rather than letting our opponents drive the narrative of the match. From Mormando we learned referee management and the courage to fight for points with our tongues as well as our blades. And fencing against Keeth and Akhi you knew if you scored a point on them that it could work against anyone in the country and be effective at a world cup, where they were now making strides.

Slow Is Fast

In the fall of 2000, I poured myself into teaching and fencing, putting one foot in front of the other to go deeper and deeper into both, hoping that dogged determination would lead to break-throughs. Three months into the school year, I finally found my textbooks—they were stacked next to the urinals in a now-defunct school bathroom that had been repurposed as a storage closet filled with supplies. Heading into that year's North American Cup season, I hoped for similar big things.

Before, I had been a college kid. Now, behind my saber were the twin forces of full-time lessons with Yury and evenings spent at the Fencers Club. Even without these additions, I was fresh from making the top eight at the Austin National Championships, and now with new skills, a new mental game, and full commitment, I was excited to take my new self for a test drive.

Through the fall, I fenced and taught and tried to stay afloat, and then finally it was December—time for the year's first tournament, a North American Cup in Ontario, California. The North American Cup series was still looking for the right format and in the year 2000, they instituted a rule that gave fencers ranked in the top sixteen a bye for the tournament's first day. Remaining fencers had to fight the six-person qualifying pools and then direct elimination matches until whittling their number down to 32. Then, strangely, on the tournament's second day, the sixteen ranked fencers were mixed back into another round of pools, meaning that 32+16=48 fencers were split into 8 pools of 6. On this second day, the pools again fenced 5-touch, round-robin matches and the bottom half was eliminated. The remaining 24 *again* fenced in pools of 6, cutting the bottom 8 until finally only sixteen fencers remained. Only at this point did the tournament switch to 15-touch, direct elimination matches, going from 16 to 8 to 4 to 2 to the winner.

In other words, despite making almost no sense whatsoever, the vast majority of the tournament was designed for me: 5-touch matches. It was an experiment and I was definitely a beneficiary.

No matter the Byzantine format, as a drowning first-year teacher now ranked in the top sixteen, I was happy to rest on the tournament's first day. At the time, registration and match mechanics were equally Byzantine. We mailed in our registration forms months in advance to the United States Fencing Association (USFA) in Colorado Springs, where they had an office near the Olympic Training Center, where (presumably) interns sliced the envelopes, entered fencers' data, and mailed confirmations. Online registration didn't come about until after 2008 and by-hand registration meant that a handful of athletes would invariably arrive on a tournament's first day to find their names suspiciously absent from the list of qualifying pools. Or on the flip side, match officials would put fencers on the strips for the qualifying pools only to find that a couple hadn't shown up. They'd have to stop the pools, re-sort the fencers, and start over, delaying the start by hours and meaning that fencers who'd warmed up now took the strip cold. This also meant that spectators and the almost nonexistent media had no idea what time the fencers they had come to watch would be on the strip. Parents packed lunches and media stayed away. We competed in a bubble.

In Ontario, there were twenty or so metallic strips running simultaneously in a huge convention hall, with fencers' equipment strewn about the hall, no seats for spectators, and fencers in all three weapons roaming around like amoebas bouncing around a water droplet. The 100-ish fencers in men's saber elbowed for position in front of a bulletin board where pools were posted in 12-point font on 8.5"x11" paper.

After blissfully wandering the hall for the first day, on the tournament's second day I fenced my way through the 5-touch pools to the round of 24, and there on the sheet of printer paper was the lineup for my next pool: Keeth Smart and Akhi Spencer-El, two top Canadian fencers, and the Italian fencer who had moved to the U.S. and was attending Columbia. A parent turned to me and said, laughing, "It's been a nice competition for you! You're not making it out of this pool!"

I fumed.

My pool of 6 gathered around the referee, who wore a blue dress jacket, a tie, and gray pants, missing only the top hat that would complete the Mad Hatter look. He held a clipboard and checked our equipment stamps to ensure that we were all wearing our underarm guard, a small, additional piece of white fabric that provides an extra layer of protection over a fencer's heart.

I lined up against Keeth Smart in my first match. Thinking about winning, I launched an attack off the line, but Keeth skittered away and riposted like a lightning strike for the touch. I wanted this with everything I had. I charged harder, but my blade found air—Keeth again predicted my lunge and accelerated backwards out of range before stepping in behind my blade to take the point. I needed to go harder. But the harder I went, the more frantic I looked and the more pronounced my tells—I was cocking my body, tensing it for a long lunge that could cover the distance to Keeth, but those milliseconds of forewarning let Keeth accelerate out of range with his fluid grace. The match ended with the *thwak* of Keeth's saber against my Kevlar jacket—I'd lost 1-5 and was never really in the match.

Next I fenced Akhi. Unlike Keeth's athleticism, Akhi is a technician. So instead of moving out of range when I charged, Akhi cut into me mid-step, hitting me under my arm when I exposed it in preparation for my attack—two different but equally effective ways to skin a cat, and unfortunately I was the cat. I lost to Akhi 1-5.

Against the two Canadians and the Italian, I fenced my heart out, sweating, panting, and when I landed a touch—and there weren't many—pumping my fists and screaming at the top of my lungs, hoping the breakthrough was happening, hoping all my hard work and determination was finally paying off.

But the payoff never came. I beat one of the Canadians and ended my pool with a dismal record of 1-4, failing to make the round of 16 and finishing the tournament in 19th position.

Back in Manhattan, our second school principal of the year had resigned, and the third took up the vacant post. I limped toward winter break at IS-90, every day slamming the throttle at the beginning of each class period to blast through the ambitious lessons I'd written that would help my students catch up. The problem was, the lessons weren't working. Every day, halfway through the class period, I would realize I'd lost my students; only I didn't have time to slow down! They were already behind and I had to keep pushing, keep cranking, keep the pedal to the metal. My test results were dismal—my students didn't understand the material. All my educational theory, classroom management strategies, lesson plans, and high expectations seemed to have flown the coop.

During winter break, I tried to put the stress of teaching and the pain of middling fencing results behind me to focus on the annual winter training camp at the Fencers Club. Along with most of the regular crew, top college and club fencers from around the country came to practice five or six hours a day and study with Yury. I told myself that focus and determination would pay off— using the camp to add strength, speed, and aggression would help me turn around my results at the next tournament, another North American Cup in Greensboro, South Carolina in January.

The camp came and went. I felt strong. I felt fierce. I felt fast.

In Greensboro I was still ranked high, so I sat the tournament's first day, then again fenced my way through pools to the round of 24, where I thankfully drew a much weaker pool than I had in Ontario. I took my line, crouched into my en garde, charged, fought… and lost. Each match, I tried to increase my determination to win, win, win. But each match, I lost, lost, lost. I finished the tournament in exactly 19th position. Again.

I stayed to watch Keeth beat a Canadian fencer for the gold, and Steve Mormando—the wily Olympic veteran—make the round of 8, dancing with his point-in-line, riposting behind the back, and arguing his way past fencers half his age. He couldn't move quickly, but he didn't have to.

In both teaching and fencing I fought and fought. But where were my results? After making the decision to leap headlong into fencing instead of getting on with law school and life, I'd actually taken a step *backwards* in my fencing results—from making the round of 8 at the Austin National Championships to finishing 19th at the year's first two NACs. I was training with Yury, I was trying to hold a strip every evening at the Fencers Club, and

I was focused on climbing the U.S. rankings toward the 2004 Olympic team. Why was I sinking to the bottom instead of rising to the top?

From Greensboro, I returned to Manhattan determined to fight my way out of the slump. At Fencers Club, I fenced harder and harder, faster and faster. I ran and trained.

One evening I found myself flying at Yury, who blocked me easily over and over. At an instructional pace, I was practicing ignoring Yury's fakes—only I was falling for every one. Finally, Yury ripped off his mask.

"Team! What are you doing!"

"What?!" I yelled back, frustrated, vibrating, focused.

He paused. "Team," he said, "let me tell you a poem." *Oh God, here we go with the bear again*, I thought. "Good speed is speed when you can control it. If you cannot control your speed, you are stu-peed." Did that qualify as a poem? "You're going too fast, Team," Yury said. "Slow down."

I tried. He lowered his mask and I took a slow step before lunging. Yury blocked me easily. "No!" he yelled. "Slow down!"

I moved slower. Yury faked and I fell for it. "Still too fast!" he yelled. I went slower, to a crawl. Yury faked. I fell for it. "Slower!" he yelled. I tried to cork my frustration, and now rage, into the bottle of snail-slow speed. Yury faked. I saw it. Of course I saw it—I was moving too slow to react! I stepped forward and Yury made a couple more fakes. Finally he started his real parry and I saw it, too, and dove into the opening to catch Yury's open target.

"Woo, woo, woo," said Yury, his noise of approval. "This is your speed, Team."

"This is my speed?" I said. "Really?"

"Good speed is speed when you can control it…"

"If not, you are stu-peed," I finished. We both laughed.

"Or *balda!*" exclaimed Yury with a laugh, using the Russian word for stupid. I'd picked up a handful of Russian words in our lessons. Most of them meant *stupid*.

"Now go practice this speed in your bouts," said Yury. The lesson was over. We saluted and Yury called up his next student. I held his voice in my head: the right distance, the right speed.

In April 2001, during IS-90's spring break, I flew to Germany for my first international competition. In fact, it was a tournament on the German national circuit, but they accepted foreign entries and it lined up with my break. It was a bit strange to register for some random national comp in another country, but so be it—I figured it would be a nice way to dip my toe in the international scene, and it had one big advantage over most international comps: double elimination. As long as I fenced my way out of the qualifying pools, I was guaranteed at least two 15-touch matches.

As a first year teacher, I was drowning along with my students and even living at home with my parents. My $29,000 teacher's salary barely paid for food, equipment, and training. The thought of whipping out a credit card for airfare and a hotel made my stomach do flips. Hopping on a plane would be lost time and borrowed money, but at least in Germany I'd get two bouts for it.

So that's what I did.

I armed myself with a fan of credit cards and showed up at the airport with my fencing bag and a duffel. Of course, you have to check sabers, but I carried on everything else—mask, metallic jacket, wires with plugs no one's seen before, one glove, whites, shoes, toothbrush, and my students' papers to grade on the plane. If my stuff went to Budapest while I went to Germany, all I'd need to borrow would be a blade.

Needless to say, even in the pre-9/11 era, airport security loved me. Who travels with a mask, wires, and a Kevlar jacket? That first trip, I sweated and checked my watch as first one security agent, then the supervisor, then the supervisor's supervisor sorted through my gear, strewn across a folding table like the Unabomber's workbench.

I arrived in Germany feeling like a zombie—tired, strung out, and wondering how I possibly thought I could teach and fence at the same time and stay sane. At the fencing hall, I was some random American guy that no one knew, and despite the Germans' perfect English, I stumbled through the mechanics of tournament registration and ended up taking the strip for the pools feeling disoriented and out of place. Without expectations, I decided that instead of trying to win, I'd use the tournament as a test run for some of the techniques I'd been working on with Yury: false temp parry riposte, false temp attack, false temp feint cut, all at the right distance and at a speed that wasn't stu-peed.

In my pool populated mostly by German youngsters, for the first time, at a slower speed, my fakes started to work. And conversely, I stopped falling for all of my opponents' misdirections. I qualified for the round of 64 and, again focusing on going slow— "my speed"—I blew through a couple lesser-known Germans to make the round of 16. In the round of 16, I faced an opponent who had just upset Wiradech Kothny, the individual and team bronze medalist at the Sydney Olympics. After his upset win over Kothny, my opponent had hugged his coach and celebrated mightily. Maybe it was the emotional pendulum swinging the other direction after the previous match's high, but in the 16 my opponent seemed flat. I parried him on the first 2 points and from then on he took pains to set up his attacks, which let me hit him in preparation—I was a step ahead in the cycle of actions.

Every once in a long while, you fence a match and it seems like everything works—you go forward and score, you go back and score—out of pure *why not*, you try something bizarre like a duck parry… and it works! This was one of those matches. I won 15-3 to make the quarterfinals, where I met Dennis Bauer, also nine months removed from winning the team bronze at the Sydney Games. The competition consolidated to one raised strip, and, with a couple hundred people watching from the bleachers, Bauer beat me 15-11. But I gave him a strong bout—when I faked, I saw his uncertainty, and when he faked, I was able to ignore his traps. Sure, Bauer was then able to recover in time to take the points he needed to win, but suddenly what I was doing was working.

After the weekend competition, I still had the full workweek of spring break to kill, so I decided to hitch a ride with a German coach to the Junior World Championships held that year in Gdansk, Poland. Actually, just as I'd mistaken Colin Clinton for his twin brother Elliott at Brandeis, I'd met the German coach's twin brother and assumed my travel companion was the same person. He must have been mighty confused when a shoestring American simply said hi and asked for a ride to Poland, but he was nice enough about it and I only discovered my mistake later.

We drove through the countryside through an old, concrete border crossing boosted directly from a Bond film, where the crossing guards checked our passports and looked in the trunk. Though we never hit anything resembling a highway, the coach seemed to know the way.

I didn't know what hotel the U.S. team was staying at in Gdansk, but after some wandering around by the fencing venue and a couple conversations in broken English and international gesture language, I found the team and talked my way into crashing on the floor of one of their rooms.

For a few days I watched the next generation of U.S. fencers, including Tim Hagamen, a Riverdale fencer now training at Fencers Club with Yury. I had started coaching two days a week at Riverdale to throw some change at my ballooning credit card bills, and Tim Hagamen was one of the students on the team. Opposite my focus on high school fencing, Tim had decided to fence clubs while keeping a toe in high school fencing to support Riverdale and the man who gave him his fencing start, Coach Schneider. Competing in the under-17 cadet division, Tim Hagamen won a silver medal. He was obviously on a steep trajectory that could soon see him rocketing past the plane on which I sat.

I connected with Jason Rogers on the trip, a young lefty from California. Jason had traded skateboarding for fencing after taking a lesson with Romanian-American coach Daniel Costin. (Costin had coached the Romanian Olympic team before moving to Los Angeles.) I admired the fact that Jason had been able to break into the rankings from outside the established fencing powers of New York, Atlanta, and elsewhere. Now with the blessing of his coach, he'd decided to attend Ohio State, where he hoped Vladimir Nazlymov could help him take his game to the next level.

But the story of the tournament was Ivan Lee from the Peter Westbrook Foundation, an African-American fencer from Brooklyn who, like Keeth, had attended Brooklyn Tech and then gone on a full ride to St. John's. He took silver in the extremely competitive junior division. With his hair dyed red after competing for St. John's at the NCAA Championships, it was obvious that Ivan had joined Keeth and Akhi as the third untouchable of U.S. fencing.

At that world championships, Ivan, Tim, Jason, and another young fencer from Arkady in Atlanta, Colin Parker, pulled off a first in U.S. fencing history: winning the junior men's saber team world championship. Surely this generation was poised to vault past even Keeth and Akhi, let alone me, into the Olympic success that U.S. fencing had never before seen.

At the Gdansk Junior World Championships, I also met and befriended Olympic foil fencer Iris Zimmermann, then on break from Stanford. Five years ago, she'd won the Cadet World Championships as a fourteen-year-old, the first world championship win of any kind in U.S. fencing history. Iris had been an integral part of the women's foil team that came within 2 points of a medal at the 2000 Sydney Olympics, losing the bronze medal match to France on a controversial penalty call. Now women's foil was United States fencing's great hope for a medal at the 2004 Athens Olympics.

Watching the competition that week in Gdansk, I realized that in order to climb from my #10 national ranking to the #4 ranking I needed to qualify for the 2004 Olympic team, I would not only need to scramble past the people ahead of me, but I would also need to climb faster than these talented young fencers behind me. Could I climb fast while moving slow? Late in the week, I caught a train back to Germany and then a flight home.

Then, after a week at school, I caught a Friday flight to the season's third North American Cup in Reno, Nevada. The tournament started in the evening and I arrived jet-lagged and exhausted, but also energized. My slower self was another new self in a series of new selves, and it's always exciting to see if a breakthrough is really a breakthrough or just a fluke—another dead-end path in the maze of improvement. I fenced my way through pools, through the rounds of 64 and 32, and then in the round of 16 I met Terrence Lasker, the Nazlymov student who had finished just behind Keeth and Akhi to miss the 2000 Olympic Team. I'd never fenced him before, but I'd seen him a hundred times. Lasker was Nazlymov's top student. He had been to Europe, was slender, black, with a relaxed style. He had a way of shimmying just out of range, tempting opponents to attack, but when they did, they found their sabers slicing through nothing but a puff of smoke where Lasker had only just been.

The first point, I moved slowly forward off my line. Lasker checked into the middle of the strip, tempting me to lunge, but I saw the fake for what it was and slowly accelerated my steps—

slower to faster, driving Lasker down the strip, my shoulder re-laxed, until he took an off-balance step and I lunged to hit. The next point, I moved forward slowly and saw his shoulder twitch. Without thinking, I stepped back and parried. There was his blade, *snick!*, off my blade, and I riposted for the touch. Next I used false temp attack: I checked into the middle, saw Lasker's uncertainty, and lunged, jumping out to a 10-5 lead. Then he turned on his speed. Even when I guessed his intent, he powered through my parries, closing the gap to 14-10. He tried to make me use the whole strip, figuring I would break down over distance. As I advanced slowly toward him, he threw a series of fakes, checking toward me. My body wanted to respond, to charge, but I didn't let it, advancing slowly, slowly, as if on a high wire, until I couldn't stand it anymore. I lunged, hit, and had beaten Terrence Lasker!

Nuts to the newly-instituted system of double elimination: Lasker won his next match and we met again in the quarterfinals where he beat me 15-10, but I'd posted a top-eight finish for the first time since Austin. From there, I went back to Manhattan, back to training, back to teaching. But I'd validated the lesson of this most recent new self: slow is fast. Only at a slow speed could I see a match objectively. Only at a crawl could I see my opponents' fakes as fakes, and only by starting slow could I set up my own fakes.

Back in the classroom, instead of blindly charging the machine gun nests that were my seventh graders, I slowed down, thought about my actions, and it helped me see what was working and what wasn't. Earlier in the year, I'd sometimes give kids detention and they simply wouldn't show up. What could I do? Now I tried something new. One day a student didn't show after school... and I went to his house. It was a two-room Washington Heights walk-up with fourteen people living in it. When his mom buzzed me up, I found my student helping take care of his younger brothers and sisters. I sat across from his mom at their kitchen table as my student listened from the other room, completely mortified that Mr. Morehouse was in his kitchen.

I slowed down. I listened. I understood something about why my student wasn't finishing assignments and I made an adjustment.

I showed up at a couple more students' doors and I started to get a rep: "Dude, Mr. Morehouse will *come to your house!*" Students started showing up for detention and we used the time not necessarily as a punishment, but to work on materials they'd missed. Subtly, I changed the classroom message from improving behavior to understanding the work, trying to hammer home the idea that the rules were in place not to create a police state but to help them learn.

Instead of focusing on discipline, I focused on my lesson plans—on my technique instead of on pigheaded repression. Better lessons kept students involved and my discipline problems decreased. Going slower in the room let me go faster through the curriculum, allowing me to focus on the things that got results and not just on a frenzy of actions that might in fact be pushing me in the wrong direction.

One day I was sick on my feet and I remember the kids suddenly acting like angels—an unspoken agreement among them to take it easy on poor, sick Mr. Morehouse. Another time, a kid from another class opened my door from the hall, cursed at me, and then ran out. Dee—one of my bright but tough students whose brother was in jail—jumped from his desk, ran into the hall, and tackled the intruder. Of course, I had to give Dee detention, but when I asked why he'd jumped the kid, Dee said, "No one makes fun of you but us!"

By the spring of 2001, I hadn't climbed past the #10 ranking with which I'd started the year and most of my IS-90 students were still reading below grade level—but on their standardized tests, they'd made a year's worth of progress and hadn't fallen any further behind. After plummeting from my starting point in both teaching and fencing, through slowing down and trusting my training, I'd fought my way back to my baseline, back to within reach of my goals. Just before the end of my first year as a teacher, I brought this upward trajectory to my first international world cup tournaments.

International Fencing
Is Not a Game

Armed with my new, wily slowness that allowed me to step back and see a match objectively, I was ready to leap into the season's last few world cup tournaments in the spring of my first year of teaching.

In fact, I'd already competed in one international world cup, which was held in Boston in the spring of my senior year at Brandeis. Representative of the attention given to U.S. fencing at the time, the world's top fencing talent competed in a tiny school gymnasium in Peabody, Massachusetts surrounded by pullout bleachers. The finals were held in the school auditorium. I had surprised myself, fencing well enough in the 5-touch qualifying pools to sneak into the tournament's round of 64 and the start of the single-elimination, 15-touch matches. There, I had been seeded exactly 64th, and so faced the tournament's top seed, the Russian world #1 ranked multiple gold medalist Stanislav Pozdniakov. It was my second time going against a Russian

World Champion, the first being in Harlem against chess champion Garry Kasparov in elementary school. I didn't fare much better than I had the first time, as Pozdniakov dismantled me 15-4. When I charged, he parried away my attacks and landed ripostes. When I tried to parry, he crashed through for points. I counted it as a learning experience.

In one of the later-round matches at that Boston World Cup, I watched the 1998 World Champion Italian Luigi Tarantino jump off the strip and try to choke an opposing team's coach for snickering at a referee's bad call that went against Tarantino. The American referee, who was wearing a Daffy Duck tie, stood by while Tarantino's Italian teammates pulled him off. After calling the match's final point against Tarantino, the ref literally ran from the venue.

Welcome to international competition.

In the spring of 2001, after fencing the German national competition, watching the Junior World Championships in Gdansk, Poland, and returning home to a strong result at the season's last NAC in Reno, I was ready for my first true world cup. Today, there are eight or ten Americans at every world cup, but not back then. Americans had only just begun to hit the circuit, and only the top Americans at that: among them Westbrook fencers Keeth Smart, Akhi Spencer-El, Herby Raynaud, and now the youngest member of the elite, Ivan Lee. They were already on the national team, whose travel expenses were paid by the U.S. Fencing Association. Because Keeth and Akhi were taking a break from the world cup circuit after the Sydney Olympics and Ivan Lee was in school at St. John's, I was the tournament's only American.

My plane landed in Frankfurt and I took a train to Bonn, riding alone with the hum of the wheels, like I had so many days between my parents' house in Riverdale, IS-90 in Washington Heights, and the Fencers Club downtown. It's what I'd always done: taking the train to fence. After an uneasy night's sleep, I found the venue was just like any other—strips on the floor, judges, bleachers, and fluorescent lights in a gym. If I squinted a bit, it was just like a college competition or a North American Cup. Fencers wore whites covered with electric jackets and beekeeper masks just like every other tournament. There were fencing bags and warm-up suits everywhere. It felt like home.

Still, I took the strip in Bonn that day nervous and jittery, expecting to get decimated. I could never beat Akhi in practice and even he wasn't doing so well internationally at this point. I imagined these fencers would be competing at an unbelievably high level and I hoped only to score enough to earn a respectable defeat.

I opened my six-person, round-robin pool with a 5-3 win. I was lunging, expecting to get parried, but somehow my blade was sneaking through. I won the next match too, finished the pools with a 4-2 record, and then won a sudden death match to make the tournament's second day—the round of 64.

Waiting for me in the 64 was former World Champion Frenchman Damien Touya. His world ranking was in the top sixteen, so he got a bye to the round of 64 instead of having to fence the pools. In 1996, he'd won a bronze medal in individual saber in Atlanta, and he'd just taken 5th in Sydney, eliminating Keeth Smart along the way.

It would be a learning experience, I told myself. It was a step on the path to closing the distance. Time and money were immaterial compared to simply basking in the superhuman glory of the world's elite fencers, even as they dismantled me. I went through my preflight checklist, dialing in my strategy for the first point. The director said *Allez!*

Touya eats newbie fencers for breakfast—we are his version of Wheaties. The reality of this match was that Touya had more than twice my ability, experience, technique, and speed. But here's the thing: while I was certainly a newbie, my technique wasn't necessarily on the newbie continuum of expected fencing skill. My ungainly technique—the funky angle of my feint cut—wasn't necessarily a less-skilled version of Touya's. It was *different*. I'm sure there were, and still are, holes in my defense and inaccuracies in my attack, but they aren't in the expected places.

It's like poker: you can trust top-notch opponents to play logically, their actions giving clues to their cards. But it can be harder to play against unskilled opponents—if they're playing willy-nilly, who knows what their hands hold?—and they certainly can't be trusted to act logically when you've played them into logical spots. Likewise, a strange fencer is sometimes a dangerous fencer. Later I would learn that an ungainly newbie fencer only succeeds until he has been "solved," at which point the initially promising results can take a nosedive. But for now, the gist is this: I took Touya to 13-13 in my first international competition. I would attack, miss, then, without really seeing his blade, raise to block my head and catch Touya's blade on the way, hitting him with the riposte. Mid-match, Touya started stretching, jumping in place a bit—he'd imagined this match would be his warm-up, the start of his tournament, and now he was trying to get the blood flowing before it was too late.

It worked. Touya took the final 2 points and the win. But I walked off the strip into a new world. Truth be told, it was mostly luck that made it such a close match. But in terms of closing the distance between being a New York City public school teacher who's asleep on his feet in the evenings and being a competitor in the world of elite fencing, it was huge. I remembered watching perfect, superhuman Olympians skate the 1984 Winter Olympics. I remember one Saturday in eighth grade meeting Olympian Peter Westbrook for the first time and being awed. Now I'd nearly beaten a recent Olympian at the top of his form in an international competition.

It gave me more than confidence—it gave me real belief. Not the kind born of ignorant bliss and wishful daydreaming, but the kind of belief brought by actually getting in the game and taking away something positive.

After I was eliminated, I watched from the stands, paying attention to how fencers at this level moved. The typical U.S. fencer tends to be immediate. We take big steps and launch big attacks, running down the strip at opponents. Until now, this is what I'd been used to seeing. I'd prepared a whole game around this speed, but at the international level, everyone seemed more patient. At international tournaments, Americans' speed makes us cannon fodder for opponents' patience—American fencers new to international competition tend to run headlong into the buzzsaws of fencers.

For example, while there are certainly French fencers who don't "fence French," on the whole the team takes shorter steps than other countries. The toes of the French front foot come up a little higher than other counties, and the foot lands with a distinctive heel-toe. Generally, this makes French fencers very strong defenders. Compact feet allow them to reverse quickly, and the emphasis on footwork makes them lithe in retreat. This allows the French to outdistance an oncoming attack and make it fall short before scoring on the riposte.

I watched the Italian fencers, who tended to be a bit more demonstrative. Didn't win the point? An Italian fencer might rip off his mask, check his equipment—surely it couldn't be his fault! Surely the equipment was to blame! The Italian fencer might scowl at his opponent as if he had done something weird, something unseemly, to take the point. If hit with a wild cut, an Italian might rub the touch as if he'd been hit really hard and look down the strip as if to say, *This isn't fencing!* That said, I could watch

Italian fencers for a straight week and not get bored. They're beautiful, and Italian fencing itself is as much art as sport, perhaps a holdover in this traditional fencing country from the time when competitors were given points for style as well as for touches. Of course, there are exceptions to the styles of Italian fencing. Luigi Tarantino comes straight at you, not dancing around with swaggering steps like other Italian fencers. He charges so aggressively you'd think you were facing a raging bull.

The Russians are the antithesis of the French footwork and the Italian artistry. You get the impression that the French and Italians are trying to touch you... but the Russians are trying to kill you. At this Bonn World Cup, the Russians were the world's top team, having earned the spot almost solely by the inhuman power of their attacks. If you went back against a Russian, he was going to score. Fencers like Stanislav Pozdniakov and Sergei Charikov would come at you down the strip, faking the whole time, putting you immediately under pressure. They were hard to block and hard to make fall short. I watched, and I wondered what I could take from these styles...

The Bonn World Cup was the first weekend of another week-long break from IS-90, a sort of second spring break. I stayed in Germany for a training camp at a storied German facility called the *Tauberbischofsheim*, a massive training center with three full-sized fencing rooms, a dozen strips in each. Pictures of German champions hung on the walls and Olympic medals were enshrined in a glass case. Many teams stayed for the camp—there was another world cup nearby the next week. After a day of training, the Russians drank vodka with the Belarusians in the dorm-style rooms. I was the only American. With no internet in my room, I passed the time between practices by grading papers and watching German MTV, which was a mix of American videos and Goth-looking German groups I'd never heard of. At night, after they turned off the lights in the complex, I would walk outside to the nearest source of food—a McDonald's. Many of the top German fencers were sponsored by Mercedes-Benz, and they'd drive off in sparkling cars. It was my first look at professional fencers: the mechanics of living and training paid by the state and the incidentals of a rather well-heeled life paid by corporate sponsorship.

At the center I met a tall, sullen German giant named Mattias Behr. Later, another German fencer told me the story of Behr's 1982 World Championship match against Russian Olympic champion Vladimir Sminrov. Behr hit Sminrov in the mask, punctured the mesh, and his foil lodged itself deep in the Russian's brain. He tried to rip back his blade, but it was too late. His foil splintered. Sminrov screamed and ripped out the protruding shard of blade before falling to the strip in a pool of blood. He would die nine days later. The accident resulted in massive changes in safety equipment, including mask strength requirements and Kevlar outfits.

Now, at the facility, German students from the city came to fence with the top international talent. Throughout the day we had lessons from an array of coaches. There was a physical therapy facility upstairs, and, next to it, a fencing store that sold equipment at much lower costs than any supplier in the U.S., which marked up equipment after import. After practice, fencers hung their uniforms in closets to dry and the rooms stunk like crazy. In the lobby of the facility, a soda machine sold beer. The Russian Stanislav Pozdniakov was there training and I watched him, imagining how I might copy him the way I'd once copied Taka Sudo. What makes someone the best in the world?

I learned that most fencers speak English. While French is the official language of fencing, English is the unofficial language of communication between countries. On the strip, fencers from Italy would scream in English at Russian referees.

One night, a handful of German fencers invited me to a club called *Airport* a short drive away. There was hip-hop music and American servicemen drinking Master Blasters—Red Bull and vodka—with young Germans. One of the German fencers, Marcus Schulz, had a fresh scar on the right side of his forehead. When I asked him about it, he told me the story of the German *Mensur*, a tradition that dates back to the Prussian officer corps.

At his German university, Schulz was a member of a fraternity, which, just like those at American universities, was rich with traditions. One of these traditions is the Mensur.

In fraternity basements, combatants stand a sword's length apart, holding blades called *schlägers*, which are a cross between a rapier and a saber—sharp, fairly heavy, and built to wound. They wear steel mesh goggles with a nose guard, a swath of cotton cloth wound around their necks, chain male on their chests, and padded leather on their right arms. Generally, Mensur is fought between rival fraternities, and next to the combatants stand allies who are armed in case of foul play.

The goal of the Mensur is to wound your opponent above the eye line. The top of the head and ears are fair game. Each round lasts four strokes, during which opponents aren't allowed to move their feet and must attack and parry while holding their head stoically still in the face of their opponent's onrushing blade. Rounds continue until there is blood, commonly lots of it, and many German fraternity members have scars on their cheeks or foreheads from these bouts. The scars are marks of honor—evidence of honorable membership in these storied societies.

A doctor—commonly a medical student—cleans the blades with antiseptic between rounds, checks blades for nicks that could cause jagged wounds, and stitches up the loser at match's end.

Compared to the Mensur, Fencers Club was like playing Parcheesi—a game—but there are places in the world where fenc-

Tiny Tim

With my dad and my grandfather in 1986

At bat at Inwood Little League Park in 1988

With Martin Schneider, my first fencing coach

Winning the Mamaroneck Invitational in 1996, my senior year of high
school—that's Mitsu Sudo to the right of me

With Taka (left) and Mitsu Sudo at a college meet at Yale in 1997

With Coach Bill Shipman

With teammate Mike Topper at Brandeis in 1999

With Brandeis teammates Brian Sirlin and Ken Shih

Taking it easy at a Brandeis meet in 1997

Making First Team All-American at the NCAA Championship, Stanford
University in 2000

With Akhi in 2000. He had just won this U.S. National Championship and was
headed for the Sydney Olympics

Celebrating my victory in a close match at a North
American Cup in 2001

With Tim Hagamen at a World Cup in Moscow in 2002

At a World Cup in New York in 2004 (I'm on the right)

The 2004 Olympic Fencing Team in Athens

With James Williams (left) and Keeth Smart at a 2006 World
Championships in Turin, Italy

With Coach Yury Gelman in 2008

Warming up with Jason Rogers for a fencing demonstration at City Hall for Mayor Bloomberg

With my mom at the 2008 Beijing Olympics

SERGE TIMACHEFF

Celebrating silver-medal victory over the Russians at the 2008 Beijing Olympics

SERGE TIMACHEFF

With Keeth, James, and Jason at the Beijing Olympics

Celebrating the bronze medal at the Madrid World Cup in
2009 with Jaime Marti, Zsolt Nemcsik, and Rares Dumitrescu

My first individual U.S. National Championship, 2010

ing isn't yet divorced from its pugilistic past. Learning about the Mensur and seeing the approach to the strip of, for example, Stanislav Pozdniakov made me realize that my training wasn't just an intellectual exercise. As the Russian champion Sminrov learned, it can be deadly serious.

While at the training camp, I watched and I tried to fence against whoever would give me a bout. Most declined—who was this impetuous, upstart American?—but I kept asking. When I got a match, I fenced my heart out, most often losing badly to far more experienced fencers who barely broke a sweat. Despite a promising result in Bonn, compared to top European talent, I still felt like a beginning high school fencer, rushing into the middle of the strip like an ill-controlled string marionette.

After spending a couple weeks in Manhattan trying to scratch my way back to an even keel at school, I took a personal day off work to make a three-day weekend. I flew with Akhi and Herby Raynaud to Romania for another world cup. Herby fenced out of Columbia University, where he'd first picked up a blade as a freshman when a gap in his class schedule lined up with a fencing class that met the university's physical education requirement. After this late start, he gained skill exponentially, earning All-American status and then moving to the Westbrook Foundation, Yury, and Fencers Club after college. He'd started getting results and, like me, was hoping to make the 2004 Olympic team.

We landed in Bucharest and Akhi, Herby, and I shared a cab from the airport to the hotel. The cabbie took to the sidewalk when the street was blocked and pulled into oncoming traffic when it seemed quicker. There were stray dogs everywhere, beggars with one arm or one leg, and kids all over the streets. It was the first time I'd thought of my Washington Heights students as privileged. These Romanian kids would have killed for my students' shoes or clothes or food.

In the morning, a bus picked us up from the hotel and drove us out to the venue. The walk from the parking lot took us through the woods—I remember barking dogs—and we hustled into an aging stadium whose color can only be described as "Cold War gray." A British fencer came in holding a big stick, saying he had fought his way through wild dogs in the forest. Everything was cement, crumbling at the joints, with rows and rows of cement benches on which sat a couple family members of the Romanian fencers.

Miraculously, Akhi, Herby, and I all made the round of 64, in which we earned all-important international points. In the 64, Akhi had an early match against one of the top Europeans, and went up 13-10, then 14-10. Then the tide started to turn. Akhi's opponent took one point, then the next, and then a third. When Akhi took off his mask, I could see he was sweating, talking to himself. He looked furious, but more than that he looked nervous. I'd known Akhi since grade school and had never seen him like that before—Akhi nervous? I didn't think it was possible. He lost the match. As cruel as it sounds, it helped me close the distance. Not only could I hang with some of the international fencers, but out here in the wide world, the domestic monsters of the sport I had grown up with didn't seem as untouchable as they did on home turf. I wasn't the only one who got nervous!

In my round of 64 match, I drew Mihai Covaliu, the Sydney gold medalist—a Romanian fencing on home turf. And I went up by 4 points! I thought, *Oh my god, I'm beating Mihai Covaliu!* But the second I thought it, something horrible happened: I stopped fencing loose and relaxed, and instead of slowing down and letting Covaliu's fakes sail past, I got jittery and started biting on every one. As soon as I realized I actually had a chance of winning and started taking the match seriously, I gave Covaliu the power to drive me. Suddenly he could fake, I would respond, and he could attack the undefended area that had been his goal all along: he started feint cutting me from the match.

It came down to the last point, tied 14-14. Covaliu took off his mask and stared at me across the strip with an expression that asked who the hell I thought I was. He followed it with a point. I lost the match. On paper finishing 60th might not have looked like a strong result, but I lost in the same round as Akhi and Herby. The distance between me and the top American fencers was closing and now, for the first time, I truly believed I could close the rest.

Filled not only with optimism but with the belief born of results, I was ready for my second year teaching, my second year truly fencing.

The New Normal

During the summer after my first year teaching, I poured myself into my twin goals—now missions—of teaching and fencing, and I realized that the melancholy I had felt on and off since starting college was gone. On the strip, fencing is an individual sport that requires and even promotes a degree of narcissism—in order to win, you have to believe you're the better fencer. But training toward this somewhat narcissistic success left a hole—a hole that I now filled with teaching. And despite the stress of being a first year teacher, working with and helping kids brought me a level of satisfaction I'd never before felt.

Ending the 2000-2001 school year with strong national and promising international fencing results, coupled with the turn-around of my classroom had me feeling accomplished and optimistic heading into my second year of being a professional teacher who was training to make the Olympics. I was a man with two missions. Nothing was going to stop me or sidetrack me. Over the summer, I meticulously planned the upcoming year's lessons and gathered my materials, and the school itself was starting to feel comparatively stable thanks to a strong new principal.

Then, on the second day of school, airplanes crashed into the World Trade Center Towers.

That morning, I was standing in front of my students, in the zone, dead set on letting *nothing* distract me from my game plan. I'm embarrassed to admit that when a teacher knocked on the door to tell me an airplane had crashed into the Towers, I shrugged it off. I remembered hearing the story of a plane that hit the Empire State Building in 1945, doing a little damage but nothing major. I think I assumed the plane that hit the Towers was the accidental crash of a Cessna or something like that—certainly a tragedy, but no reason to interrupt the second day of class. Another teacher knocked on my door and relayed the same news, this time with a bit more urgency. I thanked her for the news, but my internal reaction was still along the lines of, *C'mon already, you're interrupting my lesson!* Toward the end of the period, I happened to look out the window. Parents were streaming into the school from every direction. The bell rang and I went into another room where teachers were staring up at a TV. I stepped into the room just as news broke of the third plane crashing into the Pentagon. I watched the Towers come down.

We were over 150 blocks away—I couldn't see the smoke—but after the last student went home, I remember the eerie silence on the streets of Washington Heights. The subway was out and the streets were lined with shocked New Yorkers, wandering quietly home. It took my dad over two hours to walk home from his factory in Queens. In the silence, you could hear the sounds of far-away sirens keening through the City and fighter jets flying overhead.

All of a sudden life seemed to be turned upside down.

I spent the next day with my mom and dad, watching the news on the couch in my pajamas. It seemed like the end of everything I knew. We had no idea what would come next. What if attacks became the new norm? Would we hibernate in our city amid constant terror? Then New York City Mayor Rudy Giuliani announced that schools would open the next day. And open they did. I traded my pajamas for my teacher's uniform of a button-down, short-sleeved shirt with a tie and on September 13, 2001, we went back to school. The kids, like the people in the streets, were deathly silent. We were ready to get under our desks and cover our heads with our hands. We got ample opportunity: for whatever reason, about a week after the attacks, people started periodically calling the school with bomb threats. The police explained that they suspected copycat would-be terrorists who had found a way to create fear without the need for real bombs. IS-90 instituted an evacuation code—if in the middle of a class period the principal came on and said, "The weather's great!" our stomachs would flip, and we'd all evacuate to the yard and take attendance. When the threat was deemed over, we'd file back inside and continue where we left off. Every evacuation exercise seemed real.

We spent about a month with our hearts in our throats, seeing every pigeon streaking past as a falling jet, seeing reminders everywhere. Late in the month, the Yankees got shelled by the Baltimore Orioles and I saw the score 2-11 as 9-11. My first year of teaching had prepared me to shove aside all distractions that interfered with my twin goals of teaching and fencing, but I couldn't shove aside *this*.

New Yorkers were determined to get back to business as usual, and after school on 9/13 I went back to the gym. But I realized I was just going through the motions at the gym and at school. At Fencers Club my feet did the walking and at school my mouth did the talking, but both were on autopilot—rote versions of the missions I'd planned.

Everything seemed up in the air.

I was not among the top four American fencers scheduled to compete in October at the World Championships in Nîmes, France. It wasn't clear that *anyone* was going. Could U.S. fencers compete internationally? Could we ever travel again?

Not only did the American team travel, but the women's foil team of Iris Zimmermann, Felicia Zimmermann, Ann Marsh, and Erinn Smart avenged their disputed loss in the bronze medal match of the 2000 Sydney Games to take the bronze at the World Championships in Nîmes. With this milestone result, they were in position to compete in Athens for the first ever U.S. gold medal in fencing.

Also, the women's saber event had recently been added to the international competition circuit, and the U.S. women were putting up great results, led by sisters Sada and Emily Jacobson from Arkady Burdan's club in Atlanta and by Mariel Zagunis, who fenced in Oregon with Coach Ed Korfanty. There was even talk of adding women's saber to the 2004 Athens Games.

In the fall after 9/11, I tried, along with all New Yorkers, to find a new normal—and I found inspiration in the men and women working at Ground Zero every day and in those who volunteered to join our armed services. Certainly if they could rebuild our city and protect our country, I could stay my own course, not let terror deter me from my mission to make a difference through teaching and bring the country honor through fencing. My new normal included living at home, teaching at IS-90, training in the evenings, and coaching a few days a week at Riverdale. In addition, because New York mandated that teachers be working toward the label "highly qualified," I was also attending night classes to earn a Master's degree at Pace University.

At school, I pushed deeper into curriculum and away from

discipline and found that both learning and discipline improved. Rather than the pair of 19th-place finishes I'd earned at the previous year's first North American Cups, I finished 6th and 7th at the year's first NACs in December and January.

Now, as a second year teacher, fresh off promising results in the first two North American Cups, I was ready to hit the world cup circuit for real.

It wasn't without trepidation that I boarded my first international flight after 9/11 to a weaker world cup held in London. The competition drew fencers from Germany, Spain, Iran, the U.S., the U.K., and a smattering of up-and-coming Hungarians.

Accordingly, I won every match in my opening pool. I remained strongest in 5-touch matches.

At that point in men's saber, the countries that were respected for their fencing were Russia, France, Italy, Hungary, Poland, Spain, Romania, Ukraine, Germany, and Belarus. If you weren't fencing someone from those countries you felt like you had a chance to win. In the round of 64, I drew and beat a British fencer and then drew an Iranian fencer in the round of 32, which seemed like a gift. There were very few fencers from the Middle East. For the first time at an international competition, I felt like I should win.

The punch line is that I lost. I still remember the look on Yury's face when my Iranian opponent scored the 15th point.

Making the round of 16 would have put me within inches of the points I needed to earn a top-four U.S. ranking and consequently have my travel expenses to international competitions paid by USA Fencing. Losing to an underdog in the 32 felt like a wasted opportunity. It was still two and a half years until the 2004 Athens Games and already my credit cards were getting hot.

It was easy to feel as if the world had come crashing down and, in retrospect, I imagine the depression that followed this loss was due in part to the continuing grieving process of 9/11. If terrorists could strike at the heart of Manhattan, they could strike anywhere; if I could lose to this Iranian fencer, I could lose to anyone. Sure, it's an overblown and melodramatic comparison, but the idea that things I'd worked so hard for could be here today and demolished tomorrow made effort seem useless. Fencing and teaching and life and even New York City all seemed ephemeral.

Shortly thereafter, the International Olympic Committee added women's saber to the Olympic program to bring gender equality to our sport. But the IOC did so with a massive catch. Women's saber would be included, but fencing as a whole would get no additional medals. Fencing was left with 12 events, only ten medals, and a massive problem on our hands: we would have to cut two events. The International Fencing Federation, the FIE, did what they thought was fair and put all the events in a hat and drew two—women's foil team and men's saber team events were to be cut from the Olympics.

The very event I'd been hoping to qualify for in the upcoming Athens Olympics no longer existed. Only one, or at most two, American male saber fencers would compete in the individual event in Athens instead of four fencers qualifying for the now-nonexistent team event.

Iris Zimmermann and her women's foil team event had been cut, too. After losing the bronze medal match in Sydney on a penalty and then winning a hopeful bronze in Nîmes, the women's foil team was hoping for comeuppance in Athens—and now the event didn't exist.

That said, Iris and her sister Felicia were phenoms of American fencing, and Iris had very real hope of making one of the individual competition spots. I had no hope. But I was on a mission. I forged ahead.

To combat the decision to cut events, European fencers went on strike and we skipped the next couple world cups, not wanting to be seen as strike busters. The women's foil fencers actually showed up to their team events then simply walked off the strip without competing in protest. Finally the FIE promised to review their decision at the 2002 World Championships in Portugal and fencers called a cease-fire and returned to the strip.

In April 2002, I finished a mediocre 12th at the U.S. Nationals. We all competed in a world cup held in Boston, and then it was off to Cuba for the third and final world cup in the strike-shortened season.

Cuba has a unique fencing history. In the time before Castro, when fencing was a sport of the Cuban rich, they won gold in the 1900 Olympics and five Olympic medals in 1904. When Castro came into power, he opened the sport to the proletariat but lost almost all the established masters to defection. Then, when the proletariat of the post-Castro era gained the skills to compete internationally, many went to tournaments abroad never to return. Rather than an expression of being Cuban, fencing became a way to escape Cuba.

Akhi Spencer-El tells a story from the 1999 Pan Am Games in Canada. He defeated a Cuban fencer to make the semifinals. The fencer saluted, shook his hand as is customary, and then bolted for the door. Out he ran into the street, with no money and only the fencing outfit on his back, to build a new life in Canada.

Like Cuba itself, rumor of conspiracy and spy plots swirled around the Cuban fencing team. For example, in 1976 the twenty-four members of the Cuban national fencing team were returning from Jamaica, where they had swept the medals at the Central American and Caribbean Championships, when timed bombs ripped through their plane. All seventy-eight people on board were killed. There were whispered connections to spies, exiled Cuban militants, and even the CIA. The program miraculously recovered to win medals at the 1992 and 1996 Olympics.

But when even more athletes defected and money ran out, the team stopped traveling.

Going into this third and final world cup, Keeth, Ivan, and Akhi had the top three national rankings locked up and thus spots on that year's world championships team—also, their travel expenses would be paid next year. I was in a fight for the 4th position. Win and I would fly free; lose and I would dig deeper into credit card debt. Herby Raynaud had a slight edge over Tim Hagamen, Luther Clement, and me, with Oregon fencer Marten Zagunis still within striking distance.

As athletes, we got special permission to travel to Cuba and we flew through Cancun. I remember flying into Havana at night and thinking it must be a tiny town judging by the lack of lights. In fact, it's a city of more than two million people. We gulped as we laid down our passports, but with a stamp we were in. On the streets were cars from the 1950s and '60s and Franken-cars made of the front ends of Chevys and the back ends of Fords.

The main thing I remember about the Cuban fencing venue was that it was *hot*. At the start of the tournament, officials who had driven to the event boosted their car batteries and connected them to the electric scoring machines. When a Cuban fencer's decaying saber broke, instead of throwing it out, he saved it so that it could be welded back together later. Many athletes who had been to Cuba before brought extra equipment and supplies, which they left with the Cuban team.

I drew a Cuban fencer in the round of 64. The strip was ratty and hot and the Cuban fencer was fighting for his life. I lost, bringing my record to 0-2 against fencers from countries with oppressive dictatorships. If I had beaten either the Iranian or the Cuban fencer I would have made the 2002 national team—one of the four coveted spots for the world championships that included a fly-free ticket from USA Fencing.

Instead, I was out in the round of 64 and looking at another season of credit cards. In another twist of fate, a lucky draw by U.S. fencer Marten Zagunis matched him against an underpowered British fencer in the round of 32. The Brit had been seeded 64th of 64 in the previous round, but the world's #1 fencer at the time, the Romanian Olympic champion Mihai Covaliu, hadn't shown up and so instead of an unwinnable match, the Brit got a surprise bye to the 32. It was a gift for Zagunis and he went up 14-10. Then we watched as the Brit rattled off 5 straight points to rip the win from Zagunis. One point and Marten Zagunis would've made that year's team. A year later, he retired.

So close and yet so far away for Marten, Luther, and me: the glass seemed half empty. I was so close. Just a few touches away! How would I respond?

Searching for
the Flunge

The 2002-2003 school year was my third teaching at IS-90. It was also the fencing season prior to Olympic qualifying. My goal was clear: find the few touches I lacked last season in order to make the four-person national team so that USA Fencing would pay my travel expenses next season during Athens qualifying. Between plane tickets, tournament registrations, hotel rooms, food on the road, coaching fees, and equipment, fencing toward the Olympics turned out to be a $25,000 per year habit. I now made about $35,000 as a third year teacher. But even living at home, the $10k difference between fencing costs and my salary wasn't enough to live on in New York City.

In addition to paying travel expenses, making the senior national team would allow me to compete at the qualifying season world championships, where I could earn points that weren't open to fencers who hadn't made the team. I entered the season ranked 7th nationally and, at the very least, I needed to stay in the top eight—now with everyone traveling, only eight fencers were allowed to compete at the top international tournaments.

There's an old adage in teaching that says the best teachers beg, borrow, and steal. I had applied the lesson in the classroom, stealing from IS-90's best teachers—the way they started class, their tone at the front of the room, their successful lesson plans. After watching my teammates at the Portugal World Championships, I started the 2003 season by trying to adapt the moves of Keeth, Akhi, Herby, and Ivan.

I started with the best, so of course I tried Keeth's trademark move, the flunge. It's a variation on the lunge where instead of pushing from your back leg, you leap forward off your front foot into the air. The move and its subsequent name were created by Yury. But there's cruelty in the flunge. Because it puts you so far forward, if you miss, you have almost no hope of defending yourself against your opponent's ensuing attack. It's an all-or-nothing gambit, and you know as soon as you launch if you have the distance to reach your opponent. So when you flunge, time seems to stop for a second—either you have the touch in sight, or you realize with utter clarity that you're flying through the air, thoroughly screwed. In practice, I too often found myself the latter and I soon realized that hanging my career on the flunge wasn't for me. I don't have Keeth's legs.

Akhi had a beautiful move he'd use to hit an onrushing opponent under the wrist. I always loved its demoralizing value— a fencer would be charging forward, gaining momentum for a finishing lunge, and then—*poke!*—the point would be over and Akhi's opponent would be left baffled, standing there with the unmistakable look of *pointus interruptus*. But I couldn't quite master the precision of Akhi's under-the-wrist stop cut. My imitation of the maneuver turned into something completely unrecognizable from the original. I couldn't find the precision to hit my opponents under the wrist, but for some reason I could hit them over it. When my opponents were attacking, I'd find myself almost stumbling back, seemingly helpless and off-balance. Seeing me in what they thought was a defenseless position, my opponents would make a big swipe to what they thought was a sure point. But as they lunged, I would pull my body out of the way and, raising my hand high up in the air, drop the point down onto their wrist. Thus, my sky hook maneuver was born, in the tradition of my other off-balance move, which Coach Shipman had dubbed "dog peeing on a fire hydrant" (which I had been trying in vain to train away).

A bit like me, Keeth was climbing the rankings by slowing down, but while his feet were cautious, he used his body and head to fake, building toward the snap of an unpredictable attack—frequently his flunge. Copying Keeth, I started bobbing my head forward and back to subtly open and close distances. At Fencers Club, Peter Westbrook saw my pecking and started calling it "Morehouse's teapot attack!"

I'm not sure anyone noticed my new moves' resemblance to Akhi's under-the-wrist stop cut or Keeth's measured head fakes. But as best I could appropriate them, their moves became mine. I even added Keeth's screams—the "Go!" and "Oui!" he seemed to use when in the flow. I remember a match in which Keeth was losing 8-4. The next point, he head-faked his opponent into a lunge that came up short, drove the opponent down the strip, finished, and screamed the French, "Ouiiiii!" Sitting next to me, the fencer Ahmed Yilla smiled and said, "Here he goes!" By the end of the match, you felt sorry for Keeth's opponent.

I borrowed Coach Schneider's passion, Coach Shipman's motto ("Respect everyone, fear no one"), Yury's techniques, Mormando's mental game, Westbrook's fierceness, and Nazlymov's goals. I drew inspiration from my father's work ethic, my mother's uniqueness, and the results made by fencers like Iris Zimmer-mann. In short, I became a mishmash of the people I respected, the people I admired.

It was as this amalgam that I went into my third year teaching and competing.

Now I felt I understood the rhythm of a fencing season and how it dovetailed with a school year—the times I'd be tired, when I'd have a chance to catch my breath—I found routines that al-lowed me to work and fence more efficiently. For example, by the time I got home after practice, I was too tired to plan lessons or grade papers. So instead of working at night, I started waking up early to get to school by 6:30am so I could plan, grade, and prepare my classroom. I stayed about an hour after school each day, until about 4:00pm, then took the train to Fencers Club for the start of practice at 5:00pm. A few nights a week, Yury taught an elite class starting at 8:00pm and, on these days, I coached at Riverdale before going to Fencers Club.

I wasn't the only one working. Keeth Smart had a job in fi-nance at Verizon and would usually come in around 6:00pm in his suit and tie; Herby Reynaud had a job that usually kept him until 7:00pm. Everyone else was a student—Ivan Lee at St. John's, Tim Hagamen in high school at Riverdale, Jason Rogers at Ohio State. Akhi was coaching and working in the Home Depot Olympic program—a now-defunct program in which Olympians earned full-time wages and benefits for working part time, which gave the athletes more time to train.

At the season's first North American Cup in December, I re-member Yury telling a group of coaches and referees, "Yes, Tim is very serious now." This elite group used to ignore me completely. I remember when they started nodding "hello" very slightly, then the nods got deeper, then they would shake my hand. Finally, now, we chatted when we ran into each other at competitions.

In the round of 32 at that December NAC, I drew Mike Momtselidze, a Nazlymov fencer. I felt Nazlymov watching as I beat him. If Momtselidze came close, I was able to catch him with his arm back; if he lunged from far away, fearing my stop-cut, I was able to step back and catch him on the wrist.

In the round of 16, I beat Terrence Lasker again. In the round of 8, I drew the up-and-coming fencer Adam Crompton. Crompton had started at St. Benedict's in New Jersey, trained at the Westbrook Foundation, and was now at Ohio State with Nazlymov. He's built like a Mack Truck, about six feet tall, and looks more like a running back than a fencer. You would think someone with that kind of muscle wouldn't be able to move. You'd be wrong. Crompton was amazingly quick, and on top of his quickness, he used his muscle to hammer home painful blows. He parried so hard that your hand rattled and your shoulder shook. When he hit, he'd yell, "Bossa-LA!" and hold his fist up to his face. Fencing him was always painful and difficult—as much an exercise in courage as it was in technique and problem solving. But he did have his weaknesses: he took big steps and tended to get flustered when you scored. That day, my intuition was on, and I found the holes in his steps. Adam charged—a truly intimidating sight—but I was able to pick him off with enough ripostes to advance to my first NAC finals, where I would face Ivan Lee.

Ivan was a destroyer, tearing up opponents. He's also one of the smartest fencers I've ever fought, a master at hiding his intentions. I knew if I let Ivan dictate the mood and tried to match his tricks, he'd pick the meat from my bones. So while Ivan fenced coolly, I fenced hot, yelling and fighting.

But when I attacked, his long left arm would swing in, almost lazily, to take my saber and then the points. I went down quickly, brutally, to a score of 5-12. How relaxed he looked! Ivan barely even needed to fence in order to kill me. In this situation, I've seen fencers cede the final few touches and slink away for the convention hall exit. But I fought. I fought and I lost, coming back a bit to end at 9-15. In the match's final act, I at least managed to salvage my honor, and even losing in the finals of the season's first North American Cup was a spectacular result for me.

At the time, anonymous internet message boards were popular. For whatever reason, fencers used one called www.Fencing-Sucks.com to trash talk everything from who sucked on the strip to which female fencers were hot. Following my finals loss to Ivan, a lot of the spiteful chatter was aimed at me. Post after post held the gist "Tim might be able to fence NACs, but he'll NEVER make an international result." Actually, I counted it a minor triumph: a couple years ago nobody thought I could make *national* results, and now they'd ceded me a backhanded version of national respect. It was the first time I'd really been talked about on those boards. It meant I was officially on the radar!

The result temporarily bumped my national ranking to #5. The next NAC was in San Diego and I lost in the round of 8. Mike Momtselidze beat Ivan for the win, and then it was the start of the world cup season.

We flew to Moscow. Soviet fencing success had been built in the 1950s when the program begged, borrowed, and stole the best aspects of the French, Polish, Romanian, and Hungarian styles, combining these bits and pieces of technique into an efficient, scientific approach to farming points. *Are more points scored on attack or on defense? Where on the strip?* The Soviets built this knowledge and their borrowed techniques into medals. Nazlymov once told me that while he was a coach in the Soviet Union, "We never thought about second place. For us, a silver medal was an oops." Now in early 2003, with Stanislav Pozdniakov and Sergei Charikov leading the way, the Russians were again the most dominant force by far in men's saber fencing.

When we got off the airplane in Moscow, it was freezing. Keeth had fenced there in 1999 but, for most of us, this was our first visit. We stayed at the Hotel Russia, which has since been torn down. It was a massive cement hotel with hallways that seemed to stretch for miles, like an industrial version of the hotel in *The Shining*. Prostitutes hung out openly in the lobby and lounges. From the hotel, we boarded a rickety old bus, fumes pouring in through the windows, and drove to the fencing stadium for the first day of pools. As usual, I fenced well in the pools to make the tournament's second day, the round of 64, where (as usual) I lost and ended up finishing 52nd. Ivan Lee and Tim Hagamen went out in the round of 32. Keeth just kept on winning, flunging all the way to the finals.

The finals were held in a huge stadium and, before the final match, a Russian pop star performed. Women in skimpy dresses escorted the fencers into the stadium, in which there was a crowd of a few thousand. The Russian billionaire oligarch Alisher Usmanov was now president of the Russian Fencing Association and had flown in all the former Russian Olympic and World Champions. Nazlymov was there—he gave a televised press conference and handed out prizes.

In the finals, Keeth lost to Charikov; it wasn't even close. But seeing Keeth standing up on the podium built a belief in the rest of us that we could earn the right to stand up there, too.

Next, we went to London for the relatively inconsequential Corble Cup, the one in which I'd lost to an Iranian fencer and thus doomed myself to paying the 2003 season's travel expenses. Because so many top fencers skipped the tournament, I didn't have to fence the first day. Instead, they needed referees, so Keeth and I each refereed a pool! One of the fencers in the pool I officiated got upset by an underdog and blamed it on my refereeing—the next day, the miffed fencer refereed my round of 32 match. Of course, I lost. Only in amateur sports!

Ivan Lee went out in the 16. Again, Keeth rolled. Between matches, Keeth always changed into a dry shirt, and it was during one of these exchanges that he said to us, gathered around like acolytes, "You see? These guys are scared! We can beat these guys! They suck!" To my knowledge, it was the first time that an American saber fencer with any credibility articulated the idea that we could beat the Europeans. And not just that we could beat them, but that we were *better!* Despite the crudeness of "they suck," the idea spun our ingrained perception of European dominance on its head. Keeth had exposed them, tearing them apart 15-6 or 15-5. It was a weaker tournament, but still—watching the finals, Akhi leaned over to me and said, "Watch, Keeth is going to win this one!" And he did, beating the Spanish Olympian Medina, who was ranked in the world top ten, for the tournament gold. It was the first time I heard the U.S. national anthem play at a fencing competition, and I have to admit—I was proud.

It was back to school for a week and then I was off to Bonn for a grand prix—a special kind of world cup worth double points. I left Thursday after school and would take the red-eye back before school on Monday morning. Unfortunately for me, the tournament was a quick one: Ivan eliminated me on the first day in an unlucky draw. I watched Tim Hagamen make the round of 16 to leapfrog past Akhi and Herby into the #3 national ranking, just behind Keeth and Ivan. Tim Hagamen, who had been in seventh grade when I was a freshman in college, and whom Yury had for a brief time affectionately called "little Tim," had just blown definitively past me.

After another couple weeks of teaching, we were off to Athens for a tournament called the Coupe Akropolis, held in a building with an otherworldly, tent-like ceiling—another three-day weekend. I fenced through the pools and then, in the round of 64, drew an Italian fencer named Caputo. Up to that point, I had not beaten a fencer from any of the powerhouse European countries or made it into the top thirty-two at any of the stronger competitions. As if mirroring Yury's lesson, Caputo attacked me slowly, pushing me down the strip while holding his distance, slow enough to ignore my fakes while waiting for an opening. I quickly realized I wasn't going to win moving backward, so I turned on the move that Peter Westbrook dubbed my "teapot attack," jerking my head back and forth. I remember going up 14-11 and forcing myself to focus on fencing and not the fact that I was so close to winning. On the next point, I lunged, missed, and was suddenly on defense, scurrying away from Caputo's attack back to my end of the strip. Having been unable to stop his attack the whole match, I desperately set up Mormando's point-in-line—the fencing equivalent of Ralph Macchio's crane position from the Karate Kid. Caputo would now have to come close enough to beat my blade before he could attack me. He came forward and hit away my saber but then, instead of defending, I closed my eyes and pushed my blade into his chest, hoping to time him out before he could land his cut. In saber, if a point lands 300 milliseconds before the other arrives, the machine will "lock out" the other person from scoring. I opened my eyes and turned to the machine, where only my light now shone brightly! One light! A point not requiring a referee's call. I had won, making my first strong world cup round of 32 and reclaiming the #5 U.S. ranking!

Next, I drew the Russian Sergei Charikov. I knew I couldn't beat him fencing typically, so I leaned forward and went back to the style that had won me matches in college. I hunched forward and began circling parry-four, restricting him to a small target area, and giving myself a chance to find his blade as he came for me. It was another parlor trick; unconventional, but it worked, at least temporarily. After I parried him a few times, he actually requested a strip change—certainly my points were due to faulty equipment! He kept looking beseechingly at the ref, who looked sympathetically back at him as if to say, *Of course you're right Mr. Charikov—there's no way this American could be blocking you!*

As we changed strips, I had time to think. I was sure that, during the break, Charikov would come up with strategy to solve my parry ploy, so I decided to out-evolve him—changing to an unexpected, conventional approach. Then, on the new strip, Charikov fought through my imperfect imitation of classic fencing technique to win. Would he really have solved my clumsy chicanery? I'll never know. But one thing is certain: I couldn't fight conventionally and win.

After the tournament, our plane broke down and the airline put us in a nice hotel for the extra day. For once, I had my own room, a robe, and a nice TV. It cost me a personal day at IS-90, but it was a needed day of calm in the eye of the storm that was the world cup season. As we hung around the hotel, we checked the internet and saw something amazing: with Keeth's result, he was now #1 in the world! The first American male in U.S. history to achieve the feat.

At the next world cup in Padua, Italy, Luigi Tarantino, the fencer who had choked an opposing team's coach at the Boston World Cup I'd attended while at Brandeis, approached Keeth and said, "What? Now you want to win Olympics? Hmph!" and walked away without waiting for a response.

The tournament was sponsored by Luxardo liqueur, so we all got free booze and Mr. Luxardo paid for the preliminary rounds to be held in a small stadium, after which the finals were moved to a lavish downtown theater. A packed house of spectators dressed as if for the opera, and the grand stage was professionally lit and outfitted with one raised strip. None of us got to touch it, with Keeth finishing 9th, Ivan making the round of 32, and me exiting unceremoniously in the round of 64.

I flew home from Europe early on Monday morning and taught a half-day of school that afternoon. On Thursday, I left again for Spain.

The competitions were beginning to blur together, but not this one. It was the biggest I'd been to yet, held at the Villa de Madrid. Jason Rogers had missed most of the year due to his fencing commitment as a scholarship athlete at Ohio State, but he arrived looking good. In the round of 32, Jason beat the Spanish fencer Jorge Pina, blocking his attacks and then finishing strong. Jason beat a French fencer in the round of 16 to reach the quarterfinals, where he finally fell to Pozdniakov. Suddenly, from a rank of about 8th in the country, Jason jumped ahead of everyone but Keeth and Ivan.

And at this Madrid World Cup, Keeth met Luigi Tarantino in the finals. Keeth was on fire and it looked like Tarantino was barely fencing, as if he didn't care. Keeth flew at him; Tarantino stood there looking indifferent. I think Tarantino knew he was going to lose that match, so he tried his best to look like he wasn't trying to save face as Keeth scored point after point. It was Keeth's second world cup win, this one in a huge tournament.

Finally, I finished the whirlwind world cup season ranked #6 nationally, one place higher than the previous season, but still not on the senior national team. I had failed in my year's goal and would have to pay my expenses during the Athens qualifying season.

Flying home, I was exhausted and I started to realize that trying to fence this much while teaching and going to graduate school was just too much. Being so worn out in the classroom after these trips wasn't fair to my students, and making a run at the Olympics next year would mean even more time and travel. But what could I do? I was already living at home, my time stretched thin and my money stretched thinner. I didn't have a dollar or a minute to spare, but knew that I'd need plenty of both to survive the upcoming qualifying season. Then, just when things looked bleakest, several Riverdale Country School families and their friends offered their financial support—and I can't thank them enough. I wouldn't live lavishly, but I would live to fence the qualifying season!

Keeth, Ivan, Jason, and Tim headed to Cuba for the World Championships. I started training for the Olympic qualifying season.

The Talents of Endurance and Planning

As a senior at Brandeis, when I had talked to Steve Mormando about my goal of making the 2004 Olympics, he told me there are three things fencers need to climb the rankings: skill, endurance, and planning. First, can you pick up the tools you need to be better than the other fencers trying to do exactly the same thing? Endurance and planning are in some ways more in your control, but harder for most people than you think—Mormando said that if I stayed the course, consistently worked hard, and planned effectively, I'd eventually see other fencers in the field start to fall away.

His words were prophetic. By the fall of 2003, when qualifying started for the 2004 Athens Games, about half of the 18 people who were ahead of me in 2000 when I had first talked to Mormando had quit fencing. They thought they were too far away, had other things going on in their lives, had given up the dream and the fire. While half the field had faded away, there was still the task of building skills against others who were in it for the long haul.

The good news is that every season starts with a clean slate. So what if Keeth had touched the #1 world ranking last year? So what if Ivan had perennially planted his feet in the rounds of 16 at last year's world cups? So what if Jason Rogers and Tim Hagamen started the year rounding out the senior national team? Likewise, so what if I'd made every round of 8 at the national tournaments last year? None of that mattered. Or it mattered only tangentially—Keeth and Ivan had a bit of a head start, thanks to some points earned at the Cuba World Championships, but the majority of qualifying was about the present: your best two scores from the season's three NACs plus the points you earn at five international world cups. That's it: eight events to separate the Olympic team from the rest. The people in serious contention were Keeth, Ivan, Akhi, Herby, Jason Rogers, Mike Momtselidze, Colin Parker, Adam Crompton, and Tim Hagamen.

As is the case every year, the qualifying year's first tournament was a North American Cup in December. True to my M.O. at national tournaments, I made the top eight, edging Tim Hagamen 15-14. I drew Herby in the 8 and when I pointed out to Yury that I'd never beaten Herby, he simply said, "Well, now's the time." I beat Herby to make the 4, before falling to Keeth and taking 3rd. Keeth went on to win the event, with Ivan taking 2nd.

Another thing happened at that competition: one of the top contenders had planned his flight to arrive just before the start of the tournament, but he had missed his flight and with no leeway, he missed the tournament. Lack of contingency planning had now put him behind the rest of the field.

The first international tournament was the London World Cup I'd attended for the last couple years. In fact, despite a long history of fencing in the UK—Queen Elizabeth still has an appointed duelist who would fight for her honor in the case of a challenge—and many fencing schools, the UK doesn't tend to produce fencers that compete with top continental talent. We stayed in a small hotel and ate at a T.G.I. Friday's. The short flight from New York, the fact that the tournament was held in a school gymnasium, and hearing English made it a nice bridge between the national events and the more difficult world cups that would follow.

In London, I qualified well out of the pools and beat a couple of Brits to make the round of 16, where I lost. Somewhat surprisingly, Keeth lost in the 16 as well. Actually, after touching the #1 ranking, this had become a bit of a worrisome trend for Keeth, and it was due in part to a change in the way referees were calling his flunge. In previous years, refs had called Keeth's footwork the start of his attack—Keeth would bring his back foot forward and from that point he had right-of-way. His opponent would have to dodge or parry in order to cancel Keeth's right-of-way and earn the right to score a point. But in 2003, refs reevaluated the flunge and started calling the forward motion of Keeth's arm, rather than his footwork, the start of his attack. Now Keeth could be hit in preparation. As he cocked his feet for attack, a quick fencer could nip him before his arm came forward, earning a touch that would likely have gone Keeth's way just a couple years ago. Keeth remained a fixture in international rounds of 16, but there was a chink in the armor of his previous seasons' dominance. It made American fencers nervous: we wanted a medal, and at that point, we needed a hero to get it.

The story of the London tournament was Patrick Durkan. He made the round of 4 to jump ahead of us all in qualifying points. He wasn't even on the radar for Olympic qualification coming into that season, having scaled back his training and competitions over the past few years. Unfortunately for Patrick, the national rankings lag a couple tournaments behind current results—at that point, Patrick's ranking was still based mostly on last year's tournaments… and Patrick hadn't competed at any world cups the previous year. He'd been allowed to compete at the national qualifying events, but despite his 3rd place finish in London, he wasn't ranked high enough to be allowed to compete in the following international world cups. From London, most of the team went to Budapest, but our new frontrunner, Patrick, went home. It would be two world cups before his ranking caught up with his London results and allowed him to compete. By that point, he was irredeemably behind in international points because he had failed to plan correctly for an Olympic run. Like the fencer who missed the flight to the season's first NAC, Patrick's decision not to compete the previous year put him almost completely out of contention despite his London result.

Budapest is a common stop on the international small sport circuit not just for fencing but for speed skating, wrestling, boxing, and a host of other under-funded, primarily individual events. In part, this is due to the Stadion—a Soviet-era cement sports compound with facilities for what seemed like every little sport under the sun. When you check into the Stadion, you have to pay for your stay up front—in cash. In 2003 I forgot the rule, and so after showing up jet-lagged and ready for a bed, I remember wandering the streets of Budapest looking for an ATM.

For whatever reason, when you book a two-bed room in Europe, you tend to get two single beds pushed together in the middle of the room. So at most European tournaments, the first thing American roommates do is rearrange the room, pushing the beds apart. At the Stadion, the rooms were small enough that even with beds pushed apart, you still feel like you're sleeping on top of your roommate. So instead of just pushing for the walls, we always rotate the beds to sleep head-to-toe. By now, it's tradition—what do you do when you get a room at the Stadion? You rotate the beds. Experienced fencers just do it, walking into the room and grabbing either the foot or the head without even discussing it. Still, the Stadion is clean, not entirely decrepit, and filled with history. Peter Westbrook had stayed there on his way to Olympic qualifying, and now it was us making the two-block walk to the fenced-in stadium compound where the world's best fencers vied for spots at the Olympics.

Because I'd come straight from London, I was a couple days early for the individual event, so I watched and took score for the U.S. team event. At that point, the team was made up of the holdovers from 2003: Keeth, Ivan, Jason, and Tim Hagamen. As much as we loved Yury and appreciated the fact that it's likely none of us would be where we were without him, we joked about his motivational speeches. For whatever reason, Ukraine had our number, beating us anywhere, any time, and usually by a large margin. Maybe they fenced with a little extra fire against us, since Yury had emigrated from Ukraine to the United States. Whatever the backstory, I remember Yury's speech to the U.S. team before facing Ukraine in Budapest: he wanted us to fence loose and explained that after our fencing careers ended, we'd all go on to jobs in finance or law or whatever we chose. He told us the Ukrainians had none of that—the Ukrainians were fencing for their lives and so had everything to lose. Somehow this was supposed to take the pressure off us, make us light on our feet, add just that little bit of recklessness that fencers need to win. Instead, it made us feel like we were staring down a pack of feral dogs waiting to rip us limb from limb.

Despite Yury's speech, the team continued its streak, losing badly to Ukraine.

The day before the individual event, I came down with a nasty fever. Luckily, the 5-touch pools remained my great strength. In this qualifying season, for the first time, it really mattered. Here's how a world cup tournament works: the top sixteen fencers in the world rankings don't have to fence the first day when the pools are conducted. The rest of the fencers fight for the remaining forty-eight spots in the second day of the tournament—the round of 64. It's a good place to be, effectively gaining passage to the round of 32—a place most American fencers would kill to be.

The rest of us fence the six-person pools. You fence every other fencer in your pool—5 short matches to 5 points each—and the sixteen fencers with the best pool records go immediately to the round of 64. Say you go 6-0 in your pool—you'd make the 64 and be seeded high enough to avoid meeting one of the world top sixteen who'd gotten a bye.

Fencers with middling results in the pools have to fence a sudden-death elimination match against another middling qualifier. This match comes after pools on the tournament's first day and is fought to 15 touches. If you win, you're into the 64 against a high-seeded opponent. If you lose, you're out.

Here's the important point: you only start earning international points—the points we needed for Olympic qualifying—at the round of 64, and I was still best in 5-touch matches. So dominating my pool was by far my best chance at points—with a strong record, I could go straight to the 64 rather than having to fence a 15-point sudden-death match to get there. I'd meet a lower-seeded fencer in the 64; that at least gave me hope of making the 32.

Sick as a dog, I went 5-1 in the Budapest pools to sneak into the 64 without having to fence a qualifier. Looking at the draws for the next day, I saw that in the round of 64 I had a relatively weak Greek fencer.

It was a good spot: a day to rest before taking on a fencer I should beat. But instead of catching 16 hours of palliative rest, I couldn't sleep a wink. It was the return of Iranian/Cuban syndrome. It's easy to fence as the underdog: you show up, fence loose, and sleep well the night before knowing you have nothing to lose. Afterward, you either shrug your shoulders at an expected loss or you celebrate a triumphant win. Fencing as the favorite is different. You can stay up all night over thinking your opponent, feeling the pressure. In Budapest, making one round of 32 was likely the headline result I needed to make the 2004 Olympic team. This was it. This was my shot.

There are no sure things in sports and with me fencing sick, going on thirty-four hours without sleep, I was worried about the condition I'd be in for my match. That morning at breakfast, I tried to drink fluids and save my energy for the match. In some odd way, focusing on my health instead of obsessing over a match I "should" win may have helped me to *just fence* and not freeze up.

And as I took the strip, I *just fenced* with everything I had, not worried about the opponent standing across from me or what it all meant if I were to win or lose. I beat the Greek fencer.

Afterwards, I felt like I'd fought my way onto the 2004 Olympic team.

Until I looked at the other Americans' results. Jason Rogers had made the 32 as well. And in the 64 Keeth drew Herby. It's interesting: Herby was actually in danger of falling out of the top eight in national rankings, nixing his right to compete at world cups. At the same time, Patrick Durkan was sitting at home waiting for his London result to catapult him into the 8 and thus earn him the right to compete internationally. Keeth played to win, but for whatever reason, Herby beat him badly that day. I remember the last point: Keeth fell and Herby touched him to win 15-8. Herby had another lifeline.

So while in past years making one round of 32 would've put me ahead of the American fencers with whom I was competing for four precious Olympic spots, that wasn't the case in 2004. Suddenly American fencers were fencing better. I'd have to make another 32—or more—to qualify for Athens.

We went to Germany. I went 5-1 in the pools again to make the 64 without having to fence a direct-elimination qualifier. Unfortunately, instead of drawing a pushover, I drew the strong Ukrainian fencer Vladislav Tretiak, who for whatever reason happened not to fence well in the pools the previous day. He slew me mightily, but at least I grabbed points for the 64—Keeth and Ivan were the only ones to make the 32, where both lost. At this tournament, another fencer was eliminated from the race. Powerhouse Adam Crompton, a teammate of Jason Rogers, coached by Nazlymov, fenced for Ohio State. He was a bit of a dark horse, but running in 6th or 7th nationally with a very real chance of breaking through at any moment. If he could grab a couple 32s, he'd make the Athens team. That was his plan—he'd registered for all five qualifying world cups and was poised to make a serious run. In Germany, he realized that by competing in the remaining three world cups, he would cut into his college season and thus lose his scholarship. Jason had planned ahead and taken the year off to prevent the conflict, but Adam hadn't realized the problem and had tried to do both.

The rules were clear and there was no wiggle room. With only an outside chance at making the Olympic team, Adam chose school and was out of the race. Just like that, another fencer fell prey to circumstance and a lack of planning rather than a lack of skill. Steve Mormando's words were proving true: take care of everything around fencing while you give yourself the time to build the skills in the sport and good things will happen. The folks leading the pack were doing all three.

The rest of us in contention went to another world cup in Athens. It was six months before the Games, and everything in the city looked about half done. Traffic was a mess, as they were still adding lanes to the highway that connected the airport to the city. The qualifying pools were held at the old airport. Dust covered the ground and the fencers had to clean their shoes after every point to avoid sliding around on the slapdash metal strips. Still, the Olympics were in the air. Stores were selling Olympic paraphernalia and competitors looked at the event a little more seriously—both as a warm-up and a chance to make a statement for the real event coming up in half a year.

I slipped a bit in my pool, going 4-2 and sweating out a close victory in my direct elimination bout to make the 64. London rankings had finally caught up with Patrick Durkan and he was allowed to register for Athens, but he fell to Ivan in direct elimination. Barring a huge Cinderella run, he was out of contention.

For the round of 64, we moved from the dusty strips of the old airport to the Olympic venue itself. Strips were raised, TVs broadcast the points, and the event organizers made us wait in the tunnels until hearing, "From the USA, Tim Morehouse!" It was electric—like jacking straight into a childhood dream. I drew Giampiero Pastore, who would go on to fence strong for Italy in the Games, and I got crushed in the 64.

Ivan made the 16, so with two world cups remaining, it was Ivan far out front followed by a struggling (for his standards) Keeth, and then Jason, who I trailed by a top-thirty-two result. Mike Momtselidze and Herby Raynaud were not far behind, and the rest had fallen away through life, logistics, or not knowing the system.

In Moscow, we again stayed at the monolithic Hotel Russia. By our third day of ignoring the prostitutes in the lobby, they started shouting insults that called our masculinity into question as we walked past. The same rickety, fume-filled bus took us from the hotel to the fencing venue, which had been built for the 1980 Olympics. I had a breakdown in the pools, going 1-4 in my first 5 matches. I beat Sydney bronze medalist Wiradech Kothny to end the pools at 2-4 and earn a direct elimination match that could see me through to the tournament's second day. In direct elimination, I eked out a win against a young Russian to make the 64. On the following day, I drew Stanislav Pozdniakov, who by that time had pocketed four Olympic gold medals, including the individual gold in Atlanta. I knew I'd have to make one-light touches instead of two-light touches, where right-of-way and the point hung on referees' judgment. These two-light touches tend to swing toward the favored fencer, and a ref would be even more inclined to do so in Moscow against a Russian favorite. I started with false-temp lunges mixed with Akhi-style stop-cuts to Pozdniakov's wrist while he was in preparation. I tried with my parries to claim right-of-way and to keep his blade off my equipment entirely. Early in the match, my scoring light went on and, for the most part, his stayed off. Every time I hit Pozdniakov, he tested his equipment, flexing his saber and asking the judges to check the connections. Everything seemed to work, but just in case—as Charikov had done the previous year—Pozdniakov made us switch strips. Fencing Pozdniakov in Moscow, we went to 14-14. The referee said *En garde. Prêt? Allez!*

Pozdniakov came at me, no longer a matador playing with the bull, but one now going for the efficient kill. Where was his blade? He pushed me down the strip. I searched through the parries, and finally his lunge came, straight at me like an arrow toward my heart—and I sliced it out of the air, taking his blade. We both connected, me crashing into his mask and Pozdniakov slashing into the Kevlar of my right side. Both scoring lights went on, but it was my obvious right-of-way!

I had won! I had beaten Pozdniakov in Russia and had almost certainly secured a spot on the 2004 Athens Olympic team!

Only that's not how it happened. The referees ruled that my

touch had landed low and awarded Pozdniakov the point and thus the match. I was out in the round of 64! Keeth, Ivan, and Jason all made the 32 (where Ivan lost 14-15 to Pozdniakov on another disputed call) and so were ahead of me in qualifying points. Fencing in the last match of the 64, Herby Raynaud had a chance to pass me, fencing against another Russian upstart whom he could have beaten. You always want to win your way onto a team rather than seeing one of your competitors lose their way off, but that's what happened to Herby when he lost in the 64 to an unnamed Russian kid. It was his Cuban/Iranian syndrome.

It was a long flight home, and I spent it pacing the plane. One more tournament. I was now in 4th place, within a disputed touch of being in a virtual tie with Jason Rogers for 3rd. But I was still within the reach of those behind me, including Tim Hagamen, Herby, and Mike Momtselidze, should any one of them make a 32 without me. I spent two weeks fretting, a total wreck, in a blur of nervousness, one tournament away from knowing if I'd qualify for Athens. All the hours since middle school, all the dead-on-my-feet practices, $30,000 in credit card debt that I had no way to re-pay—it all hinged on one more world cup, where my qualification balanced so precariously on the beaded tip of my blade.

We went to Bulgaria. Or, should I say, all of us but Mike went. Mike had done well nationally and had made every round of 64 in the four qualifying world cups. If he'd made the 32 and I'd failed to make the 64, we would've been virtually tied, the qualifying coming down to a formula of touches. Maybe Mike considered himself out of the running or at least an odds-off long shot. But whatever the reason, he decided that even one more world cup was too much for his decimated bank account to bear. That's the world of small-sport athletes: endurance and commitment must be so much more than physical.

So we were one lighter in Bulgaria. Keeth, Ivan, Jason, me,

Herby, and Tim Hagamen in that order—the only ones left with a shot. After my first bout in the pools, I was so nervous I threw up on the side of the strip. But I made the 64; so did the other Tim. We both lost in the 64, leaving me ahead by a nose. Jason fenced his heart out to make the 16, solidifying his spot in 3rd place. It was nice that I didn't have to sweat my one-point loss to Pozdnia-kov, because Jason's points put him clear of where I would have been. And Herby didn't make the second day, earning exactly zero points for his trip to Bulgaria and leaving him outside the top four.

Herby and I were sharing a room. When I walked in after losing my match in the 64, but having claimed the 4th and final spot on the Athens team, Herby was sitting alone, icing his elbow, which had swollen to the size of a grapefruit. It's a wretched place that only small-sport athletes know. And I'd certainly been there.

But for me, that day was the flipside of despair. I had made the Athens Olympics! I couldn't show Herby my joy, so I put on my walkman, went to a different floor, and, with me eyes closed, enraptured, danced through the halls.

The Fine Line Between
Everything and Nothing

Our four-person team was set, but qualifying for the Olympic team event itself was still up in the air. If the team didn't qualify, two and not four of our fencers would go to Athens. Only 8 teams qualify for the Olympics—the top four teams in the world plus a team from each of the four zones: Europe, Asia, Africa, and the Americas.

Keeth, Ivan, Jason and I stayed in Bulgaria for the team event, and the night before matches, we showed up at our hotel only to find that there were no rooms left for team USA. Instead, tournament organizers drove us to a hotel that had been closed for renovations, where we stayed with the Korean team in rooms without heat in the dead of the Bulgarian winter, wearing winter coats and hats and smelling leaking gas. The next day we got trounced by Poland, Spain, and, in the final kicker, Kazakhstan, to finish 13th—and qualify for the Olympics as the top team from our rather lackluster zone. It wasn't necessarily the triumphant entrance we imagined, but it worked.

Now with everything wrapped up, we could focus on acting like a team rather than like competitors. In the season's final months of world cup competitions, we developed a USA-against-the-world attitude: a chip on our shoulder that we would take with us to the Olympics. We found that, suddenly, we were focusing on team rather than individual results and that this focus took us to close matches with some of the top teams in the world. Keeth was our rock, always tough; Ivan was our comeback specialist and brought tremendous energy to the team; Jason was the grinder, battling his heart out against the best European fencers; and I was the alternate, trying to fight and scrap as hard as I could for touches against the world's best whenever I got the chance to fence.

The final world cup before the Olympics was held in New York City. Because the city was bidding for the 2012 Games—for once there was money behind it—the initial rounds were held at Hunter College, with the finals moving to Grand Central Station. Finally we didn't have to fence jet-lagged. And with some real promotion at last, the fans came out in force.

A team event is a race to 45 touches. Every time the lead team reaches a multiple of five (5, 10, 15 touches, etc.), the fencers rotate. So each of the three fencers is guaranteed 3 bouts, one against each of the other team's three fencers. Also, instead of fencing pools or early rounds, team events start with a round of 16.

Fencing against Poland in the New York World Cup round of 16 in the basement of a Hunter College building, we took a 40-30 lead into the final bout. Then Polish fencer Kuniusz scored 10 straight before Ivan rallied back to win 45-42. We breathed a collective sigh of relief—and elation. We fenced Russia (who were so confident they rested Stanislav Pozdniakov) in the round of 8. As we took the lead, Pozdniakov kept looking to his coaches, asking if he should warm up. The coaches kept nodding no, and we again built a 40-30 lead until finally Russia put Pozdniakov into the last match against Keeth, our closer. Pozdniakov started to close the gap. Like the Poland match, the 10-point lead was thankfully enough, and Keeth held on for the win—our first in team history over Russia. We then beat France for the first time, and then Spain, to win the first team world cup in U.S. saber history. Needless to say, after this tournament of firsts, and with the Olympics now less than a month away, anything seemed possible.

Iris Zimmermann hadn't qualified for Athens, losing the second spot to Keeth's sister, Erinn Smart, by exactly 2 international points—maybe the difference of one touch. Despite knowing she hadn't qualified, Iris competed at the New York World Cup. Early in the competition, she injured her knee—her third serious knee injury—but she fenced through it to the semifinals. If the women's foil team event hadn't been cut, Iris would have been in Athens. But just as the FIE gave me my shot, they took it away from Iris.

A few weeks later, Keeth Smart, Ivan Lee, Jason Rogers, our coach Yury Gelman, and I flew to Athens and walked off the plane with the throngs of ticket-holding sports fans, ecstatic to finally be in the Olympic city. Athletes talk about the Opening Ceremonies being the event they'll remember forever, but for me the airport was equally memorable. At the end of the gangway, Olympic organizers greeted us and pointed us towards an athletes' line for expedited entry. The Athens mascots pointed the way—two puffy, cartoonish characters based on the Greek gods Athena and Phevos.

The Iraq War was in full swing and security was tight. There was some question as to how U.S. athletes would be greeted in Athens, but at the airport, it was all smiles and warm greetings. We had our cameras out, snapping pictures of everything with rings. On the one hand, I felt ready to burst with joy, and on the other, I was desperately aware that I couldn't possibly soak up *every-*

thing. At home, you might forget what you had for lunch or what you did the previous day, but I'll never forget walking through the airport with my teammates—experiencing a crystallized moment that none of us could ever exactly recreate.

Outside, the highway from the airport to the city was finished—sparkling almost—and it was an easy bus ride into town, made even smoother by a police escort. Our first stop was the American University of Greece, where Team USA had installed its headquarters and training facilities. There were Team USA signs everywhere, athletes milling around the campus, and support staff making sure we knew where to go and had everything we needed. The five of us stepped out into the sweltering Athenian heat, but were quickly whisked into the apparel room, where we were fitted with tee shirts, shoes, hats, luggage, shorts, and outfits for the opening and closing ceremonies. Really, it was too much to carry around and they gave each of us a box with prepaid shipping to send home the extra swag that we wouldn't need during the Games.

Then we took pictures for our all-important credentials. For the next three weeks, these credentials would hang around our necks, dictating where we could and couldn't go and defining the other privileges we had as athletes and coaches.

My credential was a bit different than my teammates'. Making the team had been my goal. And while I'd achieved it, it didn't mean that I got to compete. As the fourth member of the team, I was a "replacement" athlete. Unlike an "alternate," I could be subbed into the team competition, rather than competing only if someone higher on the totem pole got hurt. But my getting subbed in was only likely if we were already out of medal contention.

Everyone knows about the Olympic Village, but no one knows about the place where the alternates, replacement athletes, training partners, and second coaches stay. They come to the Games, too. Every country does something different with their "almost" athletes, and the United States put the couple hundred of us in apartments just outside the training facility. After we had our gear, our credentials, and our marching orders, Keeth, Ivan, Jason, and Yury hopped back on the bus and were whisked away to the Olympic Village, while I stayed in the "almost" village, where athletes milled about campus, passing time by working out and wondering if they'd get the chance to compete. For some, the almost village was purgatory—they'd been favored to make the team or had made it in the past only to fall one spot short in Athens, doomed to watch their teammates win as their own hopes faded away.

For some it was even worse. Because teams like women's softball were so heavily favored, the difference between the village and the almost village was more than the difference between competing and not competing—the softball alternates knew it was the difference between being an Olympic gold medalist and nothing at all, having absolutely everything if they saw one pitch and nothing if they stayed *almost*.

For others like me, it was heaven—the culmination of years of training and one long stride up the path to what we hoped would be the real thing four years later in Beijing. As a small-sport athlete, I appreciated the fact that all the food was sponsored—Power Bars and Gatorade, and unlimited Häagen-Dazs!

In the days before the opening ceremonies, my teammates arrived to train and eat outside the overcrowded facilities of the Olympic Village. Marion Jones, in the midst of the doping scandal that would destroy her career and eventually send her to prison, spent a lot of time at the campus trying to stay out of the spotlight. But every evening they'd go back to the Village, while I stayed *almost*.

I met a synchronized swimmer who told a story, similar to

mine, of watching those in front of her melt away. She'd missed the team by five spots, but the five in front of her declined the invitation to the almost-Olympic Village and she'd accepted; so here she was.

We almost athletes weren't allowed at the Opening Ceremonies. Instead, the U.S. Olympic Committee threw a toga party for the 200-ish of us at the almost village. Again, for some it was bittersweet, but I was ecstatic. I was here. In Athens. At the Olympics.

At the training track, I watched middle distance runners kick out seemingly endless laps of 4:00-ish minute miles. The men's and women's basketball teams practiced there, and I watched from the sidelines as LeBron James, Allen Iverson, and the others casually drained 3-pointers. Michael Phelps was nineteen at the time and poised to win six gold medals at these Athens Games. I was twenty-six, already old by some standards, and glowing with the energy of the Games around me—with only an outside shot at even competing.

At world cups and world championships, there are no "replacements"—the team is comprised of four members and fencers substitute in and out like basketball bench players, as Pozdniakov had done in the final round against Keeth in New York. Everywhere but the Olympics, the fourth fencer almost always fought a couple of points and was counted as an integral part of the team. But at the Olympics, three fencers—not four—were considered the official team. You couldn't substitute out and come back later: instead, to get the fourth fencer in, you had to substitute before the start of a round. Moreover, the fencer who had been replaced was permanently out.

Or one of the three fencers on the team could fake an injury. It had become almost a tradition—teams would advance to the medal rounds and then, to ensure the 4th got a medal, 1 of the original 3 would fake an injury. The French had done it in 2000 when desperately behind to the Russians in the gold medal match—their 4th fencer earned a silver for fencing 1 point, which he lost to Pozdniakov after the French closer took a dive.

Once "injured," a fencer's Olympics were over. If a fencer left the three-person team to allow the replacement to compete, the fencer would literally switch beds with his replacement, going to the almost village while the replacement took the bed in the Olympic Village. At that point, if there was another injury among the top three, the team would be disqualified. Thus, no one was subbing while in medal contention.

Our men's épée team had made a deal with each other before qualifying even began that they would draw straws to see who subbed out so that their 4th fencer could compete. But Keeth and Ivan had put up international results for years, and with Jason they'd just won New York. We had a very realistic shot at a medal, so we were going to put our very best fencers on the strip: Keeth, Ivan, and Jason.

On the morning of the individual event, I met my teammates at the venue: a hangar of the old Athens airport that had been converted into the fencing stadium. On the huge floor were red, blue, green, and yellow strips with massive scoreboards over each and TVs around the venue showing close-ups of each fencer. I helped my teammates warm up, but in truth I was probably an awful practice partner. *Just don't hurt them*, I kept thinking. Not that they couldn't have beaten me even if I fenced full speed, but I remembered hitting Keeth below the belt in Portugal years ago right before he had to fence the world championships, and I didn't want to hurt anyone's confidence (or testicles) in the seconds before the first match. So I fenced flimsy, and it was suddenly time to take the strip. Our team donned their credentials and headed to the floor while I donned street clothes and headed for the stands. I was intent on soaking up everything I could—what was happening, how people looked, how they handled themselves—trying to learn as much as possible so that when my day finally came, I would be ready.

There were fencers competing in the individual competition and in his first match, Jason drew the fiery Italian, Luigi Tarantino. Jason scored first. Then it went 1-1. Then the points started rolling away and two minutes later, Jason was out 3-15. Three points, two minutes: that was it for Jason until the team event. Later he'd tell me how hard it had been seeing all that training and travel and sacrifice blown like chaff into the wind in the space of 120 seconds.

Ivan and Keeth both won their opening matches. Ivan lost to Pozdniakov in the 16. Keeth fenced Italian superstar Aldo Montano, whose father and uncle had both fenced in the Olympics. A quick Google image search for Aldo Montano shows you the difference between the lives of U.S. fencers and that of Montano, who pops up as frequently in pictures of yachts, Milan fashion week, and underwear advertisements as he does in fencing whites.

Just before the Olympics, we'd been to a training camp in Tuscany with the Italians, Ukrainians, and a handful of other athletes who would be competing in Athens. At camp, Montano had consistently tried to parry Keeth's flunge, always seeming to be looking for just the right angle, the right velocity to take Keeth's blade in flight. In the round of 16, Keeth looked for Montano to parry. But Montano had set him up. Instead of parrying, Montano switched strategies completely, attacking into Keeth's hesitation and hitting Keeth in preparation as had become the standard counter to Keeth's flunge. Keeth couldn't adapt in time, Montano won, and the U.S. men were out of the individual. Montano would go on to take the gold.

The next day, we all watched the U.S. women's saber. Sada

Jacobson was ranked #1 in the world and her sister Emily had qualified second. It was the first Olympics for women's saber in any form, and without a women's team saber event, the U.S. was only allowed two spots. The sister story, the newness of the event, and the chance of U.S. medals brought media attention the sport had never seen before. Suddenly there were cameras set up around the fencing venue like spikes on a hedgehog.

Two short weeks before the Games, there was another story. Nigeria chose not to send a fencer and the FIE decided to fill the empty spot with the highest-ranking, non-competing fencer. That fencer happened to be Mariel Zagunis, our team's alternate, who had missed qualifying ahead of Emily with a 14-15 loss at the season's last qualifying world cup. Despite the heartbreak of missing qualifying by 1 point, Mariel had stayed committed to her training, posted some great results, and then there she was—a nineteen-year-old girl from Beaverton, Oregon, a freshman at Notre Dame—competing in her first Olympics.

Sitting in the stands with Jason, Keeth, Ivan and Mariel's mom, I predicted Mariel would win it all. I figured Mariel would be fencing without expectations, just happy to be there since it almost didn't happen, whereas Sada and to some extent Emily carried the weight of expectation. Mariel went 15-13, 15-11, 15-10, then finally 15-9 over Chinese fencer Xue Tan to claim the gold! It was an ecstatic moment. We rushed the finals strip, picked Mariel up and tossed her in the air. Then she paraded around the room, draped in the flag, while the national anthem played. In this sport dominated by Europeans, the United States had its first gold in 100 years!

And while Sada lost to Tan in the semis, she won the bronze medal match—two fencing medals for Team USA! In the aftermath of the Games, Mariel's gold would change our little sport forever, but at the time all I could see on the horizon was the upcoming team event.

The day of the event, I suited up, warmed up, and started feeling the competition jitters, even though in all likelihood I wouldn't compete. The announcers called our names and I walked through the entrance tunnel with Keeth, Ivan, and Jason and sat on the bench as my teammates stood on the strip opposite three Hungarian fencers.

To call us underdogs against Hungary was an understatement. The U.S. saber team had never beaten Hungary—never!—and our fencers' individual results against Nemcsik, Ferjancsik, and Lengyel were weak to say the least. The Hungarian team was ranked #2 in the world. We were ranked #7. We came together on the side of the strip, put our hands together and chanted "U–S–A!" But you could tell the bluster covered nerves. This is what the four of us had worked so hard for—so many hours, so much debt, so little reward up until now. For Yury, this was his shot: finally his Olympic team had the chance at a medal he'd never been given as a Jew in the USSR.

When Ivan Lee opened and went down 3-5 against Hungary, Yury started pulling his hair out. When it looked like the refs blew a call, Yury shouted, "They won't let us win!" as if he were back in the Soviet Army Championships being told to favor Moscow fencers. Ivan came off the strip with his head down, but Keeth grabbed him by the shoulders and shouted, "Come on! We can do this!" We weren't allowed to stand, but the energy was so intense that after every point we scored, we jumped screaming to our feet as the side referees scolded us and told us to sit. On the bench with us was Jeff Bukantz, our non-competing team captain, whose job was to work the politics and know the rules inside and out.

Keeth followed his strong words with a dominant performance to make it 10-8, and Jason ended his first round behind at 12-15.

When we were up, we flew and when we went down, we sank, as if we were living a lifetime of emotions in the space of minutes. We went down 26-30, then 38-40, and then Keeth took the strip as our closer against Ferjancsik, a fencer Keeth had never defeated.

On the strip that day was a Keeth I had never seen before. He looked over at the bench, smiled, and nodded. Then instead of flunging and screaming, it looked as if Keeth went inside himself, sucking into a pinprick of light in the middle of a fencing strip in Athens. Ferjancsik attacked and Keeth moved calmly back to make the hit fall short, then worked Ferjancsik methodically down the strip until landing a fluid, precise lunge. It was as if Keeth were channeling Akhi's precision. Instead of screaming, Keeth nodded, and the calm power radiated from him like heat waves off a summer street. He tied the match at 43 and then, as we all knew he would that day, scored the final 2 points. Our first team win over Hungary put us in the Olympic semifinals, with Italy, France, and Russia!

We drew France, a team we had only just beaten for the first time in New York. Between matches, we went back to the waiting area and then emerged again through the tunnel as the PA system announced our names. The winner would fight for the gold, and was guaranteed at least a silver medal. The loser would fence for the bronze.

The pain of Jason's individual performance didn't linger—he'd fenced well against the Hungarians and now fenced the French brilliantly, taking 13 points on aggregate and giving an equal 13. Ivan and Keeth fenced back and forth as well, with Keeth starting the final match against former World Champion Damien Touya, again down 38-40. Touya was big, known for his speed and his vicious attacks. His metallic lamé jacket sat bulkily on his frame and his en garde looked like a coiled slouch.

Keeth had that calmness again. The first point started and

Keeth stood close to Touya—too close?—and of course, Touya took advantage, lunging like a snake at a frozen rabbit. But Keeth wasn't there. God, Keeth's speed was awesome! He was away before Touya's saber claimed the space and then dove in behind it for the point. Down 43-44, Keeth pushed into the center of the strip. Touya responded with a long advance-lunge but again Keeth was away, Touya's saber slashing through the air an inch in front of Keeth's jacket, and Keeth riposting for the touch.

And then it was 44-44: one point for a guaranteed medal, one point to decide which team would fence for the gold. You could taste Touya's disdain—the French closer against the American upstart. Did the moment get to Keeth? Instead of pulling away to make Touya come up short and then taking a one-light touch, when the ref said *Allez*, Keeth flunged at the same time, Touya lunged and they both hit, throwing the fate of the match into the referee's hands.

The fencing world waited for the call. *Simultaneous*, said the ref—they'd both attacked and the touches had landed within the 300-millisecond lockout period. There was no right-of-way and so no point, according to the Spanish referee.

Keeth and Touya took their places on the strip. Ivan, Jason, and I were on our knees in front of the bench, holding hands, holding our breath. *En garde. Prêt? Allez!*

In a replay of the previous point, they both attacked—Keeth flunging off the line into Touya's liquid-fast lunge. The ref again called *Simultaneous!* Touya screamed and blood spouted from a hole in his sword-hand glove, where Keeth's saber had speared cleanly through his hand. Touya dropped to his knees and was immediately surrounded by teammates and trainers. Keeth cleaned his sword.

An injury timeout lasts ten minutes and Touya used them all, refusing to call in the team's substitute. In the background, Italy upset the gold-medal-favored Russians. Whoever won the next point would face relatively beatable Italy for the gold. Whoever lost would fight the nearly invincible Russians for the bronze.

At the end of ten minutes, Touya took the strip against Keeth. From the bench, we could see blood leaking through the dressing around Touya's sword hand. *Allez!* Again, they both started fast off the line and lunged, hitting in the middle of the strip like butting big-horned sheep. Both lights went on. Again, we'd put the outcome into the hands of fate and again we got ready for the call *simultaneous!*

And then the ref called the point for Touya.

Yury screamed. In the end, we hadn't been allowed to win. Keeth's calm was gone and he let out a howl at the ref. But it didn't change the call. And after beating Keeth, Touya charged past him down the length of the room, spun around, and then holding his saber like an M-16 in his bloody hand, Touya ma-chine-gunned our bench.

Later, led by Touya, the French defeated the Italians for the gold. While the French anthem played, their alternate was back-stage trashing folding chairs. In the past, the French team has had one of their fencers fake an injury so that the alternate could be brought in; that way, he would be able to stand on the po-dium. But not in Athens.

After the match against France, we sat silently outside the venue in the heat of the Athens summer as the crowd filtered out. Keeth was silent. Jason was quiet. I wasn't sure what to do and it wasn't my place to say anything. Finally Ivan spoke. He said we could do it, that we could beat Russia and take a medal. We nodded silently. Ivan said it again, and eventually we started to believe it.

We fenced in the middle of a grand hall: one strip with packed bleachers on either side. Once the fencing started, the hall went dark except for the lights on the fencing strip. TV screens above the strip showed the fencers and the score, and the action was broadcast on a huge Jumbotron screen.

Now it was Jason and Ivan who felt they could prop up Keeth. Against Russia, they tore up and down the strip, staying out of the no-man's middle, building a 40-35 lead.

Five points from a medal, Keeth took the strip against Pozdniakov. On the first point, Pozdniakov caught Keeth flatfooted and nervous with a strike that was over in less than a blink. "I should've said something more to him," said Ivan, on the bench. We screamed for Keeth and watched in horror as Pozdniakov scored a string of points, feeling the terror of facing Pozdniakov, the world #1, on a run, in front of a thousand spectators, four years' worth of work on the line.

After going down, Keeth battled back to 44-44. Again, one point was the difference between everything and nothing. Just like when Keeth fenced Touya, Ivan, Jason, and I got on our knees, holding hands in front of the bench. That final point, both fencers lunged into the middle and landed together. Again we expected *Simultaneous! Pas de point!*

Then, to our horror, the referee raised his hand to signal a point for Pozdniakov. We were all stunned. The referee called the point against us. We were so close. Keeth quietly took off his mask and turned his face to the sky as the triumphant Russian team stormed onto the stage.

Ivan, Jason, and I ran up the strip to collect Keeth. We hugged him and we cried. Of course, we realized that without Keeth, we would have lost the first match to Hungary. It was Keeth who *brought* us to the bronze medal match. But when Keeth got back to the bench, he sat there despondent. Small-sport athletes aren't used to living their wins and losses in the spotlight, but here at the Olympics, with a medal on the line, it was different. Millions of people watched as TV cameras zoomed in on Keeth's anguish while we tried to shield him. Finally, we escorted Keeth, in tears, into the back room. We were stunned.

Two points, both at 44-44, were the difference between our dream and a nightmare. It was tempting to blame the referees, and diving into the middle of the strip allows you to do that. But as underdogs, we all knew better than to fence in the middle. Later, Keeth would say that when he stood across from Pozdniakov, he questioned whether he deserved to be there and so, instead of taking control of the match as he'd done against Hungary, he'd lunged into the middle, hoping Pozdniakov might land on his guard or that the referees might give him the points, rather than pitting skill with the Russian champion. Lessons were supposed to build *toward* the Olympics and not away from them. I wondered if we could ever recover, if we would ever have the opportunity to apply the lesson, to write our destiny with active blades instead of betting for victory on a weighted coin toss.

Dealing with "Almost"

As explosive as Keeth is on attack, he's also controlled and almost clinical, on the strip and off. Other fencers routinely break down almost as part of their ritual of loss, but not Keeth. The first time I saw Keeth cry was after he lost to Pozdniakov in Athens. The second would be four years later in Beijing.

But at that moment, the team, with Keeth as its leader, was devastated. Even though he'd carried us through Hungary and brought us back against France, he felt as though he'd let the team down. But that couldn't have been further from the truth. He had fenced a spectacular Olympics; his saber introduced the U.S. team to the exclusive club of legitimacy among the sport's elite countries and, we hoped, among the judges.

Keeth had won everything but a medal.

I wished I had been a better fencer, wished I could've helped the team. But I wasn't ready yet. It wasn't my time. I hoped that my time would come at the 2008 Games in Beijing, and with that in mind, I found myself standing in the fencing training room at the American University of Greece the day after our loss to Russia. There were mats on the floor from an earlier Taekwondo training session, but I was alone—the only person in a room decorated with Olympic rings. I had on shorts, a tee shirt, my fencing shoes, and I held my saber.

Opposite me was Pozdniakov and we were in Beijing. I charged the strip and my feet on the practice mat were the room's only sound. But I heard fans in the bleachers catch their breath as I lunged, was parried, and riposted to catch Pozdniakov in the sleeve for a one-light touch. I was alone in the room, sweating through my shirt, flying against the windmills of a nonexistent opponent who could not have been more real. Standing in Athens, I was in Beijing, four years in the future, and I was fencing for a medal.

I think it was the first time I became conscious of visualizing success. Sure, I'd done it since middle school when I imagined walking into school a different person—confident and in charge and able to hit the winning jump shot at a lunch recess game of playground hoops. But projecting an opponent onto the strip of the Athens training facility was the first time I took intentional, conscious control of my fantasies. It was the first time I took my tendency to daydream and put it to good use. This is how I would spend the next four years—visualizing success, visualizing Beijing, examining myself with the goal of weeding out tendencies that blocked my success, and solidifying traits that aided it. I had reached a point where I was my saber and my saber was me, and as much as winning required looking outward to the strip, it also required looking inward.

But in Athens, in 2004, there was a *Sports Illustrated* party to attend. That's the Olympics: amid the myriad personal stories of massive triumph and devastating loss, the show goes on. And nothing was showier than *S.I.* bashes. The party was held at a

club overlooking the Mediterranean where a handful of little ca-
banas were each outfitted with a themed bar. The main party was
around the lighted pool with the eye-popping red, white, and blue
of a huge USA printed on the bottom, which seemed to magnify
through the water as if shot with a fish-eye lens. Or maybe that
was the Mai Tais. Either way, the synchronized swimming team
broke the pool's nighttime mirror, performing for the crowd and
whipping the pool into whitecaps. The women's soccer team had
just won the gold and Brandi Chastain, Julie Foudy, Mia Hamm,
and the rest of the spectacular 2004 U.S. women's team led a conga
line through the party with their medals around their necks. For
whatever reason, Evander Holyfield was there. Michael Phelps
was there, too, with half a soccer team's worth of gold medals.

There was shrimp and lobster—for a fencer it was opulence
beyond imagining, and like a bear gorging before a long hungry
winter, I took full advantage. Still, the four of us—Keeth, Ivan,
Jason, and I—couldn't kick the shock of the previous night. We
weren't alone. You could tell who'd won, who'd lost, and who had
yet to compete by their demeanor around the pool. Some winners partied like it was 1999; some losers joined them, but with
an edge to their use of the open bar that made it painfully obvious they were masking their pain with the electricity of the night,
the Mediterranean, and a couple hundred of the country's hottest
dance partners, at least for a couple of hours. The athletes who
were still to compete had a shrimp or two and left early.

I met a journalist for the *New York Sun* who thought I had an
interesting story and we did an interview a couple days later. It was
an afterthought to everything else going on.

Then it was the closing ceremonies. Alternates and the rest
of the almost crew weren't allowed in—remember, I'd spent the
opening ceremonies in a toga, watching the event on screens at
the almost village—but by that point in the Games, security had

loosened quite a bit and one of the guys inside borrowed credentials and used them to smuggle me and the other two weapons' replacement athletes into the ceremony.

You reach the stadium field through a long tunnel, and though I'd seen NFL teams bursting from the chute for years, there's nothing like being on the other end, walking out into the immensity of a packed stadium. It was disorienting, like viewing the lowest zoom level of Google Earth: you, beyond which there was the U.S. team, beyond which were the athletes on the field, beyond which were the guards ringing the pitch, then the spectators in the stands receding in stadium tiers, then Athens, and Greece, and the world—all shot from above and all magnifying with a click back to the athletes on the field. Every sport got its own Olympic commemorative pin, and U.S. fencers were given a little bobblehead figure. Trading pins was as hot among athletes as it was among fans and the fencing bobblehead had become a hot commodity. So, especially at the closing ceremony, we were constantly being approached by other countries' top athletes, who attempted in broken English to broker deals for our bobbleheads. Along with the phrases needed to argue their sport's refereeing decisions, most athletes had learned how to ask in English, *Do you have a pin?* It was the international language of Olympic commerce.

At the ceremony, many countries were in traditional garb and in addition to pins, people were trading hats. The U.S. foil guys had a competition to see who could barter his way into the funkiest hat. And so on the field was this big circulating international soup of people you'd never see in the same place ever again. We were all hugging and there was a swept-along energy that made the night seem equal parts everlasting and ephemeral.

At the ceremony's close, organizers passed the torch to Beijing. In a preview of the Beijing opening, there were deep drums and dancing. Each athlete got a little Chinese flag with the Olympic rings on it.

The day after the closing ceremony, the fencing team flew home. We visited the White House. And then as suddenly as it started, it stopped. The Olympics went quiet.

Just before Athens, I'd moved out of my parents' house. A Riverdale family whose daughters I'd coached had an extra apartment at 100th and Columbus, and they rented it cheap to an old Riverdale fencing buddy and me. A block uptown were housing projects. A block downtown were Upper West Side brownstones—one of the City's nicest neighborhoods. When I returned to the City, my roommate at work most days, I lounged around the apartment doing almost nothing while waiting for the phone to ring. We'd always been told the reason U.S. fencing had no sponsors is that we don't win medals. Now we thought that with Mariel taking the gold, Sada taking the bronze, and the men's saber team missing bronze by a point in an historic run, our little sport might blow up. We thought media and sponsorships would be breaking down our doors—or at least that we'd have some credibility when knocking on theirs. But the phone remained obstinately quiet. The Olympics were over, and the world at large seemed to be going about its business as if nothing had happened. Other than the ruby slipper of my Beijing flag, it might've all been a dream.

Keeth retired, devastated after losing the team event. Ivan retired, too, and Jason was thinking about it. I was $30,000 in debt and jobless, holding a desk flag and memories. In that first week back, I had a hard time getting out of bed in the morning, staring into the void of the post-Olympics fencing world at large, and into the void that was my life. Though I'd jumped directly into the fencing room in Athens to practice my footwork and had been teleported to the strip in Beijing, marrying that vision with the full stop of my post-Athens life was another challenge altogether. In Athens, amid all the Olympic hubbub, Beijing had seemed immediate—the sun rising on the city as the world turned from Greece to China—but at home in New York, it seemed impossibly far away.

Between Athens and Beijing was four years of footwork and blade drills, Yury and Fencers Club, NACs, world cups, nationals, Pan American games, airplanes, and hotels.

In addition to the grueling mental challenge of the long road of training and competition, I'd simply come to the end of the financial road. My credit was dried up. Before I could buy another plane ticket or register for another stay at a competition hotel, I needed a job.

It still felt like summer and I had a track record of wretched summer jobs. Between high school and college, I'd been a camp counselor and had gotten mono. After freshman year, I'd hefted never-ending stacks of paper at the book bindery. And after my sophomore year, I'd been a telemarketer for the United Jewish Appeal, working under the phone pseudonym "Jacob." It hadn't been the most farfetched name in the office. The guy at the next desk went by the name "Jaime Krolomski" (that was Julio).

The machines robo-called potential donors and when someone picked up, we'd launch into the script. Whatever they said, there was a scripted answer. If you did your job well and talked people into giving, you'd move up the ladder and get to talk with people who'd donated big in the past. These bigger calls would be "taped for training purposes" and you always had someone listening in, giving advice once the call ended. So Julio and I learned how to stay just barely in the sweet spot: do the job well enough to avoid getting fired, but not so well that you'd be promoted to the big calls and end up with someone critiquing your every move.

After work, I sometimes drove Julio home, always dropping him off at 96th Street. It turned out that Julio lived with his extended family in the projects a block north of my new apartment—I never knew he'd walked uptown from the drop-off on 96th. When I moved to the neighborhood just before Athens and then afterwards, we hung out at my place in the evenings. When my other friends would visit, they'd say, *Dude, you live a block from the ghetto!* And I'd wince because Julio lived *in it*.

Julio went to Hofstra University and then took a job in finance. Now in 2004, he was supporting his family and moving himself, and by extension all of them, up the socioeconomic food chain by leaps and bounds.

If you want a real success story, talk to Julio.

As for me, I was contemplating what time-killing job I'd land post-Athens. Going back to telemarketing wasn't a stretch of the imagination.

My parents had taken a couple of messages on the home number from Teach For America. It sounded like some sort of alumni thing and I figured they were inviting me to a dinner I couldn't afford and didn't really have the motivation to attend. Other than that, the only interesting call I got was for a substitute teaching job at Riverdale on the second day of school. I took it and pocketed $110.

After my first day of subbing, Teach For America caught me at my new number. Rather than an alumni events coordinator, on the phone was the Managing Director of Program for the New York City region. The executive director, Iris Chen, had read the article about me in the *Sun*—the one I'd given an interview for at the *Sports Illustrated* party. She'd read between the lines to correctly guess that after the Games, I had a big zero going on. There was a job open. The school year had already started and they needed a program director—a liaison and support for fifty or so TFA classroom teachers—and they needed it, like, yesterday. I interviewed a day later with three or four different people and later that evening they hired me. I went to work at the Teach For America headquarters at 9:00am a few days later.

It was a quick turnaround from the pinnacle of my sport to working seventy-hour weeks at a new job. In the year since I'd been a Teach For America teacher at IS-90, things had changed. The New York City program had gone from three program directors and 400 teachers to eleven program directors and over 700 teachers, and the office had moved to a hallway of Teach For America Corporate in an office building on 36th Street between 7th and 8th.

I took the elevator to the 7th floor and the doors opened on cubicles and offices: a bustling, professional environment, albeit still populated by idealistic, brilliant, overwhelmingly young people.

I met the team, got my cube, and put my mini Beijing Olympic rings flag on my desk.

Basically, I was the support and manager for fifty-odd TFA teachers at twenty schools in the South Bronx. During the day, I observed teachers in their classrooms, taking notes and gathering data that spoke to measurable objectives, specifically toward the goal of moving students two years in reading skills over the course of one school year. Then, commonly, the teacher and I would sit down with the school principal to discuss performance.

Like my first year at IS-90, I fenced very little that fall and then only in a perfunctory way that I hoped would allow me to stay level rather than lose ground. I remember coming into Fencers Club a couple times a week, running through a quick warm up, packing as many matches as I could into two hours, and then getting back to answering emails from my teachers on the train ride home.

I took a little swagger to the fall's first competition, the December North American Cup. Without Keeth, Jason and I were top dogs along with Ivan, whose retirement had lasted only a couple months. I figured I'd "made it" now and had whatever it was that kept top fencers on top. Besides, the NAC was populated mostly by college kids, aging lions, and the people we'd had to beat on our way to the Athens team.

Wearing my Olympic team warm-ups, I felt like I'd gone from being the hunter to the hunted. In my first bout I took my en garde with a little more shimmy than I'd brought to past comps. And in that first match, in the pools where I had learned to more than hold my own even internationally, my relatively unknown opponent ran at me, ran at me again, stayed on the attack and killed me 0-5. So much for the shimmy.

After the match, a ref who'd been watching and was a friend of mine told me that people were saying my Athens run had been a fluke, that despite the void left by Keeth and others' retirements, being the Olympic alternate would be the crowning jewel of my career.

How do you deal with toeing the edge of your dreams—Keeth's and Yury's dreams of a medal and my dream of Olympic competition? I thought that the plateau I'd worked so hard to claw my way onto before Athens would put me high above other national fencers, allowing me to coast through a season while I got my Teach For America feet under me again. But American fencers weren't on plateaus below me, they were vectoring upwards. I knew that if I didn't keep climbing, they would soon smash through the floor of my plateau and just keep on climbing, climbing, climbing out of sight. It was an exciting time in the sport but it was no time to coast.

Was touching the *almost* good enough for me? Would I be content to tell my kids someday that I'd been the alternate on the Athens Olympic team?

I rallied to make the round of 8 at that NAC. But even without Keeth and some of the other top fencers, I didn't make the 4. I was back where I'd always been— standing on the plateau of almost. If I wanted more, I was going to have to keep grinding. More than that, I was going to have to learn how to grind all over again, in a whole new way. There was something missing that I needed to turn *almost* into reality.

Fencing Pretty

Athens didn't exactly catapult fencing into the national consciousness; we were in no danger of becoming the new figure skating
or beach volleyball. Even so, our men's and women's results made
us look like medal contenders and medal contenders get stipends
from the U.S. Olympic Committee. Specifically, by the start of the
2005 season—my second school year as a Teach For America program director—in addition to travel expenses the top two fencers
in each weapon got $2000 a month and the number 3 and 4 fenc-
ers each got $1000. We were now getting more support than any
previous generation of fencers.

Our sport was growing up and so was my job.

Teach For America had taken an approach to education
very similar to the beg, borrow, and steal process the Soviets had
used in the '50s to cobble together national styles into their own,
streamlined medal machine. After interviewing successful teachers, Teach For America discovered that success in the classroom

didn't hinge on resources, curriculum, or even class size. What they found is that the best teachers were oriented toward numerical goals. Teachers who said, "I'll feel fulfilled if I help only one child succeed!" tended not to thrive. It was the teachers who threw themselves into the mass production of grade-level readers that got results.

I don't mean to proselytize a mechanistic, one-size-fits-all approach to education. Far from it! If there's anything I had learned over and over again it's that individuals use very different skills along their paths to success. But the best teachers, like the best fencers, have one thing in common: high expectations and a willingness to focus on the minutiae needed to get them.

Teach For America institutionalized this best practice, setting the goal for us: in the course of one school year, teachers would try to move their students two years in reading and in math. But rather than an abstract target, at the beginning of each year, teachers would assess their students' individual abilities and then the goal became personal—no matter where students started, they would *progress*.

No matter where I was as a fencer, I needed to progress.

After Athens, Yury and I refocused on fixing my style to make it more conventional and beautiful—to remove the oddities of my technique and smooth the rough edges that still earned me strange looks on tour. I was on a mission to fix what was wrong with me, what made me different, and we spent hours practicing the path of my shoulder, the path of my arm, the path of my wrist and of my blade; the tilt of my body toward and away from my opponent; the direction of my toes and knees, and the combination of lightness and power in my steps. Yury never let me progress through sloppiness and I counted it a measure of his belief in me.

Okay, let me admit that it sucked. This is painstaking, boring work that requires the meditative focus of a Zen master and enough repetitions to reprogram and eventually supersede your natural tendencies. That said, I knew that like my students, in order to catch up to the best in the world, I would have to outwork them. And though 2005 was a lull year between Olympics, I knew that if I wanted to improve I would have to keep traveling. Starting now, I would have to go to ten or more world cups. And so I did.

Maybe it was the allure of a medal after being so close in 2004. Or maybe (as I'd heard buzzing in the air) the fact that I'd made the Athens team made it seem like *anybody* could make the team. But whatever the reason, the number of U.S. fencers at international comps bloomed. I went to ten or eleven world cup and grand prix tournaments that season. Frequently, I wouldn't even tell the teachers I was managing that I was leaving, answering emails from Madrid and Moscow and Korea and packing meetings into the days I was in New York. And still, to co-opt a Teach For America term, I failed to make the "significant gains" I needed to solidify my leap to the top in fencing. I slipped back into the pattern of top-eight finishes at North American Cups and back into the pattern of dominating the 5-touch pools at international comps, then losing my first 15-touch match in the round of 64. There I stood on my plateau, looking down the hill at the approaching mob climbing toward me.

In front of me, Keeth, Ivan, and Jason were the talents. And nipping at my heels was the next generation of talent, including big Adam Crompton, Riverdale's Tim Hagamen, and an athletic left-hander from Sacramento named James Williams, who was now training with Yury. I was a workaholic placeholder between the two groups, keeping the seat warm until the next generation's skills matured to their inevitable potential. You should've heard the way Yury talked about Tim Hagamen. Tim was a natural, gifted—he was born with something. Yury coached the hell out of me, but he never called me talented. Hagamen did things right and I did things wrong. I was the "ugly" to his "pretty."

One day, I went to a school in the South Bronx to observe two teachers. Both teachers were up for the standard, periodic district review, and so a dynamic duo from the district office piggybacked on my observation, with the school principal joining us to make for what must have been a rather intimidating foursome sitting at the back of these poor teachers' classrooms with clipboards.

The classes couldn't have been more different. In the first room, half the class was talking and one student was under a desk. Supplies were strewn about a worktable and the stacks of papers on the teacher's desk looked tall enough to crush the sheets at the bottom to crude oil or maybe diamonds.

The second classroom was pristine. Students sat quietly at their desks. The teacher talked and students listened. Unlike the first classroom, there was no danger of it being overrun by a militant uprising of dust bunnies.

I was probably the most surprised person in the meeting that followed—that's because I had the data. Compared to their scores at the beginning of the year, the students in the messy classroom far outpaced the rate of learning of their peers in the clean classroom. Somehow, the eyesore teacher was creating *significant gains* and the clean teacher was not.

Having taught, I thought I knew the look of a talented teacher, but the day I compared the classroom of chaotic achievement with the classroom of controlled stagnation called my definition of teaching talent into question. Maybe there was a broader definition? It turned out the messy teacher had a nontraditional "talent" for using data, identifying which students needed extra work and exactly where they needed it, and then keeping pods of students with similar needs during recess or after school for this extra work. He had a talent for hard work. Apparently these nontraditional talents trumped the organized teacher's talent for classroom management and hypoallergenic excellence.

I realized that I tended to judge fencing talent similarly. When I watched Ivan or Keeth or Jason, or Akhi before them, or now the top European fencers like Touya and Tarantino and Pozdniakov, they always looked so pretty. That's why I was refocusing on how I looked when I fenced—to earn the look of this talent. But was the traditional, obvious talent for beautiful technique the only inroad to success? Was it *my* path toward significant gains in my sport?

In hindsight the punch line is obvious but, for whatever reason, I couldn't see it at the time. And so I kept doggedly trying to squeeze myself into the world's definition of talent. I kept trying to be somebody else's fencer. Maybe I had an inkling that pretty fencing wasn't the only way to win, but if not the rest of the world's technique, then what? I had no clue.

20

The Status Quo Is a
Backward Slide

The 2005-2006 season, my second year as a Teach For America program director and the second year after Athens, I again made the four-person national team with the results that had become my M.O.: top-eight national results, rounds of 64 every time I traveled, and a couple rounds of 32 at world cups. This plateau paid my travel, registration, and $1000 a month.

Keeth Smart had slowly made his return from retirement—whether he was a kicked dog coming back for the beating that would emotionally end him or a Phoenix rising from the ashes was yet to be seen. In his first tournament back, I beat Keeth to make my second finals at a North American Cup, where I lost to that young fencer from Sacramento, James Williams. Tim Hagamen spent most of that year competing for Harvard and not on the world cup circuit. It paid off with gold at the NCAA Championship, and Tim was Riverdale Coach Schneider's first student to earn the honor.

As a Teach For America program director, I was feeling competent and fulfilled. My teachers were doing well and I was happy that my work trickled down through them to reach about 5,000 children.

I was running uncharacteristically on autopilot. Slowly but surely, I was paying off the $30,000 debt I'd amassed in the lead-up to the Athens Games, and I'd struck what passed for a work-fencing balance, mostly due to working 80-hour weeks when I was in New York and scheduling the groundwork of these busy weeks while traveling. I used the fleeting equilibrium to take a breath, but instead of exhaling the contentment of two missions accomplished, an honest evaluation showed me that I was clinging to the breathless cusp in both. On one hand, I was knocking on the door of the top ranks of international fencers while the pack of hungry wolves was stalking my scent. On the other hand, I was on the doorstep of a meaningful career.

There were no extra hours in the week to push any more than I was pushing with either my career or fencing. In order to go forward with fencing, I wouldn't be able to work, and to move forward with work, I wouldn't be able to fence.

As Yury delighted in saying, "You can't sit your butt on two seats."

In that season, I traveled to thirteen world cups. But every time I got on a plane, landed somewhere new, stayed in a faceless hotel for a couple days, and competed in an equally faceless gym, it seemed to get a little more workmanlike. I'd show up, punch my card, put in my hours, and then some talented fencer would punch me out and I'd head home. At these tournaments, I started to find that it was my job with Teach For America rather than fencing that motivated me.

I knew it was time for a big move in one direction or the other. With the continuing growth of Teach For America, that spring they announced an opening for another managing program director. It was a step up the chain, managing about four people who did the job I was currently in, and thus ultimately reaching more students. Maybe it was the big move I was looking for? I sent in my resume and cover letter. If I were offered the position, I would have a decision to make: take the position and quit fencing, or decline the position and gear up for another medal run on a shoestring.

As it was, the decision was made for me. I didn't get the job. So with trepidation, I decided I would leave Teach For America, put my career ambitions on hold, apply for another stack of credit cards, and go for the team and the medal with everything I had in me. Telling my manager about my decision to leave—to leave a job at an organization I believed in and loved—was one of the hardest things I've ever had to do.

At the same time, the Riverdale family whose apartment I'd been renting needed the place back. I moved into a five-story walk-up in Kingsbridge, a neighborhood in the Bronx just north of Manhattan. My window looked into the alley where garbage was kept. I broke up with the girl I was seeing. My job gone, my house gone, my girl gone—all I needed was an old dog and a cowboy hat and I'd have myself a country song.

But it was strangely energizing—like seeing the yellow line stretch out in front of you at the beginning of a long road trip. Clarity will do that, even if it's painful. It hurts to see doors slam shut, but at least with only one open door remaining, you know which one to walk through.

Then Matt Kramer, the new CEO of Teach For America, emailed me and asked that I give him a ring. I'd taken Matt to observe one of my schools when he was trying to decide whether to leave his position as the youngest vice president at McKinsey's for the Teach For America position. We'd hit it off and had spoken a couple times since. He'd heard I was leaving and he wanted me to stay. I gave him the line about Beijing—the butt, the two seats, how I needed to train full-time, etc.—and he asked if I would consider a part-time position that would work with my training to keep me on staff. Eventually, he helped me find a thirty-hour-a-week salaried job answering admissions questions via phone and email. It was a job I could do anywhere in the world as long as there was an internet connection. If you sent an email to admissions@teachforamerica.org in 2006 or 2007, there's a good chance it was me who got back to you.

Sometimes even a fully committed small sport athlete needs a champion to smooth over some of the day-to-day details. Matt Kramer was that person for me. $30,000 with benefits, plus my fencing stipend, plus travel paid by the U.S. Fencing Association would allow me to squeak through the mechanics of the next two years.

That summer of 2006, I trained hard. I read *The Seven Habits of Highly Effective People* and *Good to Great*, among a dozen other books that helped me start to screw my head on straight for the grueling qualification ahead.

In October of 2006, I went to the World Championships in Turin, Italy. Usually, in Italian world cups and grand prix tournaments, the pools and preliminary rounds are held in a gym and the finals are moved to a theater where a huge crowd dressed for the opera watches the finals. In Turin, the World Championships were held in the Oval Lingotto, which had been built to house speed skating for the just-completed 2006 Winter Games. I was ready for my big move, but I struggled a bit in the pools. Seeded low in the round of 64, I drew German fencer Nicolas Limbach, one of the top five fencers in the world, who would go on to compete for Germany at the Beijing Games.

Limbach is 6'5" and thin, with a mechanical and methodical style. He uses his height to pick fencers off as they're start-ing their attacks or to launch his own long attacks from beyond most opponents' striking range. For a big fencer, his movements are small; he leaves only small openings and he rarely takes risks. Sure, people beat Limbach, but his losses are always 13-15, or 14-15—never blowouts. My plan against Limbach was to stay away from his deadly middle-distance game—I wasn't going to escape his attack, so my only hope was to stay close to where I could find his blade.

I quickly went down 8-3 and went into the one-minute break angry. In fact, I was angrier than I'd been in a while on the strip—the adrenaline coursing through me in a way it hadn't in the previous season. Coming out of the break, I ditched my plan and went for the kill. I wasn't even really intent on winning—I was more intent on proving I wouldn't back down and that I de-served to be on the strip with him. My sudden change in energy surprised Limbach and I started landing points! I'd charge off the line, miss, but then desperately dive back, avoiding his ri-poste before sending another attack that hit. One point, I pushed Limbach down the strip, landed a touch, and watched as he put his hands on his knees, breathing hard. I looked up to see that I was ahead—but quickly pushed the score out of my mind, not wanting to fall into the trap I'd been in many times before of let-ting the score drive me into nervousness.

At 14-13, Limbach came at me and I grabbed his blade with mine, and then we both hit. There in the crash of the middle it's a subjective call—the same one I'd lost to Pozdniakov on in Mos-cow a few years earlier. With a Mormando-like sell, I screamed and raised my arms in victory. And now for the first time, having built some legitimacy behind my game, I got the important call! I beat Limbach to make the round of 32!

But while making the 32 was great, it wasn't the big move

I was looking for. The big move was the round of 16 or beyond, and ahead 14-13 over the Korean Won Woo-Young, it looked like I was headed that way. One more touch and I'd fence Keeth Smart in the 16, who was still getting his game back together after coming out of retirement. Not only that, but the luck of the draw meant that Keeth or I would face a beatable opponent in the round of 8. One more touch and it was likely an American would be in the medal round of men's saber at the world championships for the first time ever.

I was a foot taller than Woo-Young, but he was lighting fast. At 14-13, I gave up a lazy point on a double-advance lunge that caught me in the hand and then it was 14-14. It was time for my big move. It had to be.

The final point opened and Woo-Young set a trap, checking into the center of the strip and then pausing. I didn't lunge into his trap as he'd hoped—I'd learned that lesson—but instead launched a long attack with my feet, driving him backwards as he searched furiously for my blade. Then he thought he'd found it, swinging for my saber. I moved under his blade to avoid it and then lunged. He saw it coming but there was nothing he could do—my blade was inside his defense and he tried to catch me with a quick touch to my arm. There's a small window in which two touches will register before the later touch is "locked out," and without the right-of-way, Woo-Young hoped to sneak in his touch quickly enough that it would lock out my inevitable touch. Woo-Young landed to my arm but my touch landed just after— both lights went on. Because the right-of-way was mine, so was the touch and, hence, the match!

I ripped off my mask and screamed, raising my arms in victory. My parents were there and I saw them cheering in the stands. My teammates screamed for me, too—they knew what a big deal this was. I felt like no matter what happened with

Keeth in the 16, then with a weaker opponent in the 8, I had broken through another ceiling of what I thought was possible for me to achieve. I had justified my decision to go all-in with fencing. Training full time with full commitment was exactly what I needed to restart my upward climb from the plateau that had held me level since Athens.

Then I saw Won Woo-Young making a circle with his right hand. Instant replay had just been instituted at that world championships and many close touches had seen fencers signaling for another look. Still, not a single call had been overturned and fencers were starting to imagine that instant replay was a bit of a novelty, subordinate to the tradition and the traditional arrogance of real-time refs. But in Woo-Young's case, why not try? With the match otherwise ending in defeat, I would've done the same thing.

The match's replay official was a member of the officiating committee—in fact, it was one of the members who'd pushed for the use of instant replay. The main official and the replay official watched the tape. I wondered what could be happening—they were having a long conversation, an argument even. Finally the match official returned to the strip.

He twirled his hands to show the call had been reversed. In its way, it was an historic moment—the first time instant replay had been used to overturn a call in international saber fencing. I'm sure there's a footnote somewhere about it. It sounds dry, doesn't it? Like the kind of thing you'd skip over if you were reading a history of fencing. But at 14-14 it meant Woo-Young had won. It meant I lost. I stood there stunned. Later, the match referee would say he still felt it was my point… but that he also liked his job. I challenged the call again myself, but the new call stood. Long after the match was over, I sat on the edge of the strip, stunned and listless. As the next fencers took the strip, Ivan came over, took my arm, and escorted me off the main floor. What had just happened? In the space of a replay I went from justifying a major life decision to regretting it. That's how it goes in fencing. Rules change and sometimes the implementation is brutal.

Here's another interesting footnote that sounds dry until you imagine what it means for a person's career, and thus his life. Right after Athens, the FIE had changed the "lockout" timing from 300 milliseconds to 120 milliseconds. One consequence was that an opponent could nip you as you attacked, and if your attack then landed more than 120 milliseconds later, your touch would be locked out. People said the new timing would kill the parry. Even after getting parried, a fencer often continues his stroke to land the touch. But the parry gives his opponent the right-of-way on riposte. Now, after parry, the riposte was landing more than 120 milliseconds after the first fencer's continuing attack—meaning the riposte was locked out. The parry was dead.

I had had two years to come to terms with the new timing. The parry wasn't dead—fencers simply developed quicker hands. But fresh from retirement, Keeth Smart hadn't fenced with the new timing. After beating me, Won Woo-Young ran at Keeth in the round of 16 and Keeth couldn't counter with the parry-riposte he'd honed over years and years of practice. He was catching the parry, but landing his riposte too late, giving Woo-Young one-light touches. Woo-Young went on to win 15-14 and took the bronze medal at the 2006 World Championships.

In any case, two days after my loss to Woo-Young, Keeth, Ivan, James Williams, and I were set to fence the team event. But the night before the event, Keeth had had an allergic reaction, his head swelled like a beach ball, and the trainers gave him the equivalent of Benadryl to counteract it. Keeth took the strip groggy against the Germans and that, in combination with his inexperience with the new timing, meant we were eliminated in the first round.

My big move was no move at all. In fact, it was a step backwards for our team. In the blink of a replayed touch, my validation escaped like a stomach punch.

The next tournament was a Pan American Championship—a new category of tournament the powers-that-be had introduced in hopes of boosting the legitimacy of non-European fencing. I had been going to the gym every day, fencing every evening. I was in the best shape of my life. Keeth had work commitments and so didn't attend. And in this tournament, with a weak field made weaker by Keeth's absence, Ivan Lee, Jason Rogers, and James Williams finished 1st, 2nd, and 3rd.

I didn't even make the top eight, again losing to a Cuban fencer I was highly favored to beat. I was posting *worse* results than when I had a full-time job.

And it would get even worse before it got better.

Dog Peeing on a
Fire Hydrant

There was a nightmare scenario I tried not to think about: if somehow I lost my #4 U.S. ranking, I would lose my $1000/month stipend and have to pay my travel expenses, and at the time, I wasn't making a full-time salary. Still with a mountain of debt, if I slipped from the four, I doubted I'd be able to survive long enough to take back the points I would need to ever regain it.

Then, at a world cup in Bulgaria, it happened.

In my round-of-64 match, I faced Fabrice Gazin, a French left-hander with smooth, flourishing attacks. While I'd been finding some success with my defense, once Gazin got going he seemed impossible to stop, and I didn't think my defense could measure up. So when the ref cried *Allez!* I jumped forward out of my box to launch a quick advance-lunge, which I hoped would take him off guard. Not so much. He caught me in preparation and I was down 0-1.

Back in my box, I tried to focus on the technique I'd been training so hard to perfect in practice. I would keep my back foot down and would take care of my lines. I knew I was nearly as fast and as strong as Gazin and didn't want to let him find the rhythm of his attack, so I blasted into another advance-lunge and again he found me in preparation with my arm back. Smack! I was down 0-2.

And that's how it went: he had my tempo and I simply couldn't match Gazin's attack with my own and I lost 8-15.

Ben Igoe made the top sixteen and Jason Rogers made the top four, falling to Pozdniakov in the semifinals to win a bronze medal. Both blew past me, pushing me to 5th in the national rankings, behind Keeth, Ivan, and the two of them.

The fencing life is a race against the clock. You race your body, your mind, and the pressures of the outside world for enough success to allow you to fence another day. My body was fine, my mind was sound, but without a full-time job, my finances were shot. At number 5, I would have to pay my travel expenses. The next world cup was in Tunis, which might as well have been a light year away for all my hope of paying for a ticket from JFK through Rome to Tunis-Carthage International.

But I got lucky. Just as it took a couple competitions before Patrick Durkan's spectacular results at the London competition in the Athens qualifying season affected his ranking and allowed him to compete at the following world cups, I had twenty-eight days before the rankings would catch up with my lackluster performance in Bulgaria. In that time, there was one more competition: Tunis. I had literally one more chance, fencing for my life on the international circuit. If I could take back the 4th spot, I could keep competing. If not, I would be in serious trouble.

I knew this on the plane ride home from Bulgaria with my teammates. And let me tell you, it was a long flight: buzzing along with the hum of the engines was the question of whether I might panic and break. I could hear it in Yury's tone as he explained what would happen to me now out of the top four. "I know," I said.

On the long flight home I played the match I'd lost to Gazin over and over in my mind, using it like a mantra to push away the panic while looking for what the match could teach me about the next tournament—how could I get a little faster, a little more precise, a little stronger for Tunis? It was the question I had asked since Riverdale, through college, at Teach For America: *what's wrong with me and how can I fix it?*

I saw it in my mind: I'd tried to take the initiative, attacking Gazin fifteen times. And these were the points I lost. The problem seemed clear: I had one week to shore up my weakness, plug the hole in the dam, and learn to do the thing I couldn't do—get just a little bit better so next time I could out-Gazin Gazin.

But that was a joke: there's nothing you can do in a week to get faster or stronger—nothing you can do to get *better* in such a short time. On the plane ride home from Bulgaria I finally faced a hard fact: I was *never* going to be a pretty fencer or a typical fencer. I was never going to be as fast as Keeth Smart, as wily as Ivan Lee, or as technically sound as Jason Rogers. I might never have a style that pleased Yury.

It's funny: after repressing my nightmare for so long—that despite all my work, I would never gain the technique I needed to be a pretty perennial in the top four—facing it was cathartic. I had spent countless hours chasing the goal of conventional technique and I had finally, definitively fallen short. What was the alternative? Now facing the worst, I realized that I could survive without technique—and without fencing, if need be. As a person, I'd be fine either way. Separating my self-esteem from my fencing is something I hadn't done since I got my first taste of power with a saber in my hand at Riverdale.

I thought about the 8 points I'd won against Gazin. Most were on defense and mostly on off-balance swipes I'd take at

Gazin: the dog peeing on the fire hydrant, the sky hook, and tea-pot attack. They were the weird moves that I'd been working hard to "fix" and change. Those were the ones that were working. Those were my strengths

One week between Bulgaria and Tunis.

I wasn't going to get stronger, faster, or better, but disentangling my self-esteem from achieving everyone else's idea of the correct style finally allowed me to imagine an alternative. There was one thing I did better than anybody in the world and that was land off-balance defensive swipes. I was the best at peeing on a fire hydrant. It wasn't pretty, but it worked. Or, I thought it might. That week at practice, instead of focusing on what I needed to fix, I worked on my strengths. It was a complete mental flip to be working on things that I did well rather than focusing solely on my weaknesses. To even recognize that, yes, I did have strengths (even if they looked weird) was somehow invigorating and eye-opening. I had rarely in my life reflected on things that I did and thought, *These are strengths of mine.* Seems so simple, yet it somehow wasn't. For the most part, I had walked around thinking I was someone filled with deficiencies that needed to be fixed.

There wasn't any time to test my ideas, but I figured if I was going to go down, I might as well go down doing what I do best. For the first time, I would go to a tournament not as Taka Sudo, Alex Banks, Keeth Smart, nor any of the innumerable people I admired. I would go as myself.

Oh, and the points I needed to stay in the U.S. top four to be financially able to compete in even one more tournament weren't just those of a round of 32 or even a round of 16. I needed to make the round of 8, which I'd never done before. In Tunis, I would have to fence the tournament of my life simply to live to fence another day.

Flying into Tunisia is stunning. The airport stares north across the Mediterranean at Sicily and the tip of the Italian boot. It's old stone and azure blue and the sunflower yellow of Northern Africa. Our hotel was right on the Med, and in the couple days before the start of the tournament, we thought about riding camels on the beach. Of course, we wouldn't—we'd see the airport, our hotel rooms, the fencing stadium, the airport again, and then go home—but it was nice to think that *someone* was riding camels outside our windows. And Carthage, as in Hannibal-Punic-Wars-sacking-of-Rome Carthage, was just up the street.

I'd been a history major in college and so, in terms of a place to make a last stand for my fencing career, I guessed that a couple miles from Carthage was as good as any.

I came out of the pools seeded fairly low, and my first match was against a Polish fencer named Dominik, who had destroyed me 15-4 last season in our previous meeting. I had this weird calm that seemed to put me above the action, looking down. The ref called *En garde? Prêt? Allez!* and I stood still—completely still, ready. *Come and get me!* I must have looked like a sitting duck and Dominik was happy to trot over and slaughter me for the kettle. Only that's not what happened. He lunged and I waved my body left, landing an off-balance whack to his right wrist. The second point was the same story. I watched Dominik walk back to his box, flexing his saber and checking his mask, as if going down 0-2 to me was his equipment's fault. The third point was the same—his attack sailed past and I landed a hit to his side.

When I'm fencing well, I can sense what my opponent's feeling, and I could tell Dominik felt like he was screwing up, as if something that should've been clicking just wasn't. What the hell was it? He was frustrated. I stuck with my defense and flipped the score of our last match, winning big and advancing to the 32.

My second match was against Vladislav Tretiak, the Ukrainian bronze medalist in the individual saber in Athens, who'd beaten me badly every time we'd fenced. I remembered him well—short, fast steps, and hard to hit. And this was only the round of 32—far from what I needed to stay alive. Again, I could feel him. He'd seen my first match and there was something in him that was just a bit nervous—something that knew this was a special day for me, something in him that knew I could win. The ref said *Allez!* and Tretiak drove me backwards down the strip, accelerating his pace before lunging. I backpedaled and then bent my body away from his blade and landed a flick stop-cut to Tretiak's wrist. To avoid becoming predictable, I mixed in a couple attacks and after one, I saw Tretiak rubbing his wrist where I hit him. I knew I could win. We went to 14-14— one point separating another match in Tunis from the likely end of my international career.

At 14-14, Tretiak came at me and I went back. He lunged and I connected a parry-riposte for the final touch. It was the biggest point of my career. I took Tretiak 15-14, but even that wasn't enough. I needed another win.

In the round of 16 I faced the French fencer Nicolas Lopez, who was in the top eight in the world at the time. I was hitting him with off-balance stop cuts, the slashing counterattacks of dog peeing on a fire hydrant, and I heard my teammates, standing on the side of the strip, erupt each time—cheering for me, but wondering how I was hitting this dude with lucky shots every time. Lopez would come at me, I would wave my body aside, and *whack!* I heard someone ask after one of these points, "How's Morehouse getting all these lucky touches?" And I heard Keeth Smart respond, "It's not luck!"

And he was right.

It wasn't luck. The off-balance stop cut—dog peeing on a fire hydrant—is the thing I do best. No one can pee on a fire hydrant like me. Until that point, I'd tried to train away my weaknesses until they no longer held me back—I'd tried to fence like the French or the Russians or the Chinese, like Akhi or Keeth or Ivan—but flipping the mental switch from focusing on my weaknesses to focusing on my strengths allowed me to go from almost-French to completely me. In Tunis, I took everything unique, everything ugly, and everything off-balance and *wrong* about myself—the very things I'd tried to squeeze into someone else's box, to repress and train away—and I made them my strengths. It was what I could do. So I did it.

Near the break, Lopez got so frustrated that he imagined my knickers must be the cause of his lost points. He came over between points, hit me in the leg with his saber, and looked over to the referee, as if to show that my knickers were too baggy and were catching his blade. He argued with the ref for a full five minutes and during that time, I realized that when these fencers argued—clothing violations, strip changes, and the like—it meant that what I was doing was working. I stayed focused and instead of trying to out-evolve Lopez, I concentrated on my game plan.

Again, Lopez and I went to 14-14, with me needing a win to make the top eight and retake the 4th spot in the U.S. rankings. The last point of the match, I went back, daring Lopez to come get me. He did, working toward me and then lunging for a belly cut. I went up on my tiptoes, sucking backwards, guiding his blade down with my own before swinging over the top to take Lopez in the shoulder. It was a one-light touch, definitively mine, which I had won with my own, definitive move to win the match and slash back into the U.S. top four.

Though I lost 15-14 in the round of 8 to another French national team fencer, I had earned 14 international ranking points that would let me live to fence another day.

I took the lesson: focus on my strengths, find what I do best, and do it.

The next week, I rode the lesson all the way to the finals in Algeria, earning 26 points and jumping all the way to #2 in the U.S. rankings. Remember, I'd never before cracked past the round of 32 and physically, *nothing had changed*. I'd flipped a mental switch, and this simple adjustment rocketed me into an elite space that I'd always felt I needed to fence like someone else—*be* someone else—to reach.

In the Algerian finals, I was winning 14-12 against French fencer Julien Pillet. And finally, at 14-12, after spending the match attacking into my off-balance stop cut, when the referee said *Allez!* Pillet stood still, daring me to attack. It was a direct challenge to my honor, saying, "Here I am, come get me if you can!" He waited and finally, I did. I attacked and he parry-riposted to make it 14-13. Hadn't I learned anything from the head games of Steve Mormando and Peter Westbrook at Fencers Club? I took Pillet's dare again. *He'd parried me once*, I thought, *but certainly he couldn't do it again*. He did. The score was 14-14 and when the final point started, again Pillet stood, daring me to attack. *No way could he parry me three times in a row!* No way. I charged.

And I lost the match 14-15.

I had been out-gamed. My pride had cost me a world cup victory. But in one week I had changed the entire course of my career. Instead of looking for what was wrong with me, I looked for what was *right*. And with it I was suddenly 2nd in the U.S. rankings and the road ahead looked wide open with new possibilities.

All the King's Horses and
All the King's Men

As my breakthrough spring world cup season wound down, I accepted a summer job as a school director at the Teach For America New York summer training institute. I would be in charge of an inner-city school's summer program, where new TFA recruits would attend intensive classes while teaching summer school students.

Given my track record with summer jobs, I should've known better than to take an intense summer job just before the start of Beijing qualifying. But a part of me was jealous of my Teach For America friends, some of whom were starting charter schools, others climbing the TFA ranks. I imagined myself after 2008: thirty years old and unemployable, needing to work my way into a career, again starting over at the bottom, and I wanted to keep building my professional skills, to keep myself relevant.

Just days before I reported to the job, I headed to Las Vegas for the season's last world cup. For once, the Europeans had to do the traveling. And with the draw of Vegas, teams tended to show up a couple weeks early for pre-tournament training camps and a little recreation. The comp was held in a converted ballroom—it's always surreal, carrying a fencing bag through a casino—and more than one coach didn't quite make it to the event itself. I continued my streak of strong results, making the round of 16, where I lost by one point to a strong Belarusian, Dmitry Lapkes, who had finished 4th in Athens. As soon as I was done, I traded my fencing gear for a suit and tie and grabbed my clipboard and my teaching books.

Thus attired, I watched 6'7" fencer Jingzhi Wang pull off an unbelievable comeback, beating Aldo Montano in the finals after trailing 5-14, then I headed straight to the airport to catch a red-eye to JFK. I arrived in the morning, with three days until the new teaching recruits would arrive.

I went straight from JFK to St. John's University in Queens, where Teach For America had rented space to base the headquarters of its summer institute. I walked in, dropped my bag, and got to work. I should have remembered Yury's lesson that speed is good only if you can control it. At the beginning of summer institute, I was stu-peed.

See, I was used to hitting the ground running, transitioning instantly from travel to work with my game face firmly in place, and I'd forgotten there was another way to do it. My trainers were experienced TFA teachers, themselves fresh from the end of their school years. That morning, just like me, they were arriving, checking into the dorm rooms where they'd live during the five-week institute, and maybe imagining a shower and a bite to eat before getting after it. I press-ganged my poor trainers into work at 8:00am, hitting them with more plans than we could possibly hope to accomplish in the three days before teachers arrived. My motivation and good intentions got mired in a soup of little details that I wanted handled.

Let's just say it wasn't the best first impression. I came off like a raving slave driver, whipping my trainers into the same frenzy I felt with thirty new teachers a day and a half away. It was like charging the strip focused on success, while all the lessons I had learned flew out the window.

We worked hard through the day. The next day we found out that fewer students than expected had registered for summer school at my site, so I had to give away one of my five trainers to a more populated school. Of the five, one was spectacular and one was especially difficult. Ever the altruistic idiot, I gave away the spectacular one, figuring he'd have no problem integrating with a new team and would get his new teachers up to speed no matter the setting. I was right—he was great.

But on the second day, my difficult trainer complained to my supervisor that I was pushing too hard, making the wrong choices, stumbling along pigheadedly in the wrong direction. My boss was busy, new teachers were showing up tomorrow, and with me in her office at 10:00pm, she wasn't as guarded with her words as she might otherwise have been. Really, it was a good old-fashioned chewing out, and I probably deserved it. But it took me right back to middle school hallways where something wrong with me was immediately apparent to everyone but me.

Who could I turn to? My manager thought I was a failure and so did my team. In fencing, I had finally built confidence independent of external validation, but that wasn't the case at the TFA summer institute. I needed the validation of my peers and superiors. I didn't get it.

I could've used some sleep and I didn't get any that night—tossing, turning, and then giving up on sleep and working through the night. Thirty new teachers would arrive the next morning from all corners of the country. Now awake for twenty-four hours with next to no sleep, I greeted teachers as they arrived at St. John's for the training institute.

It's disconcerting how poorly your mind starts to work after a couple nights without sleep. I mentioned that Teach For America hung its hat on data—on the handful of assessment instruments that showed how students were progressing and thus how well teachers were teaching. I had developed a little grudge against one of these assessment tools—it was cumbersome to use with students and it had a few glitches. With sleep, I might've realized this was about 1024th on the list of the moment's priorities, but I got a bit fixated on it and made it into something bigger than it was. Sleep, objectivity, and rationality lacking, I was spiraling dangerously close to the sun. I was on my own little island surrounded by staff and a manager who thought I was messing up.

I took it hard, and having made a couple mistakes, I got fixated on stopping the bleeding—making *no* more mistakes, being *perfect* from that point forward—and of course, this led to way more mistakes than I would've made if I'd just rolled with the punches of the first couple days. It got to the point that even when I did things right, my four trainers had lost enough confidence in me that they thought I still must be wrong. And having directly overseen new teachers, just as my trainers were now doing, I saw ways my trainers could improve. But at that point, offering constructive criticism was out of the question.

It got worse. By the end of the five weeks, hindsight had given me a laundry list of what-ifs—had I done this or that differently, the whole experience would've been better for everyone. But the cruel law of time, moving only forward, meant that near the end of the institute, there was nothing I could do to turn it around.

I survived that summer on Dunkin' Donuts iced coffee. The last thing on my mind was fencing, and even the life lessons I learned from the sport seemed to have flown out the window along with my confidence as a manager. Ambitious goals, data, personal strengths—it was as if I'd forgotten everything.

The last day, I met with my manager and we went over her performance evaluation of me. It's a document I've kept with me since then, like a scarlet letter. It brought everything back: maybe I wasn't good enough, maybe I had fooled everyone, tricked my way onto the Athens Olympic team. Maybe I didn't deserve it. I remember reading about the Stanford Prison Experiment, in which college students devolved into savages over the course of two weeks, and that's how I felt after the TFA summer institute. I had lost myself, lost my training and my hard-earned sense of worth. I had been stripped bare.

After institute, I went home and slept for a week, now renting a room from a work buddy and her fiancé who lived in Inwood at the northern tip of Manhattan, a few blocks from where I had played baseball as a child. They had rescued a dog—an abused boxer—and I took him on walks around the neighborhoods and into Inwood Park to face his fears of the world, trying to deprogram myself at the same time. I felt self-destructive, wanting to break my blade in half and walk away, but I kept walking, hoping I would heal.

After a week of walking, it was off to Monticello, where Yury ran a two-week summer camp at the Kutsher's Sports Academy. It was an hour and a half outside the City, and other than the camp, there wasn't much there but a Walmart, a two-screen movie theater, a video store, and a bunch of fast-food restaurants. Kutsher's is a venerable sports facility, where generations of motivated campers have trained on the football fields, gymnastics studios, pools, and basketball courts—one of which was the home of the Boston Garden's original parquet floor. In recent years, management had let the facility go—the training rooms smelled musty and we slept on rickety metal cots.

My room was on the first floor of an old wooden building that looked as if a light wind could blow it over. It felt exactly like I pictured a sanitarium, circa 1890, for those who were a bit touched in the head—a description that fit me pretty well at the moment.

With the exception of Ivan and Keeth, who had a full-time job at Verizon and couldn't take time off, all the U.S. fencers with a shot at making the Beijing team attended, along with a hundred or so high school and college athletes who used it as a traditional summer sports camp. The épée and foil fencers used the basketball gym, and the saber fencers trained in a converted gymnastics studio, where mats had been pushed to the walls to make space for rubber strips, metal fencing machines, and spools of wires that connected the machines to the fencers.

On the first day of camp, I was fencing a talented high school kid, who cut in on my wrist to take the first point. Really, I missed the parry. Suddenly the feeling of being unable to do anything right took over. I couldn't work with Teach For America or parry a high schooler. I gave in to the stress and anger and finally I freaked out—throwing my mask and smashing my saber against one of the fencing room's metal poles, the sound echoing through the room that had otherwise come to a stop to watch my tirade. I walked in circles and talked to myself and generally pulled a nutter. I'd come off a season in which I'd climbed to the top twenty in world ranking. I was the highest-ranked fencer at the camp, the person to watch. And now all the other fencers looked away—at their opponents, at the floor, at anything but me.

I really knew something was wrong when Yury didn't step in to bully me out of my funk. Remember his gregarious, "I can teach bear to stop-cut, just not you"? That was his style—in your face, pushing you just short of the breaking point. I was there already, and Yury backed off, quietly watching my tirade from the far side of the room, watching me retake the strip in a disjointed jangle of exposed nerves, but just watching. Would this next point be the one that sent me irretrievably over the edge?

One thing I'd learned the previous season was to stand on Yury's shoulders, but then jump on my own from there. In fact, a couple of years ago, Peter Westbrook had told me that there's a lot you can learn from a coach, but that when you're fencing a tournament you need to still have, and be able to fight according to, your own compass—you have to fence as yourself rather than a younger extension of your coach's saber arm. Building on Yury's guidance with my own understanding had allowed me to focus on my own funky, effective version of defense the previous season.

But there's danger in unmooring yourself from guidance—if your compass spins, there's no artificial horizon to reinforce what's level—and there I was, lost at sea without as much as a lifesaver.

In the movie *Robocop 2*, Murphy is reprogrammed into an ineffectual share-and-care flat foot. He becomes unable to retaliate, even when fired on by a man leading a Little League baseball team in robbing an electronics store. Only after Murphy grabs high voltage wires can he erase the detrimental programming to again become the hyper-violent cop we all know and love. Although it was inexplicably snubbed by the Oscar committee, *Robocop 2* holds a lesson for us all: sometimes drastic action is required to pull your head out of your hindquarters.

For me, it took whaling on a metal pole with a saber while innocent high school kids at summer camp looked on in horror. Let me be clear: I'm not necessarily recommending it.

But it helped return me to the basic lesson of fencing. In addition to teaching us the basic stance, on the first day of practice at Riverdale, Coach Schneider had explained to us that we would rarely win a match 5-0. We would always get hit. Like the bloody hand of French fencer Touya in Athens, we might even get hit hard. Coach Shipman at Brandeis explained that we should *re-*

spect everyone, fear no one, and in its way it was the same lesson: you can't fear these hits, can't fear these opponents and the brutal puzzles they present. They will hit you.

It's a fencer's job to hit back. *Master fencing, master life*—you will get hit.

That day in Monticello, my head still buzzing, disorganized, confused, I stood across from Yury. He said nothing about my tirade, about the chasm he very well knew I was staring into, about the two directions I could go from that day in the room. With his saber underneath mine, he pushed us up to ready position. Yury dropped his saber parallel to the floor and I extended my arm to his mask, double tapped, and then held steady, Yury checking my angles. We did it again. Yury sent his saber slowly to my left chest and I parried, then my lines took the tip of my saber straight to Yury's heart where we stopped, my blade arcing upwards.

"Good," said Yury. "Good."

23

Lose the Point,
Win the Idea

Two weeks passed after the Monticello training camp and then along with the U.S. team, I flew to Montreal for the Pan American Championships where, the night before the individual event, I promptly came down with a nasty fever. On the strip, I bludgeoned myself into functionality with self-talk. I had gone from chanting *I'm down, I'm down, I'm down* as I took the strip in college to *This is what I train for, it is what it is, focus on what I can control.*

Though I didn't fence spectacularly, it was enough. At this small tournament, I finished second to Keeth, nudging my world ranking into the top sixteen, which meant that at the upcoming World Championships in St. Petersburg, Russia, I would get a bye into the round of 64—now I was among the Pozdniakovs and Pillets and Montanos, who could warm up in the round of 64 against low-seeded opponents instead of fighting the pools to get there.

At the World Championships in St. Petersburg, Keeth and

I watched Jason and Ivan fight their way through the 5-touch round-robin qualifying matches. The world championships are a big deal—points count triple those of a world cup tournament, both toward your world ranking and toward the international component of the Olympic qualifying score.

In addition to resting the first day, the other benefit of a top-sixteen world ranking is being seeded high and fencing against one of the bottom sixteen qualifiers. In the round of 64, I drew a Senegalese fencer I knew I should beat. This was a mental trap I had seen before when I'd been devastated by underdogs.

The recent modernization of the theater surrounding fencing events didn't help my jitters. We'd always had a warm-up room, usually with strips laid down in a big back room amid a throng of vendors selling fencing apparel and equipment at discounts. From there, we'd wander straight out to the competition strips when the time was right. Now in hopes of making the sport a little more fan friendly, organizers of the major tournaments had installed a waiting area between the two—a little room where eight fencers stood around waiting for their names to be announced before walking through a short tunnel and taking one of the arena's four strips. Instead of warming up and then wandering out to the strip, we entered like prizefighters to the ring.

In the waiting room, some fencers chatted. Others like Pozdniakov were stoic. He'd bounce a bit on the balls of his feet and field fencers' almost reverent well wishes with a quick nod, totally focused and totally ready. I bounced a red ball. Since Tunisia, throwing my red ball had become my superstitious warm up. In the warm-up hall, I'd play catch with a teammate, usually Jason, and in the waiting room, I tossed it gently up and down to myself. Throwing the red ball calmed my brainwaves and helped me to push aside the devastating reprogramming of the TFA summer institute, to give myself over to the moment of tossing and catching in the same way I'd soon try to give myself over to the strip. You prepare and fret, but a time comes before a match when you need to simply exist, and my red ball helped me do this.

As we arrived at the world championships, the powers that be informed us of another rule change: if you started with your saber down and then cut upwards for a touch, it wouldn't count as your attack. Sure, you could still score a point this way, but only if it was a one-light point. If your opponent could get in a simultaneous touch within the 120-millisecond window, the right-of-way and thus the point would be his. At least the change in lockout timing had been announced just after the Athens Games, at a time you'd expect some reorganization! Announcing the low-saber attack rule at the world championships was like showing up to the World Series and discovering the strike zone had changed. More than anything, it created uncertainty. What angle was "down"? Would a level saber that cut upwards count as an attack? Later in the tournament, tied at 14-14, Pozdniakov launched a long attack down the strip, pushing his opponent backwards and eventually lowering his saber to cut upwards and land a touch—but his opponent had landed as well. Whose point was it? In this hugely important tournament, a call that could've gone either way would decide the match. The touch and the match went to Pozdniakov. Would the ref have given it to me, or Keeth, or a fencer from Cuba? Who knows? Despite a shortened lockout time that resulted in more one-light points, the addition of instant replay, and the sport's overall modernization, it remained good to be Pozdniakov fencing in Russia.

Jason lost in the 64. Keeth and Ivan advanced to the round of 32. And despite my jitters, I found in the back of my mind the lesson of how to fence against underdogs—the lesson I had learned while losing to them in seasons past. I put in a professional, workmanlike performance to beat the Senegalese fencer and advance to the round of 32.

There I drew French fencer Vincent Anstett. You can go to tournament after tournament and some guys you never face—now I'd drawn Anstett three times in a few months. He'd beaten me 14-15 in Tunisia and I'd beaten him 15-14 in Algeria. Really, it was with Anstett that I'd learned to decouple my self-esteem from the quest for perfect technique, so that I'd be able to leave aside that technique in favor of my strengths.

Now on the strip again with Anstett at the St. Pete's World Championships, I decoupled another form of false validation from my fencing. If you score a point, the world thinks you've fenced correctly. But you can win a point on ugly luck. Even after twenty years on the strip, a beginner will take a couple points from me in a race to 15. The opposite is true, too: you can overwhelm your opponent but still lose the point.

Fencing is unimaginably nuanced—let's say there are thirty important components of a stop cut. If you do all thirty exactly right, you'll win the point every time. If you blow all thirty, you'll never land a touch. But between these two extremes lies a tremendous gray area. Even if you do twenty-nine things right, you can lose the point. This is losing the touch but winning the idea. And if you depend only on the point for validation, you'll throw these twenty-nine things out the window.

That's what had happened to me at the TFA summer institute: I hadn't gotten the validation I needed at the time, so instead of maintaining confidence that I was doing some things right, I threw everything out and started from scratch.

This is also why I had trouble with 15-touch matches. Though I might take the first points, as the match wore on, my opponent would start to win the idea and eventually would start winning the points. By touch number 5, my opponent would have taken hold of the idea and the points would roll away from me.

This battle within a battle might sound like a technical mini-lesson, but for me it was everything. While I had already learned to distance myself from needing the validation of the fencing world, pulling away from even the validation of points allowed me to fence according to my own compass. I started looking inside points and inside myself to understand the worth of my fencing.

Going into the mid-match break against Anstett, I was up 8-7. While I wasn't winning every point, I was using my understanding to define what was working. By winning the idea, I took Anstett to 14-12, the same score at which his teammate, Julien Pillet, had goaded me into attacking him three times, thus gifting him the match in Algeria. *Stick with what you do best*, I told myself. Instead of letting ego tempt me into attack, I stuck with my game plan of defense and flick stop-cut him for the win. I was in the top sixteen at worlds!

Pozdniakov sent Ivan packing in the 32 and I faced him in the 16. I pulled down my mask and was ready to fence. *Patience, patience, patience*, I told myself. Pozdniakov came at me, lunging for the point. Again he launched and again he scored. *Patience*, I told myself. *Focus on my defense*, I said. Around the 5th point, as Pozdniakov launched attack after attack into my patience, I started noticing something in his preparation that allowed me just the time I needed to escape back down the strip, out of range of his attacks. I was fencing slowly enough to evaluate his tells. I was depending on the strength of my off-balance defense. I was turning the tide of the *idea* in my favor.

Still, Pozdniakov beat me 15-12, mostly because I hadn't turned the tide of the idea quickly enough. By the time I had solved the points, I was too desperately behind to come back against a fencer like Pozdniakov. But I knew I had something working. Again, I was starting to win the idea against the best in the world.

At the St. Pete's World Championships, Keeth showed he could evolve, too. Keeth had been getting hit in preparation for his flunge and had been unable to land the continuation of his attack within the new, shortened lockout timing, losing one-light touches to his opponents. This is partly because he'd been preparing with his arms, leaving him vulnerable. In St. Pete's, Keeth countered by building preparation into his feet. Keeping his arms ready to attack or parry, he set up his flunge with footwork hesitations, hops, and pace changes, and he rode his new focus on footwork to the round of 16 where he lost a close match 14-15.

In terms of Olympic qualifying, Keeth and I were way out front, Ivan looked good, and Jason was in 4th.

The season's first world cup was in Iran. Only the four fencers on the national team had been allowed to compete at the Pan Am and world championships, but now at the Iran World Cup the rest of the U.S. fencers joined us to begin their pursuit of an Olympic spot. We flew through Dubai and then landed on Iran's Kish Island. Kish is a tourist paradise—a free-trade enclave of five-star hotels and shopping, Middle Eastern princes, and European royalty. The airport hosts a higher percentage of small, private jets than I've seen anywhere else in the world.

Still, when we got off the airplane, men and women were split into separate lines and the women had to cover their hair. The U.S. had recently instituted a fingerprinting policy for Iranians entering the States, and Iran reciprocated with the most frustratingly thorough fingerprinting this world has ever seen. Other countries' teams joked that we were done for when the Iranian army siphoned the Americans into a side room where we spent an hour printing the various combinations of our fingers—each neighboring pair in turn, partial thumb and forefinger, partial palm print, pinky and thumb together, etc.

After Athens, we'd been advised not to wear our USA jackets

when walking around foreign countries, but then they gave us these audacious fencing bags—red, white, and blue with "Team USA" written all over them. Short of stuffing it in a trash bag, there wasn't much camouflaging it. When we walked into the fencing hall to test our equipment on the day before the start of the tournament, the Iranian equipment managers yelled in mock warning, "The Americans are here!" Later, when the lights went out during the tournament, organizers joked that the Americans had cut the power. But that's where our countries' tensions stayed—in the realm of a joke that we all shared. On the streets, the Iranian people were gracious, and even the soldiers at the airport were just following order rather than exacting on us some sort of national vendetta.

I fought my way to the round of 8, drew the strong Hungarian fencer Zsolt Nemcsik, and fought him to 13-13, 2 points to determine the match. The next point, I dodged Nemcsik's attack and nipped him with a flick stop-cut, but his sword hand was soaked with sweat—the moisture made the fingers of his glove conductive and he claimed I'd touched his fingers, which are outside the scoring zone and not the valid target of his wrist.

In March, Yury had had his spleen removed, so he didn't travel with us to Iran. Without Yury to fight for my point, the referees threw out the touch and returned us to 13-13, despite the rules clearly stating that the point should stand because it was his equipment at fault. Steadily, though, I had been learning Nemcsik's angles and pace. On the next point, I made the correct move but the referee called the point against me. Instead of feeling like I had done something wrong by not getting the point, I realized I had something right—despite the lack of validation—and decided to celebrate. The match's last point was an exact replay, and though I'd lost the point and the match, I turned around, pumped my fist, and let out a victory yell!

What an idiot I must have seemed, celebrating a loss, but in that moment I came full circle from the Teach For America summer institute, in which the lack of external validation destroyed my internal world. Here, instead, I was tallying points based on my internal evaluation of the quality of my performance.

24

Making the Team with a Whisper

So it went in Turkey (top eight) and in Budapest (top sixteen). Already, people were congratulating me on making the Beijing Games. All I needed was another halfway decent result, and given my recent track record, that looked likely. After adjusting to the new lockout timing, Keeth, too, was back in the world top ten. But just behind us was a scrap for 3rd and 4th, and with this year's breakout results for U.S. fencers as a whole, there was a very real possibility of one or even two people making a world cup finals and blowing past Keeth and me. Everyone in the U.S. top eight had made top-sixteen results at a world cup that season. James Williams had made a top eight in Moscow; Ben Igoe had put up consistent results; Jason Rogers was hanging with the best in the world; and people like Patrick Ghattas, who had spent a couple years losing in the 64, made the jump into consistent rounds of 32 and higher. Though in the previous year Ivan had climbed to #8 in the world, he was struggling this year and had fallen to #4 in the

U.S. Any of these guys would've made the U.S. team in any other year in history. But it was a different world and a different set of expectations for U.S. fencers.

Unlike the qualifying season for Athens, everyone had handled the logistics surrounding the strip, so no one was taking himself out. Going into the last two tournaments—Algeria and Tunisia—I needed one more result for a lock. Before the events, my good friend Jaime Martí from the Spanish team had been staying with me for the week in New York. On the night before we all left for Algeria, Jaime cooked a thank you dinner for Julio, some other friends, and me. He's a spectacular cook, but the next morning I woke up with what could only be food poisoning.

Surprisingly, everyone else was fine. A friend went out for anti-nausea medicine but I threw it up immediately. Still, if there's one thing you learn on tour, it's how to deal with food poisoning. No upset stomach was going to keep me from solidifying my spot at the Beijing Olympics. I called a cab.

By the time the cab arrived, I had a stabbing pain in my stomach. My friends loaded my equipment and I crawled into the back seat. Every couple blocks I had to ask the cabbie to pull over so I could vomit. I looked awful—sunken black eyes in a pale, white face—and I caught the cabbie watching me worriedly in the rearview mirror. Finally, after vomiting more than thirty times, it was obvious I needed to go to the ER. I paid the cabbie and he promised to take my luggage and fencing gear back to my apartment. When I tried to stand up out of the cab I fell over on the sidewalk outside the emergency room and was immediately mobbed by hospital staff.

A few minutes later I had a diagnosis much different than food poisoning: acute appendicitis. As I lay on a gurney shaking uncontrollably from dehydration, I waited for the surgeon to arrive. I texted my teammates to tell them I wasn't going to make the flight. My parents showed up. And then the surgeon walked in. Brandeis isn't home to many stereotypical jocks, but if they exist anywhere, they're on the baseball team. The surgeon, who told me he'd come to wheel me into the operating room, was a ballplayer I'd met in an easy-A class I'd taken as a senior. I thought, *Even the dumb jocks at Brandeis become doctors!* I asked him how long he'd been practicing. And I asked him how long I'd be sidelined: a week at best. I'd miss Tunisia and Algeria and, depending on how the guys fenced, maybe even the Beijing Games.

Fears aside, the doc did a great job—not that I remember any of it. As I came to, painkillers coursing through my veins, I started telling the nurses to call a cab so I could go to the airport. Then the pain meds wore off and I got a dose of reality real quick. I wasn't going anywhere. I couldn't even sit up, let alone fence.

When I got home the next day, my luggage and fencing gear was sitting there. True to his word, the cabbie had returned with all my stuff. A year later I ran into him. He didn't recognize me, but I tipped big.

Would my results hold up? I did the math. If any one of the half-dozen or so trailing guys made two top eights, they would pass me. Any other year I would've said it was impossible, but with the way people were fencing that season, it didn't even seem unlikely. It was in Tunisia and Algeria the year before that I'd come out of nowhere to make the top eight and then the finals in my break-through season. No one had seen it coming. Who would be the surprise story this year? I compulsively emailed Keeth for results. Ten days later I heard the news—the only top eight was Patrick Ghattas in Algeria, with Jason Rogers making the top sixteen and James Williams making the top thirty-two. Shockingly, Ivan Lee was now eliminated from qualifying for Beijing and immediately the U.S. fencing community started to worry that without Ivan's consistent blade, our shot at a medal was gone. Though the U.S.

Nationals—the last tournament that offered qualifying points—were still a month away, I was a mathematical lock.

The moment of qualifying that I had imagined—landing a winning touch and celebrating—instead came lying in bed in an empty apartment.

Almost ironically, I raised my arms and whispered, "Woo-hoo."

In the days after Algeria, Keeth Smart was having a hard time recovering from jetlag. After four days back, he was still light-headed and he started to get blood blisters on his tongue. His dentist sent him home to eat chicken soup, but soon the blood blisters spread to his neck and forehead. Like me, Keeth tried to ignore the symptoms, waiting until his tongue was swollen to the point that he couldn't talk before going to the hospital.

Covered in blisters? Just back from Algeria? An aggressive onset of symptoms? Not only did the hospital admit Keeth, but they immediately put him in a quarantined intensive care unit. Though he'd walked in under his own power, Keeth's vitals showed that he was fighting for his life.

Eventually he was diagnosed with a rare blood disease known as idiopathic thrombocytopenic purpura, or ITP, in which the immune system attacks and kills the blood's platelets. At the time he was admitted, his platelet count was 9,000—lower than a patient with full-blown AIDS. Blood needs platelets to clot, and the doctors told him that if he'd fenced that day—if he'd been touched or even bumped his toe on the way to the hospital—he would've bled to death internally before an ambulance arrived.

Through fencing connections, Keeth found Dr. John Leonard, a leading specialist on the disease. Dr. Leonard explained that the common therapy for ITP is a full blood transfusion, usually with a six-month recovery period—too late for the Games. Even if Keeth fast-tracked the recovery, in the wake of Olympic cycling's proscription against transfusions, taking new blood would disqualify Keeth from competition. So instead Keeth took the strongest dose of steroids medically allowed and hoped his body would fight the disease.

Keeth's recovery was unprecedented. Within fifty days he was cleared to train. He recovered so quickly that the doctors at Methodist Hospital wrote a journal article about his case. Still, after two months of bed rest, Keeth's body had cannibalized muscle as if he'd been in a full-body cast. He'd lost valuable speed and endurance. Adding to his trauma, in the weeks following his recovery, Keeth's mother died of cancer. Keeth was devastated, mind and body, and while he'd won the right to compete, it was unclear what that would look like.

Yury's spleen, my appendix, and now Keeth's rare blood disease—the U.S. saber team was looking like a bad episode of *E.R.*

And so it was on to the Nationals, where no matter my ranking, I had to fence pools. The 3rd and 4th spots were up for grabs, with James Williams, Ben Igoe, Patrick Ghattas, and Jason Rogers all within range. I killed myself to fence well in the pools so that I'd be seeded high enough to avoid drawing one of them in an early round, with the potential to knock a friend out of qualifying. Ben Igoe lost in the 16 and was eliminated. James Williams lost in the same round and walked out of the venue as a mathematical long shot to take the alternate spot. And Patrick Ghattas and Jason Rogers drew each other in the quarterfinals. The winner of that one match would qualify for the 3rd spot on the Olympic team and the loser would be out.

The crowd was electric—one match to determine the final Olympic spot! For half an hour they couldn't find anyone to referee. First, no one wanted to step in the middle of that much potential controversy. Additionally, Jason was from Ohio State University and Patrick fenced for Notre Dame—the schools were fencing rivals and the two fencers' coaches nixed any referee with school ties that could bias the results.

Finally, they found someone to ref, they fought the match, Jason won, and the team was set: Keeth, Jason, and me, with James Williams as alternate. In his farewell tournament, Ivan Lee won Nationals and, following the wrestling tradition, flung his shoes in the air to leave them on the strip. He retired, taking home his 5th National Championship.

By June, Keeth had come back from his illness and the loss of his mother, just two months before the opening ceremonies. Held in Vegas, the final comp would be the first time this fledgling group competed as a team. In the round of 8 we drew Hungary—we hadn't beaten them since Athens and would face Hungary in the opening round in Beijing.

Just before the 2004 Athens Games, the U.S. team had won an historic victory at the New York World Cup and had ridden the momentum to the 4th place finish at the Games, twice losing a medal by one point. In the analogous tournament before Beijing in Vegas, Hungary demolished us. Ivan had been integral to the '04 run and he was gone. Keeth was just back and obviously not in top form. I wasn't fully recovered. And Yury was barely back to his feisty self after having his spleen removed.

Fencing together for the first time, injured, without Ivan, and now with a crushing defeat against the very team we'd face first in two months, no one expected much of the 2008 Beijing men's saber team.

Being Beijing

After Vegas and with a few weeks until the Games, Keeth, Jason, James, and I finally got into a normal training rhythm including five hours a day of lifting, cardio, footwork drills, lessons, practice matches, strategy talks, and strenuous finger crossing that we didn't get hurt. Instead of going to Tuscany to train as we had before the 2004 Athens Games, before the Beijing Games we stayed home and instead imported the country's best training partners, encouraging top juniors and college athletes to fence with us those weeks in Manhattan.

These few weeks were also a rare time during which fans were interested in fencing.

I went to media day in Chicago, which at the time was still vying for the 2016 Games and so had volunteered to host anything that would increase its Olympic visibility. *The Today Show* asked me about my go-to Karaoke song, which led to me singing "Every Rose Has Its Thorn" by Poison for the camera, with the crew joining for the chorus. Bret Michaels, eat your heart out. Then I roamed the huge conference center, giving more than 100 interviews to the TV and radio stations that had gathered looking for stories. It's interesting: some athletes knew for a year or more that they'd qualified, while other competitors, like track and field athletes, arrived to media day fresh from Olympic trials. Entire ad campaigns were built in advance around people who ended up not even qualifying. For example, after winning the all-around gold in Athens, gymnast Paul Hamm fought through injury to make the Beijing team… and then withdrew in late July due to pain in his injured hand. Like Reebok's Dan vs. Dave decathlon debacle of 1992, in which after rolling out a multimillion dollar ad campaign Dan O'Brien failed to qualify, Paul Hamm's injury forced media and sponsors to scramble for storylines. But despite the obvious comeback story of our men's saber team, we didn't get much press.

Not so for the *women's* saber team, which had not only been added as a new event but featured Becca Ward, ranked #1 in the world at nineteen years old, and Mariel Zagunis and Sada Jacobson, who were both ranked in the world top eight.

There was also a second trip to Chicago for cultural training, mostly learning how not to embarrass the United States with our behavior in Beijing. We were coached on how to answer questions about the conflict in Darfur and about the air and heat in Beijing.

At the same time, Yury had decided to split from Fencers Club and open his own business: the Manhattan Fencing Center. Amid the hubbub, in practice one day at Yury's new center, I pulled my groin. My finger crossing hadn't paid off.

In the life of any Olympic small-sport athlete, there are unsung heroes. In the case of U.S. fencers that year, Lorenzo Gonzalez goes on the short list. He was a physical therapist in New York who, after his clients left for the day, opened his office to fencers.

At 7:00pm you'd find seven of us crowded in his office, maybe a couple of us doing rehab routines in the hallway. I know Keeth credits Lorenzo's rehab with getting him back in shape for the Games, and without Lorenzo, I'm not sure I would've healed in time to compete. Free of charge, and in evenings when he certainly had other places to be, Lorenzo healed the team.

And then we were off. We flew first to San Jose, where the U.S. Olympic Committee had taken over San Jose State as a launching pad for the country's athletes. We checked into dorms for a couple days, did interviews, and got our equipment while waiting for our flights to Beijing. The amount of stuff you get as an athlete is astounding—walking through a huge hall with a shopping cart, volunteers pile in tee shirts, shorts, five warm-up suits, hats, etc. Each athlete gets a FedEx box to pack with extra gear that you can mail directly home without it ever traveling to Beijing. And Keeth, Jason, and I were measured for Olympic rings and for our Opening Ceremony outfits. Decorating our dorm rooms were pictures wishing us good luck, painted by kids from around the country.

And then we were off again—as we walked to buses with hundreds of other athletes, a reporter shouted to Yury, asking him how he felt. With a huge smile Yury said, "We are ready!" It was a walking party through the airport and onto a United flight to Beijing.

When we hit the ground, everything was electric, packed with fans, media, coaches, and athletes. We were whisked through the throng and hopped on a bus to the Beijing version of the almost Olympic village—Beijing Normal University, which the U.S. Olympic Committee had taken over as the U.S. home base and training facility in China. As I had done in Athens, James Williams hopped off the bus at Beijing Normal while Keeth, Jason, and I headed to the village itself. I knew James' time would come. My time was now.

In the village, each apartment-style building was hung with

the flag of the country that was staying there. Smaller countries shared complexes, and colorful flags draped off the balconies, making apartment façades look like giant murals. Like a wedding, the village was organized with its version of a seating chart—an Eastern Bloc section here, a Europe section there. The U.S. was housed next to Israel, and due to security concerns they were the only buildings without flags. It was obvious that the flagless apartments were the U.S. and Israel, so finally they just hung the flags up after all.

We were organized in suites—I roomed with Jason in one of three or four rooms organized around a common area. Downstairs in our apartment complex, the U.S. Olympic Committee had set up a little station with a computer and a phone that called the U.S. for free. On the desk, the Committee laid out extra event tickets that you could use or could give to family and friends.

Outside, the apartments had the feel of a college quad, with grassy areas punctuated by trees and tastefully cut through with streams and small footbridges. The dining hall was unlike anything I'd ever seen—able to feed 10,000 athletes and offering everything from Italian food to Peking duck to McDonald's burgers. Milling around were seven-foot tall basketball players, obscenely muscled weightlifters, tiny gymnasts, and all in their countries' idiomatic outfits. On the first day, I lost my teammates and sat down next to a bearded guy in U.S. apparel, who turned out to be Michael Phelps.

In the village, there were people to open every door for you. There was a free barbershop, where six people worked together to cut my hair: one person welcoming, another seating, another washing my hair, another cutting, another drying it, and another person cleaning up the cut hair. Various countries' dignitaries strolled through the village—one day I ran into the entourage of France's Nicolas Sarkozy. Despite the newness and bustle, it was also a world removed, separate from the population kept outside the gates by stringent security and frequent credential checks.

It was five days until the opening ceremony and we spent it settling into the village, practicing with James at the almost village, playing *Rock Band* (I was notoriously awful), and exploring Beijing. It was muggy in the city, but people who had been in Beijing six months earlier raved about the difference in air quality. It rained in those first days, clearing out much of the remaining pollution and taking the edge off the temperature. I'm not sure how true it was, but the buzz in the village was that the Chinese government had seeded the clouds and brought the rain on purpose.

During the days, there were vans and guides to take athletes on sightseeing tours of the city. Keeth, Jason, James, Yury, and I shared a gondola up a long hill to the ramparts of the Great Wall. We talked about how lucky we were to be there together—Keeth with his blood disease, Yury with his spleen, me with my appendix, Jason winning his way onto the team in one match at the Nationals, and James grabbing the alternate spot as a mathematical long shot. There was a sign saying that people who walked a 2.5-mile section of the wall were "heroes!" So we did, taking pictures far out on the Wall at the end of the walk, in the dying light of a Beijing evening. And we felt like heroes. "We must cherish these moments, Tim," Yury said to me. "Fencing has brought many great things in our lives." It was unlike Yury. There was something else on his mind, but I didn't know until after the Games what it was.

To return to the vans we each hopped in a one-person, wheeled sled, which was mounted on a metal pipe track that wound its way at fairly death-defying speeds back down the hill.

Another day we took a bus into the middle of the city, to a park that was packed with people doing tai chi and playing board games. There was a busker in the park challenging onlookers to a game of balance. He'd stand on one box, an opponent from the audience would stand on another, the two would lock hands, and they would try to push or pull each other off the boxes like Robin Hood and Little John squaring off on the log. What the heck—I figured I'd give it a go. I was a full head taller than him and out-weighed him by at least eighty pounds. Not only that, but I was an Olympic athlete and skilled both mentally and physically in this kind of one-on-one, face-to-face competition. He beat me five times in a row, giving with his arms when I pushed, and then pulling me forward off my box, or using combinations of small fakes to goad me into straightening my arms so that he could push against them to send me toppling.

I took it as yet another lesson: skill and strategy out duel-ing strength.

We also visited the fencing arena—the biggest of its kind in the world, specially built for the Beijing Games. Despite the im-provement in air quality, the room was big enough that you could see a film of smog hanging in the air.

The Olympic Opening Ceremony started in the village. Ralph Lauren was the official clothing sponsor, so company representa-tives walked with volunteers from the U.S. Olympic Committee to make sure the U.S. athletes looked good and had dressed ac-cording to code, which included taking off any politically-loaded pins, scarves, or other apparel. The Olympics have long been held as a respite from politics, while nonetheless remaining one of the world's most potent stages for political statements—notably, the 1968 black pride salute from the podium of the 200-meter race, and Jesse Owens winning four gold medals at the 1936 "Nazi Games" to highlight the fallacy of the supposed dominance of the Aryan race. In 2008, it was the height of the crisis in Darfur, and athletes had been getting emails urging them to wear gear in the opening ceremony that called for U.S. and international intervention. Generally, athletes embraced the spirit of the Games as a respite from past and ongoing politics and so stuck to the apolitical dress code, but we elected track and field athlete Lopez Lomong as our flag-bearer—he'd been born in a small village in Sudan and fled the civil war when he was six, eventually making his way to the United States.

We boarded buses and our first stop, ironically, was the fencing stadium, where we listened to a speech by then-president George W. Bush. A number of athletes had been to a dinner at the White House earlier that summer, and as the President greeted us on the way into the stadium, he gave Erinn Smart a kiss on the cheek, smiled, and said it was good to see her again. The moment transcended politics. He was the President of our country and this was the Olympics.

After the speech, we bused to the gymnastics stadium where we sat in sections by country, waiting for our turn to start the walk toward the opening ceremony stadium, known as the Bird's Nest. It's a great moment, joining the procession of countries heading toward the stadium—the Greeks in the lead, the Chinese last, and the rest of the countries arranged alphabetically in between. You fall into step with 10,000 athletes and follow the huge American flag at the front of the contingent, aware of the people around you, but also aware of the half-mile parade—you feel simultaneously individual and special, but also feel like you belong completely to something bigger, like a nameless, faceless ant that's held by the moment, swept along by the river of the group.

It was a mile from the gymnastics stadium to the track and field complex that held the opening ceremony, but from the second we started marching, you could hear the roar. We were swept toward drums and fireworks that flashed in the night sky and the collective yell of the 90,000 people there to cheer us. Entering the stadium was like the description you hear of near-death experiences, walking through a dark tunnel and then exploding into the light of 90,000 flashbulbs amid dancers and drummers and TV cameras and everywhere your teammates being swept along just like you. Runners describe the feeling of a sprint at the end of a long race as floating above the pavement while their legs run unconsciously, and that's how I felt circling the track—both fully in the moment but somehow flooded by it to the point of disembodiment. The dancers had been whirling like dervishes for two hours in the heat and up close you could see they streamed sweat. Once we sat, huge video screens that ringed the stadium showed a montage of the torch relay, which had traveled 85,000 miles, across six continents, along the Silk Road, and to the top of Mt. Everest on its way from Athens to Beijing. Former Olympic gymnast Li Ning, suspended by wires, appeared to run the top of the Bird's Nest's walls before lighting a fuse that ran to the huge Olympic cauldron. Anything was possible. Everyone there felt they could win a gold medal. As the flame caught, firework rings exploded overhead and the Games were on.

Imperfect Perfection

I remember speed skating in my socks around apartment 5b and imagining how perfect Olympians must be—it's this perfection I had chased ever since. Finally, as I stood on the strip in Beijing opposite French fencer Boris Sanson in the individual competition, I knew the truth. We work hard and we celebrate and we cry, and along the way we gather the lessons that allow us to evolve as athletes and as people. But we're far from perfect.

I had learned to set goals and achieve them, to pick myself up after failing and to respect myself on and off the strip. And now here I was, at the Olympics... where, despite the very concrete goal of medaling in the team event, I hadn't set a goal for the individual. As I learned my freshman year at Brandeis, instead of setting a goal, the goal set me. Instead of winning, the goal became *Don't embarrass yourself at the Olympics.*

Standing there with Boris Sanson, I couldn't stop myself from thinking I didn't want to get blown out and look like a total idiot.

Instead of focusing on success, I focused on lack of failure. I was like a skier, focusing on not hitting trees instead of focusing on threading the snowy spaces between them.

Two days earlier, in the Games' first day of competition, the U.S. saber women had gone 1, 2, 3, with Mariel Zagunis taking the gold, Sada Jacobson taking silver, and Becca Ward taking bronze. There was a feeling in the air as if the U.S. squad had won its karmic allotment of medals, and in the wake of the attention that went to the women's saber medal sweep on the Games' first day, the men's competition seemed almost an afterthought. Jason won in the round of 64 and then in an unlucky draw faced Keeth in the 32, who, like me, had reached the 32 on a bye due to world ranking. Keeth was on his game—no hint of lingering effects from his illness—and he was a focused buzz saw. Jason fenced his heart out, but it wasn't nearly enough to counteract the laser-like Keeth. Keeth went on to rip through Hungarian fencer Áron Szilágyi in the 16, and I saw it as a hopeful sign for our match against the Hungarians in the first round of the team event. Keeth went ahead against French fencer Julian Pillet in the round of 8, but that day it wasn't meant to be for Keeth. He lost momentum and eventually the match.

Likewise I roared out to a 7-3 lead against Boris Sanson. But instead of keeping my foot on the accelerator for an Olympic win, I let my subconscious non-goal creep into the driver's seat. I can remember thinking, *Thank God I'm not going to lose 15-2!* With a Don't-Embarrass-Yourself sewn up, I breathed sighs of relief and Sanson sliced those sighs out of the air and added them to his score sheet. He beat me 15-12 and I was out of the Olympic individual competition. I realize now that my failure to set a concrete goal for the individual competition was a holdover of my lack of confidence. I had beaten some of the best fencers in the world, and a Cinderella run to the medals wasn't out of the question. Who knows what would've happened had I pushed for the podium? Maybe I would've walked away with a win or two.

As it was, I left the individual with a vague sense of disappointment at a missed opportunity, but also the feeling that I'd done respectably well and broken in the strip in preparation for the real task at these Beijing Games: winning a medal in the team event.

A team medal isn't objectively more important or prestigious than an individual medal—only it was to *us*. It had been our goal four years ago in Athens when we'd fallen a touch short, and it was again our goal in Beijing. And despite having been demolished by Hungary in Las Vegas, Keeth, Jason, James, and I had an energy that made anything seem possible. Each of us, through a combination of strength, commitment, and pure luck, had overcome bizarre obstacles to be able to stand on the strip together. If my appendix had flamed out a couple of weeks earlier, I wouldn't have made the team. Keeth's blood disease could have killed him, and the timing of his illness fell in the short window that both allowed him to qualify and gave him just enough time for a miraculous recovery before the Games.

Yury didn't tell any of us, but his spleen had been cancerous, and when it was removed earlier in the year, doctors found the cancer had spread. While we fenced in Beijing, cancer coursed though Yury's lymph system, which explained his reflective mood on the Great Wall a couple days earlier. He knew he was fighting for his life. We didn't: Yury delayed the start of his chemotherapy to avoid distracting the team and hadn't told anyone. For Keeth, it was the end of his fencing career; for Yury, it might be the end of his life. It was his last chance for the medal he craved since he first held a saber as a child in the former USSR. "The bronze, *at least* the bronze!" he must have thought.

I don't remember the day before the individual competition,

but I clearly remember the day before the team event. You can't be sure you'll sleep the night before you compete, so you try to sleep as much as possible *two nights* before. This way you bank those hours against the next nerve-wracked night. So the day before our saber event, I rolled out of bed late and stumbled to a computer to check the women's foil results. Like us, they were not predicted to go very far. None of the foil women had made it past the round of 32 in the individual, and they had drawn a strong Polish team in the first round of their team competition. But here's the thing about team fencing: you can't predict team results from the way the individuals perform. For example, our women's saber fencers that swept the individual medals then settled for the bronze in the team event. There's an energy certain teams bring to the strip that allows the whole to be greater than the sum of the parts. That was our women's foil team in 2008.

As I sat bleary-eyed at the computer, the screen told me that the women had beaten Poland to make the round of 4! The news jolted me awake. I grabbed Jason and we hit the dining hall so we could make the women's team's next match.

Jason and I joined Keeth and James in the stands to watch Keeth's sister, Erinn, and the other U.S. foil women take on Hungary for a spot in the finals. They didn't disappoint. The women's foil team ripped into the Hungarian team to open a huge, early lead. Unlike men's saber, women's foil matches are timed, and a fencer's segment ends either at a multiple of 5 points (like the men's), or it can end with the expiration of three minutes.

With a massive lead going into the last bout, Keeth's sister, Erinn, started to falter. Her Hungarian opponent started to go on a run and Erinn looked out of sorts. Keeth screamed from the stands, "Don't worry! Stay calm!" but the points started to slip away in a trickle that became a waterfall. It was a replay of the men's semifinal match in Athens, with Keeth taking the strip with the lead before falling in a deluge of points to Pozdniakov. The points fell, the clock ticked, and Erinn couldn't seem to counter her onrushing Hungarian opponent. It was a race against the clock with Erinn hoping time would expire before she did. The clock ticked away—three, two, one—with the score 35-33 and the U.S. on top!

Erinn fell to the strip and her teammates celebrated as much in ecstatic relief as in triumph. Keeth, Jason, James, and I stood and screamed in the stands. The finals were that night, but I couldn't take another emotional roller coaster ride the night before our own team event. I watched the women's foil team face Russia while eating dinner with Jason and our families at the Bank of America House, where friends and family of the U.S. team can eat for free. The women ran into a focused Russian team, led by a thirty-six-year-old closer in her sunset Olympics. The U.S. lost 28-11 and never really seemed to find their feet, but they had taken the silver after everyone counted them out. I thought that boded well for men's saber.

Everyone has his own way of preparing the night before a big event. You get used to it on the circuit. Time seems to creep or fly. By far the best thing to do is to beat back thoughts of the upcoming match. Otherwise, you risk visualization becoming obsession as you pre-play points in your head through a sleepless night. I obliterated all thought by watching the movie *You Don't Mess with the Zohan* and slept like a baby. I woke up rested and thought to myself: *This is it.*

In the early morning, the Olympic village is a tale of two athletes. If you've been out partying, it's an unwritten rule that you stay out of the village until morning so that you don't return rowdy and disturb the other athletes who are sleeping before their events. So the morning brings two passing crowds: one waking energized, nervous, and ready for their Olympic moment; and the other returning hungover or still drunk from a night out, celebrating their events already fought.

On the way to the dining hall, Jason and I passed a contingent of the latter, stumbling back into the village still very obviously intoxicated, wearing the clothes of a Middle Eastern country. As they reached us, one of the athletes stumbled toward me in what I imagined was an attempt at a drunken bear hug. Then he cocked an imaginary gun with his thumb and forefinger and squeezed it against my temple. His horrified teammates hauled him off, presumably for a cup of coffee and a slap in the face.

After the bronze medal loss in Athens, the bench of the U.S. team had been on the receiving end of Damien Touya's imaginary machine gun, delivered with his saber and a bandaged hand. This time I took an imaginary bullet to the temple. I kept it to myself—talk about fodder for an international incident! With our team competition in a matter of hours, I shoved the whole thing into that black box reserved for things you think about later. Keeth, Jason, and I ate breakfast and then headed to the fencing venue where we met James and began warming up for the biggest matches of our lives.

As I stood on the strip, my parents sat in the stands. My dad didn't know all the rules of fencing—sometimes my mom had to explain the points—but he was there, just as he had been there for every Little League game I ever played. From the strip, when I looked up into the stands and saw my father, I saw myself in him—his work ethic had become mine, and without it, I never would have survived teaching and fencing. My mom had given me her individualism and with it the ability to pour my heart into a sport that the mainstream didn't know existed. My parents' pride filled me with determination.

As my Hungarian opponent Szilágyi bounced on his toes before our match, I thought about Yury. The day before, at the practice facility, we had fenced on a strip next to the Hungarian team, stealing glances at each other while trying to look strong and confident. Maybe the Hungarians were as confident as they looked while they stretched and went through a standard workout. They had dominated us in Vegas and the only U.S. saber team win in history over Hungary had been the upset at the Athens Games.

In the past, Szilágyi had beaten me by circling his sword to find my blade, parrying it away, and scoring on riposte. Yesterday, standing fifteen feet from the fencer himself, Yury had mimicked Szilágyi's parry. We all knew Yury had slowed a second or two in the last year, but he pushed the lymphoma down deep while we were in Beijing to give me and the rest of the team what we needed. Yury helped me find the angle that sliced through Szilágyi's parry and, just as important, Szilágyi *saw* that I could solve his parry. As much technical expertise as Yury has, he is also a master at the head game surrounding the sport. More than practice, it had been theater—a show of strength and confidence that, at that moment, tilted the strip between Szilágyi and me to my advantage. Now with our respective infirmities and our uncertain futures, we were the culmination of Yury's fencing dream.

Warming up before the team event, we had talked about our loss in Athens—how we had met our opponents in the middle of the strip and landed simultaneous touches in that confusing blur of double attack that can be called anyone's point. In Beijing, we vowed to stay out of the middle. We would win or lose on clear touches. We vowed to wait for our opponents to come to us, and to stay out of the middle even if it meant letting some of the world's best attacking teams come at us.

I took the strip after Jason and Keeth had given points in their opening matches; we were down 7-10 with the momentum slipping away from us. I had watched in Athens and now was my first opportunity to help the team. Szilágyi dared me to attack and, with Yury's skill, I did. Apparently he didn't believe I had actually solved his parry, but point after point, I found a way to disengage from his searching, sweeping, circling blade. Just as Montano had gamed Keeth into expecting defense before Athens, our match history gamed Szilágyi into expecting an inept attack. On that day, I took 8 points to Szilágyi's 2 and ended the segment ahead at 15-12.

I won my 3 matches by a combined 3 points, but Keeth came into the final segment down 36-40 to Zsolt Nemcsik, the Athens silver medalist. Then Keeth roared back to 44-44, and it was Athens all over again. Keeth had lost at 44-44 to Damien Touya in the bloody match to miss the finals, then lost at 44-44 to Russia's Pozdniakov to miss the bronze by a point. Now, in 2008, we are at 44-44 with Hungary—Keeth's third straight 44-44 touch at the Olympics. Missing those 2 touches in Athens had nearly crippled Keeth. Now this moment would define Keeth's career, and, by extension, all of our careers. Would Keeth be the also-ran, always toeing the medal platform without setting foot on it?

Keeth had flunged at Nemcsik in the past, but it left open the danger that Nemcsik would attack at the same time and the fencers would meet in the middle of the strip where we had vowed not to let referees decide the match. This time, instead, Keeth dropped back, waiting. Nemcsik advanced—and here came his attack! But in the milliseconds before Nemcsik landed, Keeth stabbed in to take Nemcsik's wrist. Nemcsik's touch was too late—locked out—and it was a one-light touch for Keeth!

It was our second team win over Hungary in U.S. history.

Of course we celebrated! But we had more work to do. The path to the medal led through Russia in the semifinals, who, like Hungary, was a team we had beaten exactly once in our long history—at the New York World Cup just before the Athens Games. In Beijing, the Russian team was stacked with talent. Pozdniakov,

Yakimenko, and Kovalev were numbers 1, 5, and 26 in the world, respectively. Pozdniakov had four gold medals. Yakimenko had the bronze from Athens and ended the 2007 season ranked 1st in the world. Kovalev was a wunderkind with speed, flexibility, and strategy far beyond his twenty-two years.

The U.S. team was comprised of a kid from Brooklyn working full time at Verizon (Keeth), two recent college graduates (Jason and James), and a public school teacher (me). We were up against full-time professionals who had been training their whole lives to win the gold. Nobody expected us to win anything… except us.

Keeth opened 5-3 against Yakimenko—focused, fast, aggressive, smart. Keeth tore down the strip and made us believe the impossible is possible. I followed, going 5-5 with Pozdniakov and then 5-4 with Kovalev. In a beautiful, brilliant performance, Jason took Pozdniakov 5-1 and we went ahead of the Russians 20-13 in the race to 45. Then things started to unravel: Keeth gave 1-5 to Kovalev and Jason gave points to Yakimenko, putting us down 28-35. Fencing second-to-last, I faced Alexey Yakimenko, a fencer I had never beaten.

The ref said *Allez!* and I stepped into the middle, but it was a tentative move and Yakimenko speared in for the touch. Had I even moved? *Stick with your strengths*, I said to myself. On the second point, I made Yakimenko come after me, circling my saber to find his blade as he advanced, looking for the parry-riposte. But he was too fast—Yakimenko knifed around my defense to make a touch in my side. It was 28-37. Our hopes were slipping away. I could barely see Yakimenko coming—a blur of sinew and speed.

I started to wonder why I was there. Not why as in what did I have to gain, but why as in how did a fencer without talent on a team from the United States expect to compete against Yakimenko on the world's biggest fencing stage? I was a picked-on kid from Washington Heights, from a Division-III college, a train-commuting teacher. I wasn't supposed to be there. None of us—Keeth, Jason, Yury, nor I—was supposed to be here.

But there we were. There I was. It was my moment. If I could gain ground, I could give Keeth a chance. If not, we were finished. In the short time between the second and third points, I had another thought: *Why not?* The idea of people separated into two silos—talent and no talent—suddenly seemed like an artificial barrier that people erect in their minds to excuse or explain failure. In Washington Heights, I had been trapped behind a similar mental barrier that blinded me to the fact that my life could be different and better. My students at IS-90 were trapped behind the barrier of the low expectations born of socioeconomics and stereotypes. Some of the eighteen fencers who had fallen away ahead of me in the lead-up to the Athens Games had been trapped behind a similar barrier of disbelief. The U.S. team itself had forever been trapped by the world's consensus that *we just didn't have the talent.*

But in fact, on the strip that day we were the tip of an iceberg, and below the surface were all the U.S. fencers who had come before us. Peter Westbrook had sent his protégés to national championships and trained them to qualify for Olympic teams. Vladimir Nazlymov had told the world the U.S. could win medals. Terrence Lasker and Jeremy Summers changed the culture of U.S. fencing by jumping on planes to compete internationally. Akhi Spencer-El, Ivan Lee, and Keeth had earned the respect of the international fencing community and, with Jason, had built that success to within one point of an Olympic medal in Athens.

The mental chasm that divides talent from no talent is the same divide I had fought against all my life. *Was an iron bar my only reality? Was I smart enough? Could I succeed? Was I Whorehouse or Morehouse?* I had already given up on the fencing world's traditional definition of talent. I had decoupled my worth on the strip from the validation of points. *Master fencing, master life.* I knew in that moment the opposite is equally true: in order to master fencing, you have to master life. You must master the way you think. And I realized that, mirroring the shift that had taken place in me since living in apartment 5b, a glacial shift had taken place in the expectations of U.S. fencing. Now we believed we belonged on the strip with the Russians. And it was up to me to prove it to the world.

In the silence between heartbeats, I stood motionless before the start of the point, just as I had stood motionless before the start of the first 2. But I wasn't the same person behind the mask. In the years since I first picked up a saber to get out of gym class, I had proven my talents for hard work, for perfecting the mental game, for leaping into the unknown, for endurance and longevity, for teamwork, for reflection, for monasticism, for hope. These are my personal talents, which, in this space between heartbeats, I saw as fully equal to Yakimenko's grace and power on the strip.

"*En garde!*" said the referee. "*Prêt?*" Yakimenko raised his hand and reset his feet. "*Prêt?*" asked the ref, and Yakimenko again raised his hand, reset his feet. "*Prêt?*" asked the ref, then, "*Allez!*" We both moved forward, but my advance was an attack without hesitation. We both landed, but right-of-way was mine and so was the point. The next point, I pushed Yakimenko down the strip, coming up short on my first lunge but avoiding his riposte and then landing my redoubled attack. "*En garde! Pret? Allez!*" On the third point we both came forward and I landed hard on Yakimenko's mask, with Yakimenko almost on his knees in a low lunge.

I went 7-3 in the final 10 points and left the strip behind by 5 at 35-40. I had scored 17 points in the race to 45. Jason had scored 13. Keeth would need to score 10 to Pozdniakov's 4 to win. The momentum had swung in our favor and the crowd, overpopulated with Americans, cheered us on. But the task before Keeth was monumental: Stanislav Pozdniakov, the best fencer in the world for the past decade, staked to a 5-point lead.

It was a battle between aging lions in the twilight of their fabled careers. Pozdniakov had the Olympic hardware to show for it. Keeth didn't. In the Athens semifinals, they'd met at the same score, reversed, with Keeth ahead and Pozdniakov turning momentum into a flood of points and the win.

Now in Beijing, Pozdniakov took the first point to make it 35-41. Keeth and Pozdniakov reset for the second point. Both attacked and both landed: "*Rien!*" called the ref, "*Pas de touche.*" No point. They restarted and attacked and again the ref says: "*Même chose! Rien. Pas de touche.*" Same thing! Nothing. No touch.

Fencers come to a rest before a point starts—it's in the rules—but I've always thought Keeth has a special stillness. I might flex and clench my back hand in these moments. Pozdniakov shows the nonchalant stillness of an ancient gladiator who can get away with a pre-start slackening. But in the half second before the start of a point, Keeth could be an engraving. Or a cocked gun.

Keeth took the second point, then traded points with Pozdniakov.

Something was in the air.

Keeth was a shark on attack and a cobra on defense, ripping powerfully or counterstriking with fearsome precision. Against this onrush, Pozdniakov clawed for points, trying to outpace the rising tide of momentum, too experienced to be swallowed, to passively sink in a tide turning against him. Even as points slid away from him, Pozdniakov refused to go gently. Instead, he thrashed and fought his way to a 44-43 lead. Keeth had taken 8 points to Pozdniakov's 4, but it was far from enough.

They stood en garde. Keeth held up his hand to quiet the chanting American crowd. "*En garde, prêt, allez!*" said the ref. Pozdniakov attacked, driving Keeth backwards down the strip.

Then after an awkward step, Keeth turned the corner and pushed Pozdniakov back past the center point as Pozdniakov circled his blade, searching for Keeth's saber or the tiniest hitch in Keeth's step that could signal an opening. There it was—Keeth hesitated and Pozdniakov struck, connecting with Keeth's blade to take the right-of-way and following with a slashing cut to Keeth's body. A light flashed for Pozdniakov and he raised his arms in celebration, yelling to the roof.

Many people watching in the United States clicked off the broadcast or shut down their computers. Jason, Yury, James, our non-competing team captain Jeff Bukantz, and I walked from the box toward the strip to collect Keeth. But he was waving frantically at the side referee. "No!" Keeth argued, "No, no, no!" He waved his hand at the ref who was gathering the other officials around the replay machine.

On the Jumbotron screen, we saw what Keeth saw. As Keeth transitioned from defense to attack, he had stepped off the strip, out of bounds. The side ref called, "Halt, halt!" That's when Keeth hesitated, allowing Pozdniakov's touch. It had been a dead point!

Time stood still. No one in the stands knew what was happening. Our captain argued the call. Yury stood with Keeth. "Stay ready, stay ready, whatever happens you stay ready!" One minute became two, became ten.

Finally, the refs came back with their decision: *Rien, pas de touche!*

We were back to 44-43. Pozdniakov was stunned and furious, a wounded animal, but still with the upper hand. They faced off.

The next point opened and both fencers checked into the middle. Keeth retreated and, in a beautiful move, reversed in less than a blink to take the onrushing Pozdniakov.

It was 44-44 again. Four U.S. saber team matches in a row, dating back to the Athens Olympics, would be decided on the final touch. A single touch would send one of the teams to the gold medal match and the other to fight for the bronze.

Keeth lined up opposite Pozdniakov.

"*En garde*," the ref said. "*Prêt?*"

Keeth held up a hand, asked for a second, reset his feet.

"*Prêt?*" the ref asks, then, "*Allez!*" Again, they both checked into the center, then Keeth retreated back past his own starting line. Pozdniakov hesitated, unsure if he wanted to follow Keeth down the strip. Seeing Pozdniakov's hesitation, Keeth flew, launching his flunge—the move that had made his career. No other fencer in the world could have pulled it off. From eight feet away down the strip, he landed a flying one-light touch to Pozdniakov's visor. Keeth landed on his feet, saw the light, spun and somersaulted on the mat, then came up running toward our bench, howling, his sword raised high in his right hand.

This vision of Keeth is the last thing I remember. As I rose up to charge over to him in jubilation, my world suddenly went black and I passed out on the floor. The online video shows all of us coming together in a team hug. Jumping. Screaming. Crying in disbelief. We step apart… and I drop to the ground. I remain on the ground, unmoving, my toes pointing straight up, passed out cold. Everyone seems to think it's my unique way of celebrating— taking a short nap on the floor.

Then, when I came to several seconds later and saw everyone celebrating, I realized where I was, that we had won, and simply rejoined the party.

As we celebrated, Pozdniakov took off his mask, shrugged his shoulders, and walked off the strip into retirement. Later, he would lose 44-45 to Italy in the bronze medal match, and Russia would go without a team saber medal for the first time in many, many years.

Keeth hugged me, crying. He grabbed for Jason, James, Jeff,

and Yury. We all piled together over and over in delirious con-
flagrations of tears and hugs. I was crying and saying, "Oh my
god, oh my god!" over and over. Yury grabbed Keeth, locked his
hand behind Keeth's neck, and pulled him close enough to say
the equivalent of *I told you so*. Jeff handed me an American flag. I
raised it above my head with two hands and shook it out toward
the cheering crowd. Keeth and I embraced again and again.

Over the stadium sound system blared *Did you ever know that
you're my he-ro!* In that moment, the song seemed appropriate. Finally, after hundred-hour weeks of work and practice, decades of
our lives given to the sport, all the airports and debt and stalled
careers placed on the back burner—we were Olympic medalists.

If our story were a movie, it would end here. But it's not.
The French had beaten Italy, and while we celebrated, the calm
and collected French team got ready to meet us in the gold
medal match.

Four hours later—9:00pm in China and 9:00am on the U.S.
east coast—in front of a sold-out crowd and on television around
the world, I stepped onto the strip against Julien Pillet. I was completely calm. The first point, I got impatient and launched a lunge
from a step too far away. Pillet parried and riposted for the touch.
The right distance! On the second point, I feinted into the middle
and then retreated, but again I was half a step slow and instead
of setting up to wave my body out of the way of Pillet's attack,
his slash caught me across the chest. The next 2 points were exact
repeats of the first 2 and I went down 0-4 before salvaging a point
and eventually leaving the strip down 1-5.

Against Boris Sanson, Keeth went 6-5. For the gold medal
match we substituted James Williams for Jason Rogers so that
James could earn a medal and the title Olympian, and in his first
Olympic appearance, James went a respectable 3-5 with Lopez.

Our second round wasn't any better than our first, and by the time we'd fenced 7 of our 9 bouts, we were down 23-35. *Wake up!* I told myself. I knew if I could get us close, with Keeth as our closer, we still had a chance. Finally the underdog aggression I'd had since high school kicked in and I got my head in the match, taking Lopez to 5-2, the momentum turning in our favor. The next point, he caught me in the hand—an off-target area—but with my glove soaked with sweat, his scoring light went on. I changed to a dry glove, but when we tested my hand, Lopez's light came on again. At most tournaments we would have stopped to fix the technical glitch, but with the TV cameras rolling, officials pressured me back onto the strip.

My brain, just barely in the match to begin with, was now preoccupied with keeping my scoring-zone hand away from Lopez—allowing him to roar back and finish the segment 5-5. To Keeth's credit, he went 9-5 with Pillet, but it wasn't enough and we fell to France in the gold medal match 45-37. Looking back, we were never really in it. Leaving the strip, I took another lesson: setting a goal places the finish line. It will pull you toward it, but it's hard to go beyond. You only reach the bar you set. What would our finals match against France have looked like if we had set the finish line at a *gold* medal?

Still, taking the silver medal was the greatest triumph in the history of U.S. men's saber fencing—a dream that had been our goal from the start. Standing on the podium with Keeth, Jason, and James was surreal. With Yury and our families looking on, we were each hung with a silver medal. Then we grasped hands and stepped forward in unison to raise our arms.

EPILOGUE

Following the gold medal match, we had four days before the closing ceremony and every morning, I woke up in a panic. "Did we win a medal, Jason?" I would yell across to the other bed. "Yes, Tim. Go back to sleep," Jason would mumble. But I would have to get up and shuffle through my bag until I found the medal: silver, cool, and surprisingly heavy.

For every athlete who medals, the U.S. Olympic Committee throws a party at one of the sponsored "houses". Ours was at the Volkswagen House. My parents were there, as were Jason's and James', along with Keeth's sister and aunt. Afterward, we went to a bar on NBC's tab.

The network was filming a segment about the karaoke culture of China and chose us because they imagined that riding the tide of our many fencing medals, the combined men's and women's fencing teams would make idiots of ourselves onstage. We didn't disappoint. I reprised my go-to karaoke favorite, Poison's classic "Every Rose Has It's Thorn." Then Erinn Smart joined me on stage for A-Ha's "Take on Me." Let's just say we were everything the camera crew hoped for and more, karaoke gods and goddesses for the night.

During the days before the closing ceremony, we gave interviews to the U.S. television networks that had sent news teams to Beijing. We were on *The Today Show,* and because most of us were based in New York, the whole host of NYC affiliate stations had us on. James' mother was convinced he would lose his medal, so she made him give it to her for safekeeping. The four of us stood there on camera, James without his medal, and when the journalists invariably asked what happened to the missing medal, James had to explain over and over again that his mom had taken it away.

At the closing ceremony, I tried to soak up as much Olympic spirit as I could. At the end of the ceremony, Beijing passed the torch to London. The flame was driven out of the stadium on a red double-decker bus and I wanted to jump on that bus right then and there. I wanted to run up to the top deck and ride straight to the next Games. I knew I wasn't finished and I knew what the next four years would look like.

On the long flight back to the U.S., I drifted in and out of sleep and over and over I saw the hand of a Chinese athlete passing the Olympic torch to an English athlete. At the closing ceremony I had been so far away I could barely see the flame; now I was at super close-up, inside the flame as it passed from Beijing to London.

My first competition after Beijing, I won a North American Cup and then went on to win the 2010 and 2011 National Championships. I finished the 2009, 2010, and 2011 seasons ranked #1 in the U.S.

After Beijing, I also bounced rent checks and ate more Ramen noodles than any person probably should. Our scrappy, grassroots system had allowed the U.S. saber team to build twenty years into silver medals, but to compete for the gold with France, Italy, Russia, Hungary, and Ukraine, we needed another push. We needed what swimmers and figure skaters had: the support that allows these athletes to be professionals. Deciding all of a sudden to be a professional meant some rather exquisite financial suffering, but I blazed the way into food and training sponsorships and helped solidify the link between fencing and fashion. I hoped that like Peter Westbrook starting his foundation, or Steve Mormando teaching U.S. fencers to rule the headspace needed to compete, or Akhi Spencer-El being the first golden child to earn the world's respect, or Nazlymov telling the world that U.S. fencers could win medals, and Keeth helping make it happen—that my clawing for sponsorships would make it easier for those behind me.

Just like the fencing world said I didn't have the talent to make the Olympics and that the U.S. didn't have the talent to win a medal, the world said that no one in the States would ever pay for a ticket to watch a fencing event, and that fencing would never be on TV in the U.S. As I had been at Riverdale, fencing was a sport with low self-esteem, so I tried to pull it up by its bootstraps. After the Olympics, after a medal, after proving the impossible was possible, I thought to myself, *Why not this?*

We held the inaugural Fencing Masters tournament in New York City in 2010 and we proved everyone wrong—1,800 fans paid for tickets, packed a ballroom, and the event was televised. As I finish this book, Fencing Masters: Kick-Off to London is being planned with expectations for an even larger crowd and televised audience.

I started the foundation Fencing-in-the-Schools, which will create new fencing programs in economically challenged areas, uniting my passion for fencing with my passion for education.

Keeth went to Columbia business school, got an MBA, and works in finance. Jason fenced a few more years before leaving the sport for a job in marketing. As I had done after being the alternate in Athens, James continues fencing with an eye on London.

In the year after Beijing, Yury battled lymphoma. He coached through chemotherapy and a full bone marrow transplant. For a year, he was almost docile, but by the fall of 2009, he was back to telling me he could teach a bear to feint cut better than me. Did he treat me differently after I helped win an Olympic medal? Not at all. "Fencing is life, life is fencing," he continued to tell me, "and if you're not pushing forward, you're falling backward."

In their own way, Yury and Peter Westbrook had always been friends and rivals, with Westbrook finding and motivating the kids who Yury eventually trained, the relationship accompanied by periodic upheavals in turf and politics. Apparently, their rivalry extended to medical one-upmanship. After Westbrook complained to his doctor that he couldn't muster the energy to fence in practice, his doctor told him it was all in his mind. But after losing forty pounds, Westbrook was diagnosed with lymphoma, too. He brought the same passion and enthusiasm to beating the disease that he brought to holding a strip at Fencers Club, saying that for his morning and afternoon chemotherapy sessions, he was always the first to arrive and the last to leave. Like Yury, Peter beat the disease.

At the 2009 Dallas World Cup, I lost 15-13 to Yakimenko in the semifinals and one of the older Olympic U.S. fencers sincerely congratulated me on a strong showing. But I was pissed that I'd lost. There was a new normal—a new set of expectations for American fencing. A good showing against the best in the world was no longer a victory.

U.S. junior fencers are now winning world championships.

Partly due to our performance in Beijing, they *expect* to win. We have redefined the culture of U.S. fencing to include the expectation of winning. In men's saber, Daryl Homer made the rounds of 32 and then 16 in his inaugural world cups, and, within two years, he has moved into the top sixteen in the world. In 2010, the foil fencer Miles Chamley-Watson reached the #2 ranking in the world. Foil fencer Gerek Meinhardt won bronze and our men's épée team took silver at the 2010 World Championships. The following year, at the Catania World Championships, seventeen-year-old Lee Kiefer won a bronze medal in the women's foil and eighteen-year-old foil fencer Race Imboden made it all the way to the quarterfinals as his teammate Alex Massialas, at the age of seventeen, earned two bronze medals at difficult world cups before graduating high school.

And one day at Yury's new club, Manhattan Fencing, I found myself across from a middle schooler, new to the club, who was trying to get his feet right for advancing and retreating. If he was Fred Astaire, Ginger Rogers would've had bruised toes. He was frustrated and quickly slipping into that headspace that makes golfers throw putters into water hazards. I could've taught a bear to advance and retreat better than him. Was he hopeless?

The next week he was back.

Though I'm going for the gold in all aspects of my life, I don't know if I'll win a gold medal in London. But I know that someday a USA fencer—this kid or a kid just like him—will win the gold. You build these pyramids, with each generation pushing through barriers of expectations, and talent, and goals. The middle schoolers at Manhattan Fencing, Fencers Club, and the numerous new clubs popping up around the country start a handful of blocks higher than they used to. Ivan, Keeth, Erinn, Akhi, Jason, Terrence, Jeremy, Jason, Iris, Felicia, Ann, Buckie, Ed, Arkady, Mariel, Sada, James, Peter, Steve, Yury, and so many others fought to drag these blocks into place. We have yet to win a gold medal in men's fencing, but I know now some U.S. fencer—maybe today or tomorrow or next year or the next Olympics—will stand on top.

Acknowledgments

The journey of this book in many ways reminds me of my path to the Olympics. And like my Olympic journey, I needed the support of many people along the way—there are many books about individual achievements and this isn't one of them. Instead, just as I'm indebted to my fencing teammates, I'm equally indebted to my writing team.

First, I'm supremely grateful for the help of writer Garth Sundem, author of books including *Brain Trust* and *The Geeks' Guide to World Domination*, who helped me turn my ideas for a manuscript into words on the page. This book wouldn't be the same without him. Garth, I can't thank you enough for helping this dream turn into a reality.

As you can guess, there aren't many books about small-sport athletes and most of them haven't made any best-seller lists. With fencing being one of the smallest of the small, I feel extremely lucky to have found my literary agent, Jennifer Miller of Miller-Bowers-Griffin Agency, who recognized this book's potential and helped me run with it.

I'd also like to thank Paige Stover-Hague of Acanthus Publishing, who picked us up and helped us get to the finish line of publication, and I thank her for her work on the book.

And a special thank you to David Lee for his amazing graphic design work on the cover and for all his hard work and belief in me and my projects.

I also want to acknowledge a few others: my coach Yury Gelman and my teammate Keeth Smart, who were gracious enough to sit down with me for many interviews and to allow me to tell their stories, since they are so intertwined with my own. I hope I did you both proud. Thanks to author, Richard Cohen, and USA Fencing Hall of Fame curator, Andy Shaw, for providing me with countless great stories about the history of fencing, and to Vitali Nazlymov for sharing so much of his father Vladimir. Thanks to Jeff Imrich, Wendi Jill-Adelson, Jeff Spear and Rachael Kun for reading early versions of the book and providing me helpful insight. Thanks also to my early coaches, Martin Schneider at Riverdale for helping me when I needed it most, and Coach Bill Shipman for helping to foster my growth as a person and fencer at Brandeis.

Thanks to Ed Cederquist and his great company, BistroMD, for sponsoring my Olympic dream as well as to Scott Weiss at Bodhizone Fitness for supporting my goals with his tremendous staff and personal skills as a physical therapist.

And thanks to all my Olympic teammates, Teach For America family, and my friends for their constant encouragement throughout this four-year process! Thanks to the fencing community as a whole for all their support throughout the years and for being a part of my journey!

Finally, thanks to my family for supporting me every step of the way and for giving me the values of determination and individuality I've needed to pursue and achieve my dreams.